addition word problems: pp. 40,

HBJ MATHEMATICS

0 1 2 3 4 5 6 7 8 9
1 2 3 4 5 6 7 8 9 0
2 3 4 5 6 7 8 9 0 1
3 4 5 6 7 8 9 0 1 2
4 5 6 7 8 9 0 1 2 3
5 6 7 8 9 0 1 2 3 4
6 7 8 9 0 1 2 3 4 5

LOLA J. MAY
Mathematics Consultant
Winnetka Public Schools
Winnetka, Illinois

SHIRLEY M. FRYE
Mathematics Coordinator
Scottsdale Unified School District
Scottsdale, Arizona

DONNA CYRIER JACOBS
Director of Publications
Winnetka Public Schools
Winnetka, Illinois

HBJ MATHEMATICS

CONSULTING EDUCATORS

DWIGHT COBLENTZ
Curriculum Coordinator—
  Mathematics
Department of Education
San Diego County, California

MARJORIE H. COLEMAN
Amherst Elementary School
Amherst, Virginia

CHARLES DAUD
Special Education
Intermountain Inter-tribal School
Phoenix Area, Bureau of Indian
  Affairs
United States Department of the
  Interior

JUNE J. FINCH
Elementary Mathematics
  Coordinator
Chicago Public Schools
Chicago, Illinois

ANN HOLMAN
Lu Sutton School
Novato, California

KAREN LIEBERMAN
Harry L. Bain School
West New York, New Jersey

HBJ **HARCOURT BRACE JOVANOVICH**
New York   Chicago   San Francisco   Atlanta   Dallas   *and*   London

PHOTOGRAPH ACKNOWLEDGMENTS

KEY: T, Top; B, Bottom; L, Left; C, Center; R, Right.

HBJ PHOTOS by Rick Der: 2, 5, 7, 9, 11, 12, 15, 16, 21, 28, 43, 52, 57, 58, 66, 69, 73, 78, 79, 81, 84, 85, 92, 93, 100, 104, 105, 106, 108, 112, 113, 125, 153, 154, 162, 173, 180, 183, 193, 200, 217, 234, 237, 248, 250, 251, 252, 255, 261, 263, 274, 277, 278, 279, 294, 295, 309, 312, 320, 332, 333.

HBJ PHOTOS by Elliott Varner Smith: 116, 136, 152, 174, 212, 310.

HBJ PHOTOS by Phil Toy: 129, 151 (Courtesy Jim Grant, artist, and San Francisco Downtown Community College Center), 169, 198, 241, 316.

HARBRACE PHOTO by P. C. and Connie Peri: 298.

RESEARCH CREDITS: Focus on Sports, J. DiMaggio, J. Kalish: 1. The Image Bank, © Erik Leigh Simmons: 27. Black Star, Oscar Buitrago: 65. © Elliott Varner Smith: 91. © 1978 Barrie Rokeach: 115, 233. FPG, Angabe A. Schmidecker: 120. Image Bank, © Pete Turner: 135. Bruce Coleman Inc.: 164. FPG, Peter Gridley: 168. © 1979 Barrie Rokeach: 211. Roy King: 218, 271, 300. Black Star, © 1979 Andy Levin: 224. Royden L. Hobson: 227. Dennis Anderson: 272. © Roy King: 287. Grant Heilman: 290. Woodfin Camp, © Jeffrey Foxx: 303. Focus on Sports: 311. Sports Illustrated, © Time Inc., Walter Iooss Jr.: 321.

COVER CREDITS

HBJ Photo by Rick Der. Background © Pete Turner, Image Bank-West. Numbers by Walter Gasper.

ART ACKNOWLEDGMENTS

Robert Bausch: 59, 96, 97T, 111, 131, 155, 158, 159T, 160, 163, 179, 195, 213R, 215B, 221, 225C, 226, 228, 266–267, 283, 297, 305, 318R, 327R. Nancy Freeman: 20, 44, 45R. Walter Gasper (constructions): 93, 100B, 153R, 162, 169, 217. Barbara Hamlin: 3, 8, 14, 19, 40, 50–51, 60–61, 142, 146, 184, 188C, 206, 207, 223, 254, 288, 289, 291, 302, 313TR. Susan Jaekel: 31, 33, 37, 38, 39, 53, 68, 74, 75, 117, 118, 119, 123R,.124B, 126, 127, 143, 144–145, 147, 182R, 190, 200B, 202, 236TR, 243, 259, 265, 280–281, 296, 315T, 322, 324TR, 324BR, 325C, 329TL, 330TR. Tony Naganuma: 5, 6C, 9, 11, 15, 17, 29, 30, 32, 45C, 48, 49, 67, 70, 72, 75C, 78TR, 78C, 79, 80R, 81, 82, 83L, 86C, 87C, 88, 89, 94R, 95, 97B, 98, 99, 101B, 102, 103, 104, 105, 106, 107C, 108, 109C, 110, 112C, 112B, 113C, 113B, 120, 121, 122, 123L, 124T, 128, 130, 153L, 154, 157L, 157C, 159B, 161, 162, 164, 165, 166, 167, 169, 170, 171, 172, 175, 177, 178T, 180, 181, 182L, 186, 187L, 188T, 191T, 192, 198, 199, 200C, 202, 203, 213L, 214T, 215T, 217C, 218, 219, 220, 224, 225T, 236, 239C, 260, 261C, 268, 269, 270, 274, 275, 276T, 279, 282, 298, 299, 300, 306, 307, 311, 313, 315C, 316, 317, 320, 321, 323, 324TL, 325T, 326TR, 328, 329, 330, 331, 334, 339, 342, 352, 353, 354, 355, 357, 358, 360, 362, and all Challenge, Review, and Calculate graphics, and Chapter Review, Chapter Test, and Brush-Up borders. Cathy Pavia: 86, 87, 238, 239. Don Petersen: 4, 6, 10, 22–23, 36, 42, 55, 56, 71, 80L, 83TR, 98R, 101, 137, 138, 139, 167R, 176, 178C, 187R, 191C, 205, 222, 228TR, 229, 256, 257, 276B, 285, 286, 292, 293, 301, 314, 318L, 326TL, 327L. Julie Peterson: 34, 46, 47, 140, 141, 240. Mark Schroeder: 168. Ed Taber: 13, 35, 76–77, 94L, 107, 109T, 156R, 157B, 214B, 216, 244, 245, 246, 273, 319. Marta Thoma: 177R, 196, 197.

ISBN 0-15-352051-5

Contents

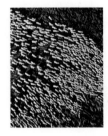

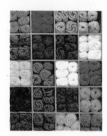

CHAPTER 1

Warm Up

Using Addition at Work

John Nelson is a truck driver. This morning John made a 35-kilometer trip and a 41-kilometer trip. To find the total number of kilometers he traveled, he adds 35 and 41. He has traveled a total of 76 kilometers.

Addition Facts

Add.

1. 3 + 8 11	**2.** 9 + 6	**3.** 5 + 7	**4.** 8 + 9	**5.** 2 + 9	**6.** 8 + 4	**7.** 3 + 6
8. 8 + 8	**9.** 9 + 5	**10.** 5 + 9	**11.** 6 + 6	**12.** 8 + 7	**13.** 4 + 5	**14.** 5 + 8
15. 7 + 8	**16.** 9 + 7	**17.** 3 + 9	**18.** 7 + 7	**19.** 6 + 7	**20.** 5 + 6	**21.** 9 + 9
22. 9 + 4	**23.** 7 + 4	**24.** 8 + 6				

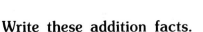

Write these addition facts.

25. Three addition facts with sums of 13.

$$7 \atop + 6 \atop 13 \qquad 8 \atop + 5 \atop 13 \qquad 9 \atop + 4 \atop 13$$

26. Four addition facts with sums of 12.

27. Two addition facts with sums of 15.

28. Four addition facts with sums of 11.

29. Three addition facts with sums of 14.

30. One addition fact with a sum of 18.

31. Two addition facts with sums of 16.

Finding Sums

5	addend	4	1 less than 5	6	1 more than 5
+ 5	addend	+ 5		+ 5	
10	sum	9	1 less than 10	11	1 more than 10

Write the sums.

1a. 6
 + 6
 12

1b. 6
 + 5
 11

1c. 6
 + 7
 13

2a. 8
 + 9

2b. 9
 + 9

2c. 7
 + 9

3a. 7
 + 7

3b. 8
 + 7

3c. 6
 + 7

4a. 5
 + 5

4b. 6
 + 5

4c. 7
 + 5

5a. 6
 + 8

5b. 6
 + 9

5c. 6
 + 7

6a. 8
 + 4

6b. 8
 + 3

6c. 8
 + 5

7a. 1
 + 9

7b. 2
 + 9

7c. 3
 + 9

⭐ Challenge

8. When 0 is an addend, what do you know about the sum?

9. When 1 is an addend, what do you know about the sum?

Making Addition Facts

These are addends.   This is a sum.

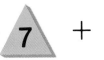
7 + 5 = 12

An addend plus
an addend
equals a sum.

Use two addends and a sum to make each fact.
You can use the addends more than once.

1. Write four addition facts.

6   5   7
13 12 11

7 + 5 = 12   6 + 7 = 13
6 + 5 = 11   5 + 7 = 12

2. Write four addition facts.

7   6   8
13 15 14

3. Write three addition facts.

9   7   6
13 16 15

4. Write three addition facts.

8   9   7
15 17 16

5. Write four addition facts.

9   5   7
12 14 16

6. Write three addition facts.

8   4   7
11 15 12

7. Write four addition facts.

4   6   9
10 15 13

Finding Sums

Add.

1. 8
   + 2
   ____
   10

2. 5
   + 6

3. 9
   + 5

4. 6
   + 7

5. 7
   + 4

6. 8
   + 3

7. 6
   + 6

8. 9
   + 4

9. 8
   + 6

10. 8
    + 9

11. 8
    + 4

12. 5
    + 8

13. 9
    + 9

14. 6
    + 9

Code	g	d	c	w	o	t	a	h
	11	13	12	16	14	18	15	10

Crack the code to answer the riddle.

What is the best kind of dog for keeping time?

15. 8
    + 8
    ____
    16, w

16. 8
    + 7

17. 9
    + 9

18. 4
    + 8

19. 7
    + 3

20. 5
    + 8

21. 8
    + 6

22. 9
    + 2

23. The answer is a __ __ __ __ __ __ __ __
                    15. 16. 17. 18. 19. 20. 21. 22.

Fact Families

Fact family for 5, 6, 11:

$$6 + 5 = 11$$
$$5 + 6 = 11$$

$$11 - 5 = 6$$

$$11 - 6 = 5$$

Use these numbers to write four facts.

1. 8, 7, 15 $8 + 7 = 15,$ $7 + 8 = 15,$ $15 - 8 = 7,$ $15 - 7 = 8$

2. 8, 9, 17   **3.** 6, 7, 13   **4.** 5, 9, 14   **5.** 8, 6, 14

6. 7, 9, 16   **7.** 3, 8, 11   **8.** 7, 5, 12   **9.** 9, 3, 12

10. 9, 6, 15   **11.** 8, 4, 12   **12.** 9, 4, 13   **13.** 9, 2, 11

 **Calculate**

14a. $3 + 4 + 8 + 6 + 7 + 5 + 2 = $ ▢
  b. $2 + 5 + 7 + 6 + 8 + 4 + 3 = $ ▢
  c. What do you notice about the sums of 14a. and 14b.?

Subtraction Facts

Subtract.

1. 13 − 6 = 7	**2.** 14 − 8	**3.** 15 − 7	**4.** 16 − 9	**5.** 11 − 5	**6.** 9 − 4
7. 13 − 8	**8.** 14 − 5	**9.** 15 − 6	**10.** 16 − 7	**11.** 11 − 4	**12.** 10 − 3
13. 13 − 4	**14.** 14 − 7	**15.** 15 − 8	**16.** 11 − 3	**17.** 18 − 9	**18.** 12 − 9
19. 11 − 7	**20.** 13 − 7	**21.** 12 − 6	**22.** 11 − 6	**23.** 15 − 9	**24.** 16 − 8
25. 10 − 6	**26.** 17 − 8	**27.** 12 − 7	**28.** 17 − 9	**29.** 12 − 3	**30.** 14 − 9

 Challenge

31. Write six subtraction facts using 13 as one number.

32. Write four subtraction facts using 15 as one number.

33. Write three subtraction facts using 16 as one number.

Making Subtraction Facts

This is a sum.   These are addends.

$$17 - 8 = 9$$

A sum
minus an addend
equals an addend.

Use the sums and addends to make facts.
You can use the addends more than once.

1. Write four subtraction facts.

9   7   8
17 18 16

$17 - 8 = 9$ $18 - 9 = 9$
$16 - 8 = 8$ $17 - 9 = 8$

2. Write five subtraction facts.

7   5   6
11 13 12

3. Write six subtraction facts.

8   7   6
13 15 14

4. Write five subtraction facts.

8   7   6
14 16 15

5. Write six subtraction facts.

8   7   6
13 14 12

6. Write six subtraction facts.

5   7   9
12 14 16

7. Write six subtraction facts.

7   8   9
15 17 16

Forest Problems *(addition and subtraction)*

First decide to add or subtract.
Then write a fact to solve each problem.

1. Alice sees 3 rabbits eating and 9 rabbits running. How many rabbits in all? $3 + 9 = 12$

2. Eric watches 16 birds in a tree. 9 fly away. How many are left?

3. Last year there were 15 fires in the forest. 7 were caused by lightning. How many were not caused by lightning?

4. The forest ranger spends 6 hours putting out fires and 2 hours planting young trees. How many hours does he work?

5. There are 9 pine trees by the pond. Elena plants 8 more. How many pine trees in all?

6. Kim took 11 pictures of deer. She gave away 4 of them. How many pictures did she have left?

7. There are 14 small ponds in the forest. 7 of the ponds have fish. How many ponds do not have fish?

Finding Sums and Differences

Add or subtract.

1. 6
   + 4
   ⎯⎯
    10

2. ·10
   − 3

3. 11
   − 7

4. 8
   + 2

5. 7
   + 4

6. 15
   − 7

7. 5
   + 6

8. 16
   − 9

9. 17
   − 8

10. 13
    − 6

11. 8
    + 5

12. 14
    − 5

13. 9 + 6

14. 12 − 4

15. 9 + 8

16. 8 + 7

17. 17 − 9

Crack the code to find the answer.

What is the difference between an old dime and a new penny?

Code	t	e	i	s	n	c
	9	3	17	8	12	5

18. 4
   + 8

19. 8
   + 9

20. 7
   + 5

21. 12
   − 9

22. 14
   − 9

23. 11
   − 8

24. 9
   + 3

25. 15
   − 6

26. 16
   − 8

27. The difference is __ __ __ __   __ __ __ __ __
                     18. 19. 20. 21.   22. 23. 24. 25. 26.

Adding Three Numbers

Add two numbers at a time.

Pick a place to begin.

$$\begin{array}{r} 6 \\ 3 \\ + 7 \\ \hline \end{array} \;\Big\rangle\; 9$$

$$\begin{array}{r} 9 \\ + 7 \\ \hline 16 \end{array}$$

$$\begin{array}{r} 6 \\ 3 \\ + 7 \\ \hline \end{array} \;\Big\rangle\; 10$$

$$\begin{array}{r} 6 \\ + 10 \\ \hline 16 \end{array}$$

Find the sums.

1. $\begin{array}{r} 8 \\ 1 \\ + 6 \\ \hline 15 \end{array}$
2. $\begin{array}{r} 5 \\ 4 \\ + 3 \\ \hline \end{array}$
3. $\begin{array}{r} 6 \\ 4 \\ + 7 \\ \hline \end{array}$
4. $\begin{array}{r} 4 \\ 3 \\ + 8 \\ \hline \end{array}$
5. $\begin{array}{r} 7 \\ 3 \\ + 8 \\ \hline \end{array}$
6. $\begin{array}{r} 9 \\ 8 \\ + 1 \\ \hline \end{array}$
7. $\begin{array}{r} 3 \\ 9 \\ + 5 \\ \hline \end{array}$

8. $\begin{array}{r} 5 \\ 2 \\ + 9 \\ \hline \end{array}$
9. $\begin{array}{r} 2 \\ 8 \\ + 7 \\ \hline \end{array}$
10. $\begin{array}{r} 4 \\ 2 \\ + 7 \\ \hline \end{array}$
11. $\begin{array}{r} 5 \\ 3 \\ + 9 \\ \hline \end{array}$
12. $\begin{array}{r} 6 \\ 2 \\ + 7 \\ \hline \end{array}$
13. $\begin{array}{r} 5 \\ 4 \\ + 9 \\ \hline \end{array}$
14. $\begin{array}{r} 8 \\ 4 \\ + 6 \\ \hline \end{array}$

 Challenge

15. $3 + 4 + 2 + 8$
16. $5 + 3 + 2 + 7$
17. $7 + 2 + 1 + 8$

18. $6 + 1 + 3 + 5$
19. $4 + 4 + 2 + 4$
20. $9 + 0 + 1 + 8$

21. $7 + 4 + 3 + 7$
22. $6 + 8 + 9 + 2$
23. $5 + 6 + 7 + 8$

Two-Step Problems

( ) mean **Do me first.**

Step 1

$5 + (\underbrace{15 - 8}_{7}) = \boxed{?}$

Step 2

$5 + (\underbrace{15 - 8}_{7}) = \boxed{?}$

$5 + \quad 7 \quad = 12$

Solve each problem.

1. $(6 + 7) - 8$ 5
2. $(8 + 7) - 9$
3. $(5 + 6) - 7$

4. $(12 - 5) + 8$
5. $(13 - 9) + 8$
6. $(17 - 8) + 4$

7. $(6 - 2) + 9$
8. $(6 - 4) + 7$
9. $(6 + 7) - 9$

10. $8 + (13 - 6)$
11. $3 + (17 - 9)$
12. $6 + (16 - 7)$

13. $(7 + 9) - 8$
14. $8 + (14 - 5)$
15. $(9 + 6) - 8$

16. There are 5 people on the bus. 6 more people get on. 3 people leave. How many people on the bus now?

 Review   (pp. 3–13)

1. $6 + 7$
2. $14 - 5$
3. $5 + 8$

4. $17 - 9$
5. $4 + 9$
6. $16 - 8$

County Fair Problems

Write a fact to solve each problem.

1. There were 11 rides at the fair. Sam did not ride 4 of them. How many did he ride?
   11 − 4 = 7

2. At the animal show 6 horses won blue ribbons. 5 cows won blue ribbons. How many blue ribbons in all?

3. Walt won 12 prizes. He gave 3 of them away. How many did he have left?

4. There were 14 animal shows. Diane saw 8 of them. How many shows did she miss?

5. Diane knocked down 6 bottles with a softball. Gail knocked down 4 and Sam knocked down 3. How many did they knock down in all?

6. Gail rode the roller coaster 7 times in the morning and 6 times in the afternoon. How many roller coaster rides in all?

Tens and Hundreds

Tens Chart

0	10	20	30	40	50	60	70	80	90
100	110	120	130	140	150	160	170	180	190
200	210	220		240	250	260	270	280	290
300	310	320			350	360	370	380	390
400	410	420				460	470	480	490
500	510	520			550	560	570	580	590
600	610	620			650	660	670	680	690
700	710	720			750	760	770	780	790
800	810	820							890
900	910	920							990

Go right to count by tens.
Go down to count by hundreds.

Which number is 10 greater than each of these?

1. 240 250
2. 380
3. 470
4. 780
5. 550

Which number is 100 greater than each of these?

6. 670
7. 510
8. 850
9. 740
10. 490
11. 90

12. Start with 700. Count by tens to 790. Write the numbers.

13. Start with 150. Count by hundreds to 650. Write the numbers.

Numbers in Order

Use 3, 8, 2. Make six three-digit numbers.

382 283 823

238 328 832

least number   greatest number

The numbers in order from least to greatest are:
238, 283, 328, 382, 823, 832.

**Write six different three-digit numbers.
Put them in order from least to greatest.**

1. Use 2, 8, 5. 258, 285, 528, 582, 825, 852

2. Use 6, 7, 4.   3. Use 8, 7, 6.   4. Use 3, 9, 1.

5. Use 9, 8, 7.   6. Use 5, 9, 4.   7. Use 1, 2, 3.

**Write six different three-digit numbers.
Put them in order from greatest to least.**

8. Use 4, 5, 7. 754, 745, 574, 547, 475, 457   9. Use 8, 1, 3.

10. Use 4, 7, 3.   11. Use 1, 6, 4.   12. Use 7, 5, 2.

13. Use 1, 6, 9.   14. Use 5, 8, 4.   15. Use 2, 9, 3.

Place Value and Sums

Number: 7936

Th	Thousands	7
H	Hundreds	9
T	Tens	3
O	Ones	6

```
  7000 ⎤
   900 ⎥
    30 ⎥ ─ values of the digits
+    6 ⎦
───────
  7936   sum
```

Write an addition problem to show the sums for each chart.

1.

Th	4
H	9
T	0
O	6

```
  4000
   900
     0
+    6
──────
  4906
```

2.

Th	6
H	7
T	4
O	2

3.

Th	3
H	5
T	2
O	0

4.

Th	2
H	0
T	6
O	5

5.

Th	8
H	4
T	3
O	6

6.

Th	7
H	0
T	4
O	3

7.

Th	9
H	5
T	0
O	8

8.

Th	3
H	8
T	9
O	1

Write the sum.

9. 1000 + 900 + 80 + 2

10. 4000 + 700 + 30 + 4

Ordering Numbers

Compare digits to put numbers in order.

Step 1
Compare thousands digits.

6714   8912

6 thousand is less than 8 thousand.
6714 is less than 8912.

Step 2
If thousands are the same,
compare hundreds, compare tens,
compare ones.

4385   4358

4385 is greater than 4358.

**Write is greater than or is less than
between the two numbers.**

1. 5000 ___ 7000   5000 is less than 7000

2. 4111 ___ 2817

3. 7219 ___ 9384

4. 5019 ___ 3148

5. 2347 ___ 2511

6. 6817 ___ 6571

7. 7851 ___ 7859

8. 5671 ___ 5680

9. 1176 ___ 3014

10. 9903 ___ 9930

11. 7778 ___ 7770

12. 4450 ___ 4445

13. 3907 ___ 3970

14. 6789 ___ 6879

15. 2153 ___ 2513

16. 4070 ___ 4770

17. 9976 ___ 9997

 **Review**   (pp. 3–18)

1. 6 + 7

2. 560 + 10

3. 560 + 100

4. 1000 + 300

Adding Large Numbers

Step 1
Add ones.

```
  4231
+ 2547
─────
     8
```

Step 2
Add tens.

```
  4231
+ 2547
─────
    78
```

Step 3
Add hundreds.

```
  4231
+ 2547
─────
   778
```

Step 4
Add thousands.

```
  4231
+ 2547
─────
  6778
```

Find each sum.

1. 53
  + 26
  ─────
    79

2. 80
  + 17

3. 432
  + 25

4. 523
  + 265

5. 603
  + 294

6. 411
  + 225

7. 32
  + 604

8. 612
  + 134

9. 123
  + 651

10. 26
  + 473

11. 2357
  + 1321

12. 1132
  + 344

13. 412
  + 1325

14. 9431
  + 435

15. 5643
  + 3326

16. 4692
  + 4203

17. 3732
  + 6135

18. 2042
  + 5837

 Challenge

19. Bill has 341 pennies. Amy has 1627 pennies. How many pennies in all?

20. Lucy Fong saved 122 pennies in May, 135 pennies in June, and 131 pennies in July. How many in all?

Subtracting Large Numbers

Step 1
Subtract ones.

```
  5897
- 2341
------
     6
```

Step 2
Subtract tens.

```
  5897
- 2341
------
    56
```

Step 3
Subtract hundreds.

```
  5897
- 2341
------
   556
```

Step 4
Subtract thousands.

```
  5897
- 2341
------
  3556
```

Subtract.

1.
```
  68
- 23
----
  45
```

2.
```
  79
- 50
----
```

3.
```
  987
- 423
-----
```

4.
```
  897
- 256
-----
```

5.
```
  437
- 200
-----
```

6.
```
  269
-  25
-----
```

7.
```
  599
- 186
-----
```

8.
```
  768
-  43
-----
```

9.
```
  987
- 234
-----
```

10.
```
  867
-  25
-----
```

11.
```
  5297
- 3064
------
```

12.
```
  3886
-  341
------
```

13.
```
  2479
- 1026
------
```

14.
```
  7732
- 4100
------
```

15.
```
  8679
- 2134
------
```

16.
```
  9799
-  256
------
```

17.
```
  8888
- 4823
------
```

18.
```
  9999
- 5299
------
```

19.
```
  7854
- 2312
------
```

20.
```
  6423
-  200
------
```

21. Tom Ortega cut 467 pieces of wood for his fireplace. In one winter he used 335. How many pieces left?

Adding and Subtracting Large Numbers

Change from long to tall.

Be careful.
Keep digits in their places.

$$234 + 64 + 401 \qquad 589 - 103$$

$$
\begin{array}{r}
234 \\
64 \\
+\ 401 \\
\hline
699
\end{array}
\qquad
\begin{array}{r}
589 \\
-\ 103 \\
\hline
486
\end{array}
$$

Write the tall form. Find the answer.

1. $83 + 14$
$$
\begin{array}{r}
83 \\
+\ 14 \\
\hline
97
\end{array}
$$

2. $79 - 39$

3. $362 + 25$

4. $497 - 253$

5. $537 + 252$

6. $9836 - 7230$

7. $23 + 34 + 42$

8. $230 + 55 + 3414$

9. $780 - 230$

10. $7 + 41 + 21$

11. $683 - 52$

12. $20 + 8 + 671$

 Calculate

13. Find four numbers whose sum is 20. Use trial and error.

14. Find five one-digit numbers whose sum is 30.

Bowling Problems

Margie and Ed bowled three times one week and three times the next week. These charts show their bowling scores.

Week 1	Margie	Ed
Game 1	101	110
Game 2	111	101
Game 3	112	100

Week 2	Margie	Ed
Game 1	113	121
Game 2	120	103
Game 3	102	122

1. What was Margie's total score for the first week? 324

2. What was Ed's total score for the first week?

3. Who had the higher score the first week? How much higher?

4. What was Margie's total score for the second week?

5. What was Ed's total score for the second week?

6. Who had the higher score for the second week? How much higher?

APRIL 6 - 14

SHOE RENTAL

7. What was Margie's total score for the two weeks?

8. What was Ed's total score for the two weeks?

9. Who had the higher score for the two weeks? How much higher?

10. Janice's score for two weeks was 123 less than Ed's. What was Janice's score?

11. Greg's total score for each week was 324 and 315. What was his score for two weeks?

12. Julio's score for two weeks was 30 more than Margie's. What was Julio's score?

Chapter Review

Add or subtract. (ex. 1–9: p. 3) (ex. 10–18: p. 8)

1. 8 + 8	2. 2 + 9	3. 4 + 5	4. 6 + 7	5. 8 + 4	6. 7 + 7
7. 9 + 9	8. 5 + 6	9. 8 + 9	10. 15 – 7	11. 13 – 4	12. 11 – 7
13. 16 – 9	14. 17 – 8	15. 12 – 8	16. 11 – 4	17. 15 – 9	18. 14 – 7

Write six different three-digit numbers. Put them in order from least to greatest. (ex. 19–21: p. 16)

19. Use 2, 4, 6.   20. Use 4, 5, 1.   21. Use 9, 7, 8.

Add. (ex. 22–24: p. 17)

22. 2000 + 400 + 9   23. 400 + 70   24. 1000 + 100 + 10 + 1

Add or subtract. (ex. 25–32: p. 21)

25. 4206 382 + 2101	26. 986 – 524	27. 34 253 + 4202	28. 6895 – 2320	29. 5000 343 + 254

30. 1063 + 221 + 600   31. 840 – 20   32. 224 + 32

Chapter Test

Add or subtract.

1. 8
 + 6

2. 9
 + 8

3. 7
 + 6

4. 6
 + 9

5. 7
 + 8

6. 9
 + 7

7. 8
 + 4

8. 8
 + 5

9. 7
 + 7

10. 9
 + 4

11. 6
 + 6

12. 5
 + 7

13. 5
 + 9

14. 9
 + 6

15. 17
 − 9

16. 13
 − 7

17. 15
 − 6

18. 14
 − 8

Find each answer.

19. Use 3, 7, 1. Write six different numbers. Give them in order from least to greatest.

20. Count by tens from 470 to 540. Write the numbers.

21. Write four facts with 7, 4, and 11.

22. 3000 + 600 + 70 + 8.

Add or subtract.

23. 28
 370
 + 5201

24. 6479
 − 2356

25. 5768
 − 536

26. 321
 345
 + 5232

27. 7671
 − 2361

28. 3 + 42 + 251

29. 573 − 231

30. 42 + 210 + 30

Brush Up

Add.

1. $6 + 4$ 2. $9 + 4$ 3. $8 + 6$ 4. $7 + 4$

5. $5 + 6$ 6. $7 + 8$ 7. $8 + 9$ 8. $7 + 5$

9. $4 + 3$ 10. $6 + 5$ 11. $6 + 2$ 12. $8 + 7$

13. $8 + 2$ 14. $9 + 3$ 15. $8 + 3$ 16. $9 + 8$

Subtract.

17. $9 - 4$ 18. $12 - 7$ 19. $13 - 8$ 20. $9 - 3$

21. $14 - 6$ 22. $12 - 5$ 23. $15 - 7$ 24. $16 - 9$

25. $16 - 7$ 26. $14 - 8$ 27. $17 - 8$ 28. $13 - 6$

29. $8 - 3$ 30. $17 - 9$ 31. $12 - 3$ 32. $11 - 9$

Add or subtract.

33. $9 + 1$ 34. $9 + 7$ 35. $14 - 5$ 36. $15 - 8$

37. $10 - 3$ 38. $9 + 2$ 39. $11 - 7$ 40. $13 - 9$

41. $8 + 8$ 42. $6 + 7$ 43. $13 - 4$ 44. $13 - 7$

45. $5 + 4$ 46. $9 + 6$ 47. $15 - 6$ 48. $9 + 9$

49. $7 - 2$ 50. $8 + 5$ 51. $13 - 6$ 52. $17 - 9$

CHAPTER 2

Addition and Subtraction

Using Subtraction at Work

Ray Alberts is a librarian. He had $95 to spend
on books and maps. He spent $78. To find how
much he has left, he subtracts $78 from $95.
He has $17 left to spend.

Using an Addition Chart

Move across to add ones. Move down to add tens.

0	1	2	3	4	5	6	7	8	9
10	11	12	13	14	15	16	17	18	19
20	21	22	23	24	25	26	27	28	29
30	31	32	33	34	35	36	37	38	39
40	41	42	43	44	45	46	47	48	49
50	51	52	53	54	55	56	57	58	59
60	61	62	63	64	65	66	67	68	69
70	71	72	73	74	75	76	77	78	79
80	81	82	83	84	85	86	87	88	89
90	91	92	93	94	95	96	97	98	99

```
  27   Start.
+  8   Move across 8.
----
  35   Land.
```

```
  63   Start.
+ 25   Move across 5.
       Move down 2.
----
  88   Land.
```

Use the chart. Find the sums.

1. 53
  + 8
  ────
    61

2. 27
  + 6

3. 27
  + 30

4. 27
  + 36

5. 45
  + 16

6. 39
  + 24

7. 65
  + 9

8. 65
  + 29

9. 34
  + 6

10. 34
   + 46

11. 73
   + 19

12. 45
   + 28

13. 56
   + 8

14. 56
   + 38

15. 18
   + 49

16. 75
   + 8

17. 75
   + 18

18. 29
   + 66

19. 42
   + 37

20. 39
   + 16

21. 47
   + 9

22. 88
   + 11

23. 66
   + 17

24. 23
   + 48

Trading Ones

Step 1
Add ones.
Trade 10 ones
for 1 ten.

$$\begin{array}{r} \overset{1}{2}9 \\ + 34 \\ \hline 3 \end{array}$$

Step 2
Add tens.

$$\begin{array}{r} \overset{1}{2}9 \\ + 34 \\ \hline 63 \end{array}$$

9 ones + 4 ones = 13 ones
13 ones = 1 ten + 3 ones

Add and trade.

1. $\begin{array}{r} 29 \\ + 14 \\ \hline 43 \end{array}$

2. $\begin{array}{r} 28 \\ + 34 \\ \hline \end{array}$

3. $\begin{array}{r} 29 \\ + 24 \\ \hline \end{array}$

4. $\begin{array}{r} 29 \\ + 33 \\ \hline \end{array}$

5. $\begin{array}{r} 28 \\ + 33 \\ \hline \end{array}$

6. $\begin{array}{r} 46 \\ + 46 \\ \hline \end{array}$

7. $\begin{array}{r} 17 \\ + 66 \\ \hline \end{array}$

8. $\begin{array}{r} 45 \\ + 16 \\ \hline \end{array}$

9. $\begin{array}{r} 58 \\ + 12 \\ \hline \end{array}$

10. $\begin{array}{r} 55 \\ + 39 \\ \hline \end{array}$

11. $\begin{array}{r} 27 \\ + 19 \\ \hline \end{array}$

12. $\begin{array}{r} 35 \\ + 15 \\ \hline \end{array}$

13. $\begin{array}{r} 36 \\ + 27 \\ \hline \end{array}$

14. $\begin{array}{r} 41 \\ + 49 \\ \hline \end{array}$

15. $\begin{array}{r} 23 \\ + 68 \\ \hline \end{array}$

16. $\begin{array}{r} 44 \\ + 46 \\ \hline \end{array}$

17. $\begin{array}{r} 72 \\ + 19 \\ \hline \end{array}$

18. $\begin{array}{r} 27 \\ + 58 \\ \hline \end{array}$

19. 35 + 26

20. 23 + 28

21. 14 + 58

22. 79 + 15

23. 53 + 17

24. 18 + 37

25. 39 + 53

26. 31 + 39

27. Betty and Jack have 44 cows.
They buy 39 cows. How many
cows do they have in all?

28. There are 13 white horses and
17 brown horses. How many
horses in all?

Trading Ones to Add

10 ones
equal 1 ten.

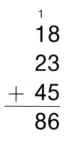

```
    1
   18
   23
 + 45
 ────
   86
```

Add.

1. 47 + 9 ── 56	**2.** 63 + 8	**3.** 74 + 6	**4.** 39 + 8	**5.** 38 + 27	**6.** 45 + 5
7. 64 + 29	**8.** 47 + 39	**9.** 56 + 17	**10.** 72 + 19	**11.** 64 + 7	**12.** 36 + 8
13. 59 24 + 15	**14.** 23 38 + 17	**15.** 46 19 + 3	**16.** 34 7 + 42	**17.** 6 34 + 18	**18.** 8 20 + 36
19. 5 24 + 34	**20.** 49 + 16	**21.** 38 14 + 23	**22.** 53 + 39	**23.** 39 16 + 23	**24.** 53 8 + 62

25. $16 + 14 + 3$ **26.** $42 + 28$ **27.** $63 + 13 + 14$ **28.** $77 + 57$

Trading Tens

Step 1	Step 2	Step 3
Add ones.	Add tens. Trade.	Add hundreds.

$$\begin{array}{r} 171 \\ +\ 153 \\ \hline 4 \end{array}$$

$$\begin{array}{r} \overset{1}{1}71 \\ +\ 153 \\ \hline 24 \end{array}$$

$$\begin{array}{r} \overset{1}{1}71 \\ +\ 153 \\ \hline 324 \end{array}$$

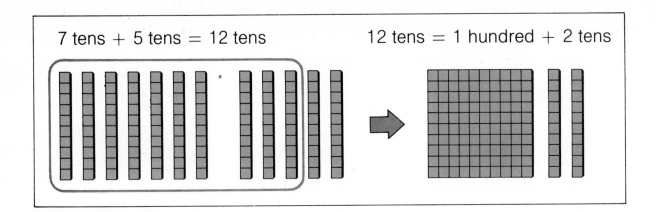

7 tens + 5 tens = 12 tens   12 tens = 1 hundred + 2 tens

Add.

1. $\begin{array}{r} 181 \\ +\ 345 \\ \hline 526 \end{array}$
2. $\begin{array}{r} 271 \\ +\ 345 \\ \hline \end{array}$
3. $\begin{array}{r} 281 \\ +\ 245 \\ \hline \end{array}$
4. $\begin{array}{r} 281 \\ +\ 335 \\ \hline \end{array}$
5. $\begin{array}{r} 181 \\ +\ 335 \\ \hline \end{array}$

6. $\begin{array}{r} 172 \\ +\ 254 \\ \hline \end{array}$
7. $\begin{array}{r} 122 \\ +\ 396 \\ \hline \end{array}$
8. $\begin{array}{r} 152 \\ +\ 453 \\ \hline \end{array}$
9. $\begin{array}{r} 162 \\ +\ 292 \\ \hline \end{array}$
10. $\begin{array}{r} 132 \\ +\ 486 \\ \hline \end{array}$

11. $\begin{array}{r} 493 \\ +\ 243 \\ \hline \end{array}$
12. $\begin{array}{r} 364 \\ +\ 351 \\ \hline \end{array}$
13. $\begin{array}{r} 570 \\ +\ 189 \\ \hline \end{array}$
14. $\begin{array}{r} 658 \\ +\ 151 \\ \hline \end{array}$
15. $\begin{array}{r} 862 \\ +\ 177 \\ \hline \end{array}$

More Trading Tens

Step 1
Add ones.
Add tens.
Trade.

Step 2
Add
hundreds.

$$\begin{array}{r} {\scriptstyle 1} \\ 473 \\ 284 \\ +\ 101 \\ \hline 58 \end{array}$$

$$\begin{array}{r} {\scriptstyle 1} \\ 473 \\ 284 \\ +\ 101 \\ \hline 858 \end{array}$$

10 tens equal
1 hundred.

Add.

1. $\begin{array}{r} 361 \\ +\ 895 \\ \hline 1256 \end{array}$

2. $\begin{array}{r} 473 \\ +\ 154 \\ \hline \end{array}$

3. $\begin{array}{r} 583 \\ +\ 264 \\ \hline \end{array}$

4. $\begin{array}{r} 160 \\ +\ 459 \\ \hline \end{array}$

5. $\begin{array}{r} 543 \\ +\ 296 \\ \hline \end{array}$

6. $\begin{array}{r} 377 \\ +\ 51 \\ \hline \end{array}$

7. $\begin{array}{r} 894 \\ +\ 93 \\ \hline \end{array}$

8. $\begin{array}{r} 341 \\ +\ 78 \\ \hline \end{array}$

9. $\begin{array}{r} 463 \\ +\ 372 \\ \hline \end{array}$

10. $\begin{array}{r} 671 \\ +\ 190 \\ \hline \end{array}$

11. $\begin{array}{r} 272 \\ 321 \\ +\ 35 \\ \hline \end{array}$

12. $\begin{array}{r} 481 \\ 125 \\ +\ 42 \\ \hline \end{array}$

13. $\begin{array}{r} 682 \\ 104 \\ +\ 123 \\ \hline \end{array}$

14. $\begin{array}{r} 731 \\ 94 \\ +\ 403 \\ \hline \end{array}$

15. $\begin{array}{r} 541 \\ 60 \\ +\ 321 \\ \hline \end{array}$

16. $\begin{array}{r} 81 \\ 341 \\ +\ 266 \\ \hline \end{array}$

17. $\begin{array}{r} 637 \\ +\ 103 \\ \hline \end{array}$

18. $\begin{array}{r} 55 \\ 434 \\ +\ 240 \\ \hline \end{array}$

19. $\begin{array}{r} 412 \\ +\ 394 \\ \hline \end{array}$

20. $\begin{array}{r} 63 \\ 81 \\ +\ 554 \\ \hline \end{array}$

21. $34 + 193 + 472$

22. $83 + 45 + 260$

23. $381 + 264 + 12$

Add and Match Game

A game for two players.

Get ready:
Make 15 letter slips, one for each letter **A** to **O**.
Mix up the slips. Put them face down. Get a
sheet of paper and a pencil for each player.

To play:
Each player takes a slip. Find your letter in the
box below. Copy the problem for the letter onto
your sheet of paper. Add.
Take another slip. Copy. Add. Are both of your
answers the same? If so, you have a match.
Keep playing. The player who gets two matches
first is the winner.

A. 228 + 501 729	**B.** 613 + 153	**C.** 471 + 75	**D.** 184 + 501	**E.** 341 + 476
F. 384 + 243	**G.** 447 + 282	**H.** 393 + 292	**I.** 131 + 351	**J.** 262 + 365
K. 290 + 192	**L.** 230 + 316	**M.** 292 + 190	**N.** 495 + 271	**O.** 234 + 582

Trading Twice

Step 1	Step 2	Step 3
Add ones. Trade ones.	Add tens. Trade tens.	Add hundreds.

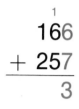
$$\begin{array}{r} {\scriptstyle 1} \\ 166 \\ +\ 257 \\ \hline 3 \end{array}$$

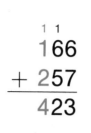
$$\begin{array}{r} {\scriptstyle 1\ 1} \\ 166 \\ +\ 257 \\ \hline 23 \end{array}$$

$$\begin{array}{r} {\scriptstyle 1\ 1} \\ 166 \\ +\ 257 \\ \hline 423 \end{array}$$

Add.

1.
$$\begin{array}{r} 166 \\ +\ 157 \\ \hline 323 \end{array}$$

2.
$$\begin{array}{r} 167 \\ +\ 257 \\ \hline \end{array}$$

3.
$$\begin{array}{r} 166 \\ +\ 258 \\ \hline \end{array}$$

4.
$$\begin{array}{r} 156 \\ +\ 257 \\ \hline \end{array}$$

5.
$$\begin{array}{r} 166 \\ +\ 247 \\ \hline \end{array}$$

6.
$$\begin{array}{r} 486 \\ +\ 294 \\ \hline \end{array}$$

7.
$$\begin{array}{r} 795 \\ +\ 56 \\ \hline \end{array}$$

8.
$$\begin{array}{r} 581 \\ +\ 249 \\ \hline \end{array}$$

9.
$$\begin{array}{r} 657 \\ +\ 299 \\ \hline \end{array}$$

10.
$$\begin{array}{r} 244 \\ +\ 387 \\ \hline \end{array}$$

11.
$$\begin{array}{r} 286 \\ +\ 179 \\ \hline \end{array}$$

12.
$$\begin{array}{r} 342 \\ +\ 179 \\ \hline \end{array}$$

13.
$$\begin{array}{r} 568 \\ +\ 374 \\ \hline \end{array}$$

14.
$$\begin{array}{r} 237 \\ +\ 86 \\ \hline \end{array}$$

15.
$$\begin{array}{r} 783 \\ +\ 197 \\ \hline \end{array}$$

Now do these.

16. $265 + 49$

17. $457 + 368$

18. $285 + 37$

19. $345 + 165$

20. $355 + 46$

21. $286 + 248$

22. $623 + 87$

23. $59 + 588$

24. $342 + 99$

25. $576 + 134$

26. $485 + 35$

27. $267 + 469$

Post Office Problems

The Post Office sorts letters, postcards, and packages.

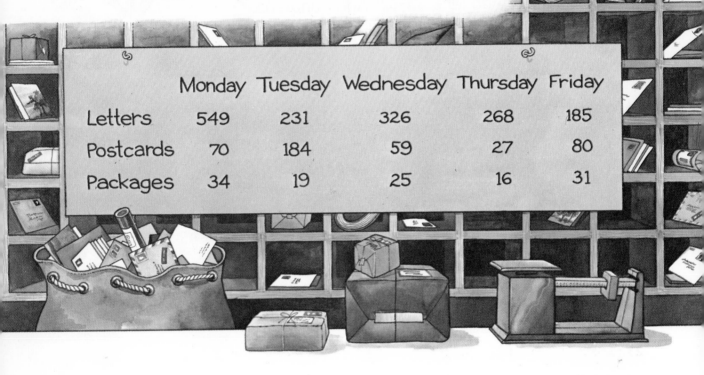

	Monday	Tuesday	Wednesday	Thursday	Friday
Letters	549	231	326	268	185
Postcards	70	184	59	27	80
Packages	34	19	25	16	31

1. How many letters and postcards were sorted Monday? 619

$$\begin{array}{r} 549 \\ +\ 70 \\ \hline 619 \end{array}$$

2. How many letters were sorted Monday and Tuesday?

3. How many letters, postcards, and packages were sorted Friday?

4. How many letters and postcards were sorted Thursday?

5. How many letters and postcards were sorted Wednesday?

6. How many letters were sorted Wednesday and Thursday?

7. How many letters and packages were sorted Thursday?

8. How many postcards and packages were sorted Wednesday?

Adding

Add.

1.	386	2.	459	3.	769	4.	834	5.	257
	+ 78		+ 83		+ 78		+ 97		+ 398
	464								

6.	437	7.	567	8.	456	9.	477	10.	631
	+ 283		+ 399		+ 174		+ 286		+ 179

11.	312	12.	406	13.	298	14.	201	15.	89
	54		42		314		433		203
	+ 544		+ 264		+ 75		+ 89		+ 231

16.	738	17.	254	18.	878	19.	536	20.	478
	+ 195		+ 397		+ 56		+ 195		+ 299

21.	643	22.	478	23.	296
	+ 86		+ 35		+ 194

24. Pam Jensen is a florist.
She sells 347 roses one week
and 495 roses the next week.
How many does she sell in all?

25. In her store Pam has 239
plain pots for plants and 174
painted pots. How many pots in all?

26. In May Pam has 463 customers.
In June she has 458 customers.
How many for May and June?

Adding Thousands

10 hundreds equal
1 thousand.

$$\begin{array}{r} \overset{1\ 1\ 1}{4569} \\ +\ 2976 \\ \hline 7545 \end{array}$$

Find the sums.

1. $\begin{array}{r}2678\\+\ 5597\\\hline 8275\end{array}$	2. $\begin{array}{r}3954\\+\ \ \ 687\\\hline\end{array}$	3. $\begin{array}{r}2675\\+\ 2869\\\hline\end{array}$	4. $\begin{array}{r}4883\\+\ 1479\\\hline\end{array}$	5. $\begin{array}{r}6645\\+\ \ \ 385\\\hline\end{array}$
6. $\begin{array}{r}4678\\+\ \ \ 556\\\hline\end{array}$	7. $\begin{array}{r}2546\\+\ 4794\\\hline\end{array}$	8. $\begin{array}{r}5887\\+\ 3149\\\hline\end{array}$	9. $\begin{array}{r}7358\\+\ \ \ 875\\\hline\end{array}$	10. $\begin{array}{r}8944\\+\ \ \ 196\\\hline\end{array}$

11. $1648 + 853$

12. $2438 + 2664$

13. $3468 + 852$

14. $2495 + 1617$

15. $1889 + 394$

16. $5276 + 543$

17. $647 + 2975$

18. $7557 + 1854$

19. $498 + 1972$

 Calculate

20. Here's a way to use addition and eight 8's to
make the number 1072: $88 + 888 + 88 + 8 = 1072$.
Use addition and seven 7's to make 1561.

Same Ones Digits

Find the sums. The ones digits in each row are always the same.

1. 9
    + 7
    ___
    16

2. 69
    + 7
    ___

3. 849
    + 67
    ___

4. 9539
    + 247
    ___

5. 6
    + 8
    ___

6. 46
    + 8
    ___

7. 526
    + 48
    ___

8. 7586
    + 1458
    ___

9. 5
    + 7
    ___

10. 45
    + 17
    ___

11. 345
    + 597
    ___

12. 6935
    + 2487
    ___

13. 5
    + 8
    ___

14. 35
    + 18
    ___

15. 175
    + 428
    ___

16. 3175
    + 1428
    ___

17. 7
    + 8
    ___

18. 27
    + 28
    ___

19. 747
    + 28
    ___

20. 6397
    + 728
    ___

21. 6
    + 9
    ___

22. 36
    + 29
    ___

23. 466
    + 119
    ___

24. 9236
    + 379
    ___

25. 8
    + 9
    ___

26. 58
    + 9
    ___

27. 158
    + 339
    ___

28. 2658
    + 339
    ___

Grocery Store Problems   *(addition)*

1. Watson's grocery store uses 3421 paper bags and 2729 plastic bags. How many bags are used altogether? ~~6150~~ $\begin{array}{r} 3421 \\ +2729 \\ \hline 6150 \end{array}$ bags

The grocery store used 6,150 bags.

2. The grocery store sells 1500 heads of lettuce in May and 2947 in June. How many altogether?

3. The grocery store orders 5374 cans of chicken soup and 4278 cans of beef soup. How many cans altogether?

4. The grocery store buys 3536 oranges one month and 3487 oranges the next. How many altogether?

5. Watson's grocery store orders 400 cartons of large eggs, 550 cartons of medium eggs, and 660 cartons of small eggs. How many cartons altogether?

6. The grocery store sells 2476 loaves of white bread and 1784 loaves of wheat bread. How many altogether?

Practicing Addition

Watch for these kinds of addition.

$$\begin{array}{r} \overset{1}{}29 \\ +\ 34 \\ \hline 63 \end{array}$$

$$\begin{array}{r} \overset{1}{}171 \\ +\ 153 \\ \hline 324 \end{array}$$

$$\begin{array}{r} \overset{1\ 1}{}166 \\ +\ 257 \\ \hline 423 \end{array}$$

$$\begin{array}{r} \overset{1\ 1\ 1}{}4569 \\ +\ 2976 \\ \hline 7545 \end{array}$$

Trade ones.   Trade tens.   Trade ones   Trade ones, tens,
                                  and tens.   and hundreds.

Find the sums.

1. $\begin{array}{r} 57 \\ +\ 9 \\ \hline 66 \end{array}$
2. $\begin{array}{r} 16 \\ +\ 27 \\ \hline \end{array}$
3. $\begin{array}{r} 27 \\ +\ 45 \\ \hline \end{array}$
4. $\begin{array}{r} 361 \\ +\ 494 \\ \hline \end{array}$
5. $\begin{array}{r} 472 \\ +\ 93 \\ \hline \end{array}$

6. $\begin{array}{r} 235 \\ +\ 424 \\ \hline \end{array}$
7. $\begin{array}{r} 4978 \\ +\ 2163 \\ \hline \end{array}$
8. $\begin{array}{r} 456 \\ +\ 398 \\ \hline \end{array}$
9. $\begin{array}{r} 1027 \\ +\ 989 \\ \hline \end{array}$
10. $\begin{array}{r} 276 \\ +\ 130 \\ \hline \end{array}$

11. $\begin{array}{r} 37 \\ +\ 483 \\ \hline \end{array}$
12. $\begin{array}{r} 213 \\ +\ 141 \\ \hline \end{array}$
13. $\begin{array}{r} 6456 \\ +\ 267 \\ \hline \end{array}$
14. $\begin{array}{r} 68 \\ +\ 437 \\ \hline \end{array}$
15. $\begin{array}{r} 5511 \\ +\ 3386 \\ \hline \end{array}$

16. $\begin{array}{r} 3457 \\ +\ 2564 \\ \hline \end{array}$
17. $\begin{array}{r} 892 \\ +\ 4309 \\ \hline \end{array}$
18. $\begin{array}{r} 5484 \\ +\ 1806 \\ \hline \end{array}$
19. $\begin{array}{r} 4466 \\ +\ 2954 \\ \hline \end{array}$
20. $\begin{array}{r} 7686 \\ +\ 1842 \\ \hline \end{array}$

Review (pp. 29–41)

1. $\begin{array}{r} 78 \\ +\ 9 \\ \hline \end{array}$
2. $\begin{array}{r} 482 \\ +\ 235 \\ \hline \end{array}$
3. $\begin{array}{r} 627 \\ +\ 198 \\ \hline \end{array}$
4. $\begin{array}{r} 67 \\ +\ 374 \\ \hline \end{array}$
5. $\begin{array}{r} 426 \\ +\ 57 \\ \hline \end{array}$

Subtracting

Subtract.

1. 17 − 9 **8**	**2.** 15 − 4	**3.** 12 − 6	**4.** 14 − 8	**5.** 16 − 5	**6.** 13 − 7
7. 18 − 10	**8.** 36 − 15	**9.** 49 − 32	**10.** 56 − 23	**11.** 24 − 23	**12.** 75 − 54
13. 414 − 404	**14.** 362 − 221	**15.** 460 − 40	**16.** 790 − 350	**17.** 561 − 200	**18.** 895 − 293
19. 578 − 102	**20.** 629 − 29	**21.** 498 − 253	**22.** 973 − 542	**23.** 125 − 14	**24.** 477 − 315

 **Challenge**

25. Victor Diaz owns a tropical fish store. He has 379 fish. He sells 71 fish in one week. How many does he have left?

26. Victor has 525 packages of tropical fish food. He sells 221 packages in one month. How many left?

Checking Subtraction

Subtract.

```
  478
- 213
─────
  265
```

Check.

```
  213
+ 265
─────
  478
```

Check subtraction by adding.

Write the check.

1.
```
  49      18
- 18    + 31
────    ────
  31      49
```

2.
```
  86
- 14
────
  72
```

3.
```
  949
- 415
─────
  534
```

4.
```
  847
- 212
─────
  635
```

5.
```
  786
-  65
─────
  721
```

Subtract. Add to check.

6.
```
  68
- 13
```

7.
```
  44
- 23
```

8.
```
  86
- 53
```

9.
```
  59
- 16
```

10.
```
  58
- 27
```

11.
```
  37
- 26
```

12.
```
  98
- 46
```

13.
```
  543
- 221
```

14.
```
  65
- 22
```

15.
```
  899
- 355
```

16.
```
  76
- 34
```

17.
```
  837
- 503
```

18.
```
  78
- 24
```

19.
```
  866
- 234
```

20.
```
  67
- 20
```

21.
```
  585
- 211
```

22.
```
  97
- 36
```

23.
```
  752
- 531
```

Subtracting Ones

Look closely.
Are there enough ones to subtract?

$$\begin{array}{r} 71 \\ -\ 29 \\ \hline \end{array}$$
no

$$\begin{array}{r} 57 \\ -\ 23 \\ \hline \end{array}$$
yes

No, you cannot subtract 9 ones from 1 one.

Yes, you can subtract 3 ones from 7 ones.

Are there enough ones to subtract?
Write yes or no. Do not subtract.

1. 47 – 19 no	2. 35 – 20	3. 94 – 48	4. 71 – 28	5. 68 – 23	6. 49 – 37
7. 80 – 52	8. 28 – 9	9. 87 – 52	10. 94 – 60	11. 63 – 17	12. 70 – 50
13. 50 – 24	14. 90 – 36	15. 45 – 18	16. 81 – 46	17. 79 – 36	18. 29 – 19
19. 98 – 29	20. 83 – 57	21. 63 – 28	22. 70 – 54	23. 51 – 14	24. 84 – 25

Trading Tens to Subtract

Step 1
Trade 1 ten
for 10 ones.

$$\overset{3\ 13}{\cancel{43}}$$
$$-\ 17$$

Step 2
Subtract ones.
Subtract tens.

$$\overset{3\ 13}{\cancel{43}}$$
$$-\ 17$$
$$\overline{26}$$

Check.

$$\overset{1}{17}$$
$$+\ 26$$
$$\overline{43}$$

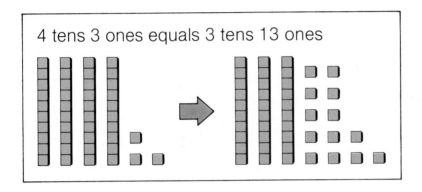

4 tens 3 ones equals 3 tens 13 ones

Trade and subtract. Check the first row.

1. 53 − 17 = **36**	**2.** 43 − 26	**3.** 42 − 27	**4.** 33 − 27	**5.** 53 − 27	**6.** 64 − 28
7. 94 − 38	**8.** 55 − 27	**9.** 84 − 56	**10.** 62 − 24	**11.** 91 − 44	**12.** 48 − 19

13. 24 − 9   **14.** 43 − 28   **15.** 52 − 26   **16.** 33 − 19

17. 64 − 28   **18.** 42 − 24   **19.** 45 − 16   **20.** 28 − 19

Trading to Subtract

Subtract.

1. 64
    − 19
    45

2. 83
    − 57

3. 50
    − 24

4. 91
    − 68

5. 44
    − 29

6. 21
    − 5

7. 46
    − 19

8. 70
    − 42

9. 34
    − 9

10. 65
     − 7

11. 91
     − 38

12. 63
     − 26

13. 80
     − 54

14. 94
     − 68

15. 81
     − 7

16. 77
     − 49

17. 56
     − 29

18. 40
     − 12

19. 62
     − 19

20. 47
     − 28

21. 70
     − 6

22. 81
     − 54

23. 93
     − 68

24. 66
     − 8

25. 74 − 26

26. 93 − 67

27. 26 − 19

28. 58 − 39

29. 35 − 27

30. 44 − 38

31. 43 − 19

32. 63 − 54

 Challenge

33. 83 people eat lunch in the cafeteria. 40 eat sandwiches. The rest eat hot lunches. How many eat hot lunches?

34. Before lunch there were 65 salads. After lunch 16 salads were left. How many salads were sold?

Subtracting Tens

Subtract ones.
Can you subtract tens?

$$627$$
$$- 483$$
$$\overline{\quad 4}$$ no

$$486$$
$$- 141$$
$$\overline{\quad 5}$$ yes

No, you cannot subtract 8 tens from 2 tens.

Yes, you can subtract 4 tens from 8 tens.

The ones are done for you. Are there enough tens to subtract? Write yes or no.

1. 876
    $- 243$
    $\overline{\quad 3}$ yes

2. 564
    $- 291$
    $\overline{\quad 3}$

3. 487
    $- 212$
    $\overline{\quad 5}$

4. 523
    $- 290$
    $\overline{\quad 3}$

5. 949
    $- 602$
    $\overline{\quad 7}$

6. 807
    $- 234$
    $\overline{\quad 3}$

7. 776
    $- 231$
    $\overline{\quad 5}$

8. 986
    $- 403$
    $\overline{\quad 3}$

9. 528
    $- 173$
    $\overline{\quad 5}$

10. 463
    $- 210$
    $\overline{\quad 3}$

11. 883
    $- 590$
    $\overline{\quad 3}$

12. 236
    $- \ 54$
    $\overline{\quad 2}$

13. 789
    $- 425$
    $\overline{\quad 4}$

14. 608
    $- 213$
    $\overline{\quad 5}$

15. 409
    $- 203$
    $\overline{\quad 6}$

16. 867
    $- 294$
    $\overline{\quad 3}$

17. 869
    $- 742$
    $\overline{\quad 7}$

18. 738
    $- 495$
    $\overline{\quad 3}$

19. 547
    $- 234$
    $\overline{\quad 3}$

20. 858
    $- 573$
    $\overline{\quad 5}$

Trading Hundreds

1 hundred equals 10 tens.

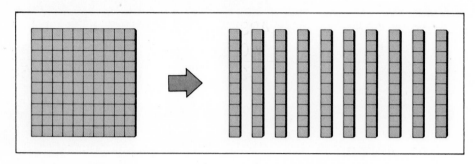

Step 1
Subtract ones.
Trade 1 hundred for 10 tens.

$$
\begin{array}{r}
\overset{3\ 12}{\cancel{4}26} \\
-\ 261 \\
\hline
5
\end{array}
$$

Step 2
Subtract tens.
Subtract hundreds.

$$
\begin{array}{r}
\overset{3\ 12}{\cancel{4}26} \\
-\ 261 \\
\hline
165
\end{array}
$$

Check.

$$
\begin{array}{r}
\overset{1}{}165 \\
+\ 261 \\
\hline
426
\end{array}
$$

Subtract. Check the first row.

1. $\begin{array}{r}326 \\ -\ 163 \\ \hline 163 \end{array}$	2. $\begin{array}{r}326 \\ -\ 151 \\ \hline \end{array}$	3. $\begin{array}{r}326 \\ -\ 171 \\ \hline \end{array}$	4. $\begin{array}{r}336 \\ -\ 161 \\ \hline \end{array}$	5. $\begin{array}{r}327 \\ -\ 161 \\ \hline \end{array}$
6. $\begin{array}{r}726 \\ -\ 253 \\ \hline \end{array}$	7. $\begin{array}{r}967 \\ -\ 583 \\ \hline \end{array}$	8. $\begin{array}{r}314 \\ -\ \ 80 \\ \hline \end{array}$	9. $\begin{array}{r}427 \\ -\ 192 \\ \hline \end{array}$	10. $\begin{array}{r}713 \\ -\ \ 51 \\ \hline \end{array}$
11. $\begin{array}{r}617 \\ -\ 242 \\ \hline \end{array}$	12. $\begin{array}{r}428 \\ -\ 163 \\ \hline \end{array}$	13. $\begin{array}{r}839 \\ -\ 542 \\ \hline \end{array}$	14. $\begin{array}{r}739 \\ -\ 382 \\ \hline \end{array}$	15. $\begin{array}{r}517 \\ -\ 383 \\ \hline \end{array}$

Trading to Subtract

Write the check.

1. 647   261
   − 261   + 386
    386   647

2. 918
   − 532
    386

3. 423
   − 180
    243

4. 719
   − 242
    477

5. 344
   − 194
    150

Subtract.

6. 836
   − 293

7. 905
   − 342

8. 528
   − 193

9. 628
   − 263

10. 518
   − 172

11. 581
   − 390

12. 238
   − 61

13. 767
   − 83

14. 624
   − 381

15. 446
   − 192

16. 858 − 262
17. 625 − 142
18. 583 − 291
19. 228 − 142

20. 555 − 163
21. 382 − 202
22. 427 − 385
23. 836 − 274

 Calculate

24. Subtract. What pattern do you see? Write the next subtraction problem in the pattern.

    121 − 99
    132 − 99
    143 − 99
    154 − 99

Park Problems

Add or subtract
to solve each problem.

1. Watengo State Park has 347 places to camp. 294 of them are taken. How many are not taken? 53

2. One day 960 people visited the park. 445 of them were children. How many were adults?

3. There are 235 painted picnic tables in the park. There are 187 that need to be painted. How many picnic tables are in the park?

4. There are 231 bicycles to rent in the park. There are 184 canoes to rent. How many bikes and canoes together?

5. One day 180 of the 231 bicycles were rented. How many were not rented?

6. There are 219 adult deer in the park. There are 178 babies. How many more adults are there?

7. One weekend 54 of the 347 places to camp were closed. How many places were open?

8. There are 347 places to camp. 129 are in the woods. How many are not in the woods?

9. On Saturday 347 people went swimming in the lake. On Sunday 272 people went swimming. How many more people went swimming on Saturday?

10. On one weekend 146 people went fishing in the park. The next weekend 86 people went fishing. How many people went fishing?

11. The ranger planted 363 pine trees in the forest. He planted 146 oak trees. How many more pine than oak?

12. In one day, people fishing caught 129 trout and 92 catfish. How many fish in all?

Trading Tens and Hundreds

Not enough ones or tens. You trade two times.

Step 1
Trade 1 ten for 10 ones. Subtract ones.

$$\begin{array}{r} \overset{4\ 16}{3\cancel{5}\cancel{6}} \\ -\ 189 \\ \hline 7 \end{array}$$

Step 2
Trade 1 hundred for 10 tens. Subtract tens. Subtract hundreds.

$$\begin{array}{r} \overset{\ \ \ 14}{\overset{2\ \cancel{4}\ 16}{3\cancel{5}\cancel{6}}} \\ -\ 189 \\ \hline 167 \end{array}$$

Write the check.

1.		2.	3.	4.	5.
813	279	611	924	512	375
− 279	+ 534	− 237	− 576	− 235	− 199
534	813	374	348	277	176

Subtract.

6.	7.	8.	9.	10.
634	847	954	438	713
− 265	− 259	− 475	− 279	− 434

11.	12.	13.	14.	15.
963	812	545	922	411
− 574	− 345	− 286	− 283	− 137

16.	17.	18.	19.	20.
837	935	724	431	862
− 489	− 567	− 267	− 158	− 498

Trading to Subtract.

Subtract. Check by adding.

1.
```
  637     289
- 289   + 348
─────   ─────
  348     637
```

2.
```
  734
- 569
─────
```

3.
```
  326
-  78
─────
```

4.
```
  564
- 189
─────
```

5.
```
  223
-  94
─────
```

Subtract.

6.
```
  847
- 648
─────
```

7.
```
  913
- 278
─────
```

8.
```
  837
-  59
─────
```

9.
```
  652
- 278
─────
```

10.
```
  544
-  79
─────
```

11.
```
  545
- 386
─────
```

12.
```
  726
- 278
─────
```

13.
```
  317
- 258
─────
```

14.
```
  614
- 179
─────
```

15.
```
  723
-  68
─────
```

16. 842 − 166

17. 371 − 80

18. 246 − 195

19. 753 − 54

20. 521 − 342

21. 262 − 86

22. 734 − 573

23. 845 − 68

 Challenge

24. Rachel and Tom are building a brick wall. They have 323 red bricks. They use 238. How many left?

25. Rachel and Tom buy 825 white bricks. They use 635 of them to make a path to their garden. How many white bricks left?

Subtracting with Zeros

Step 1
Look at ones.
Look at tens.

$$
\begin{array}{r} 407 \\ -\ 239 \\ \hline \end{array}
$$

Not enough ones.
You cannot trade
0 tens for ones.

Step 2
Trade 1 hundred
for 10 tens.

$$
\begin{array}{r} {}^{3\ 10}\!\!\!\not{4}\not{0}7 \\ -\ 239 \\ \hline \end{array}
$$

Step 3
Trade 1 ten for 10 ones.
Subtract.

$$
\begin{array}{r} {}^{\ \ \ \ 9}{}_{3\ \not{1}\not{0}17}\!\!\!\not{4}\not{0}\not{7} \\ -\ 239 \\ \hline 168 \end{array}
$$

Subtract. Check the first row by adding.

1. $\begin{array}{r} 708 \\ -\ 299 \\ \hline 409 \end{array}$

2. $\begin{array}{r} 301 \\ -\ 183 \\ \hline \end{array}$

3. $\begin{array}{r} 503 \\ -\ 87 \\ \hline \end{array}$

4. $\begin{array}{r} 600 \\ -\ 134 \\ \hline \end{array}$

5. $\begin{array}{r} 405 \\ -\ 189 \\ \hline \end{array}$

6. $\begin{array}{r} 703 \\ -\ 249 \\ \hline \end{array}$

7. $\begin{array}{r} 607 \\ -\ 198 \\ \hline \end{array}$

8. $\begin{array}{r} 900 \\ -\ 54 \\ \hline \end{array}$

9. $\begin{array}{r} 706 \\ -\ 89 \\ \hline \end{array}$

10. $\begin{array}{r} 500 \\ -\ 63 \\ \hline \end{array}$

11. $\begin{array}{r} 205 \\ -\ 136 \\ \hline \end{array}$

12. $\begin{array}{r} 700 \\ -\ 234 \\ \hline \end{array}$

13. $\begin{array}{r} 800 \\ -\ 618 \\ \hline \end{array}$

14. $\begin{array}{r} 900 \\ -\ 374 \\ \hline \end{array}$

15. $\begin{array}{r} 400 \\ -\ 189 \\ \hline \end{array}$

16. $\begin{array}{r} 309 \\ -\ 74 \\ \hline \end{array}$

17. $\begin{array}{r} 502 \\ -\ 145 \\ \hline \end{array}$

18. $\begin{array}{r} 106 \\ -\ 38 \\ \hline \end{array}$

19. $\begin{array}{r} 610 \\ -\ 202 \\ \hline \end{array}$

20. $\begin{array}{r} 807 \\ -\ 791 \\ \hline \end{array}$

Review (pp. 29–54)

1. $\begin{array}{r} 66 \\ -\ 58 \\ \hline \end{array}$

2. $\begin{array}{r} 52 \\ -\ 34 \\ \hline \end{array}$

3. $\begin{array}{r} 559 \\ -\ 278 \\ \hline \end{array}$

4. $\begin{array}{r} 760 \\ -\ 290 \\ \hline \end{array}$

5. $\begin{array}{r} 810 \\ -\ 241 \\ \hline \end{array}$

Practicing Subtraction

Subtract. Check the first row.

1. 783
    − 251

    532

2. 526
    − 273

3. 871
    − 236

4. 817
    − 493

5. 597
    − 134

6. 934
    − 408

7. 767
    − 213

8. 628
    − 271

9. 781
    − 409

10. 806
     − 370

11. 563
     − 180

12. 873
     − 260

13. 701
     − 280

14. 587
     − 259

15. 614
     − 481

16. 600 − 35

17. 748 − 215

18. 981 − 58

19. 838 − 264

20. 666 − 71

21. 400 − 155

22. 746 − 83

23. 809 − 602

24. 542 − 129

25. 237 − 108

26. 940 − 875

27. 590 − 299

 Challenge

28. Joan Becker has 945 books in her bookstore. She sells 270 of them. How many left?

29. The store has 844 paperback books. 165 are about animals. How many are not about animals?

30. The store had 235 books about sports. Joan ordered 138 more. How many sports books in all?

Marine Animal Problems

Some scientists took a boat trip to count marine animals.
Add or subtract to solve these problems.

1. On the first month of their trip the scientists saw 103 gray whales. The next month they saw 97. How many did they see in all? 200

2. On their first ocean trip, the scientists found 546 starfish. Next time they found 398. How many more did they find the first time?

3. On one week the scientists saw 37 seals. The next week they saw 108. How many did they see in all?

4. The scientists counted 149 pelicans and 357 seagulls. How many more seagulls than pelicans?

5. In one day, the scientists counted 139 dolphins and 438 tuna. How many more tuna than dolphins?

6. During the whole trip the scientists saw 203 gray whales and 109 blue whales. How many did they see altogether?

Subtracting Thousands

You trade three times.

Step 1
Trade. Subtract ones.
Trade. Subtract tens.

$$\begin{array}{r} \overset{\overset{13}{7\,\cancel{3}11}}{48\cancel{4}\cancel{1}} \\ -\ 2969 \\ \hline 72 \end{array}$$

Step 2
Trade.
Subtract hundreds.
Subtract thousands.

$$\begin{array}{r} \overset{\overset{17\ 13}{3\,\cancel{7}\,\cancel{3}11}}{\cancel{4}8\cancel{4}\cancel{1}} \\ -\ 2969 \\ \hline 1872 \end{array}$$

Subtract. Check the first row of problems.

1.   8201
  − 3518
    4683
	2. 9523
	  − 6784
		3. 8200
		  − 4728
			4. 5303
			  − 2759
				5. 6452
				  − 1653

6.   7215
  − 2486
	7. 3304
	  − 1507
		8. 6100
		  − 3585
			9. 8606
			  − 1789
				10. 9250
				  − 6465

11.   5330
  − 463
	12. 8405
	  − 1606
		13. 3400
		  − 455
			14. 7664
			  − 5788
				15. 9432
				  − 3649

Write in a column. Subtract.

16. 3417 − 1394

17. 1600 − 185

18. 4803 − 2495

19. 2634 − 1875

20. 8200 − 624

21. 9001 − 6172

Adding and Subtracting Money

$2.84

$$
\begin{array}{r} \$5.00 \\ -\ 2.84 \\ \hline \end{array}
$$

$$
\begin{array}{r} {}^{9} \\ {}^{4\ \cancel{10}\ 10} \\ \$\cancel{5}.\cancel{0}\cancel{0} \\ -\ 2.84 \\ \hline \$2.16 \end{array}
$$

Add or subtract. Remember to use $ and . in your answer.

1. $4.25
   − 1.08
   $3.17

2. $6.73
   + 2.91

3. $3.45
   + 1.89

4. $5.00
   − 2.98

5. $2.83
   − 0.72

6. $8.70
   + 3.47

7. $7.00
   − 3.29

8. $6.15
   + 3.80

9. $8.35
   + 4.76

10. $5.29
    − 3.08

11. $5.82
    + 3.57

12. $6.17
    − 4.89

13. $9.47
    + 0.60

14. $6.07
    − 2.89

15. $8.00
    − 7.35

16. Suki has a stamp collection. She pays $2.89 for some stamps from South America and $3.49 for some stamps from Africa. How much does she pay in all?

17. Carlos has $4.56 to spend on stamps. He pays $3.05. How much does he have left?

18. Sandra buys stamps for $3.79 and gives the clerk $5.00. How much change does she get?

Letter Sums

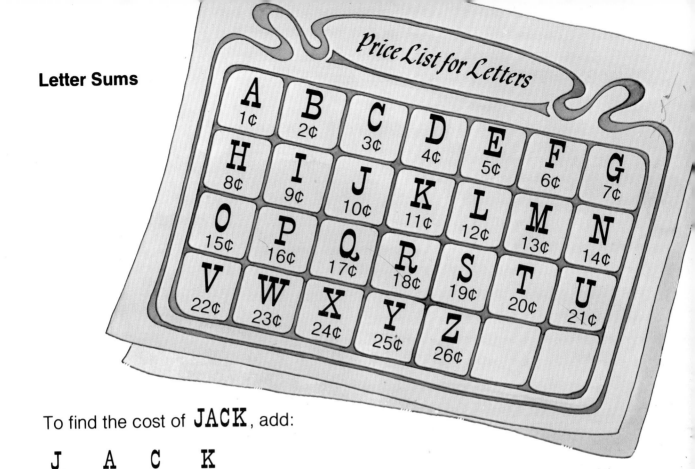

Price List for Letters

A 1¢	B 2¢	C 3¢	D 4¢	E 5¢	F 6¢	G 7¢
H 8¢	I 9¢	J 10¢	K 11¢	L 12¢	M 13¢	N 14¢
O 15¢	P 16¢	Q 17¢	R 18¢	S 19¢	T 20¢	U 21¢
V 22¢	W 23¢	X 24¢	Y 25¢	Z 26¢		

To find the cost of **JACK**, add:

J   A   C   K
10¢ + 1¢ + 3¢ + 11¢ = 25¢

Find the cost of each.

1. **READING**   58¢
2. **MUSIC**
3. **SCIENCE**
4. **BROWN**
5. **YELLOW**
6. **PURPLE**
7. **TIGER**
8. **ELEPHANT**
9. **GIRAFFE**

Which costs more?

10. **MATH** or **READING**
11. **TEXAS** or **MAINE**
12. **HOCKEY** or **BASEBALL**
13. **LEMON** or **GRAPE**

Toy Store Problems

Kite
$1.75

Ball
$0.58

Book
$2.65

Jump rope
$0.95

Bear
$4.25

Model car
$2.35

Use the price tags on the toys. Add or subtract.

1. How much more does a bear cost than a kite? $2.50

2. Beth buys a kite and a book. How much does she spend?

3. Mark buys a ball and a yo-yo. How much does he spend?

4. Ted has $3.00. He buys a kite. How much does he have left?

5. Ann buys a model car, a book, and a kite. How much does she spend?

6. Andrew buys a bear, a book, and a kite. How much does he spend?

Paint set $5.50

Yo-yo $1.49

7. Sara has $2.00. Which toy can she buy and have $0.25 left?

8. Mark has $3.00. What toy can he buy and have $0.65 left?

9. Rose has $5.00. What toy can she buy and have $3.51 left?

10. Tim has $4.75. What toy can he buy and have $3.00 left?

11. Bob has $2.00 and wants to buy a paint set. How much more money does he need?

12. Pam has $1.50 and wants to buy a book. How much more money does she need?

Chapter Review

Add.   (ex. 1–10: p. 30),   (ex. 11–15: p. 33),
      (ex. 16–18: p. 35),   (ex. 19, 20: p. 38)

1.   73
  + 48

2.   99
  + 42

3.   58
  + 34

4.   87
  + 35

5.   77
  + 23

6.   44
  + 46

7.   51
  + 29

8.   35
  + 25

9.   48
  + 17

10.   56
  + 29

11.   293
    162
  + 341

12.   82
   372
  + 465

13.   453
    81
  + 235

14.   25
   30
  + 843

15.   94
  263
  + 472

16.   489
  + 457

17.   569
  + 473

18.   605
  + 197

19.   4459
  + 2587

20.   2778
  +   367

Subtract.   (ex. 21–24: p. 45),   (ex. 25, 26: p. 48),
         (ex. 27–29: p. 52),   (ex. 30–32: p. 54),   (ex. 33–38: p. 57)

21.   73
  − 48

22.   90
  − 42

23.   63
  −   8

24.   84
  − 35

25.   747
  − 352

26.   639
  − 493

27.   945
  − 576

28.   734
  − 467

29.   725
  − 197

30.   600
  − 245

31.   700
  − 476

32.   520
  − 364

33.   3145
  − 1286

34.   4324
  − 2267

35.   2334
  −   567

36. $4200 - 285$

37. $3315 - 2406$

38. $6479 - 3491$

Chapter Test

Add.

1. $\begin{array}{r} 37 \\ + 48 \\ \hline \end{array}$	**2.** $\begin{array}{r} 57 \\ + 34 \\ \hline \end{array}$	**3.** $\begin{array}{r} 89 \\ + 39 \\ \hline \end{array}$	**4.** $\begin{array}{r} 48 \\ + 41 \\ \hline \end{array}$	**5.** $\begin{array}{r} 41 \\ + 59 \\ \hline \end{array}$
6. $\begin{array}{r} 26 \\ + 44 \\ \hline \end{array}$	**7.** $\begin{array}{r} 85 \\ + 67 \\ \hline \end{array}$	**8.** $\begin{array}{r} 73 \\ + 38 \\ \hline \end{array}$	**9.** $\begin{array}{r} 69 \\ + 15 \\ \hline \end{array}$	**10.** $\begin{array}{r} 58 \\ + 66 \\ \hline \end{array}$
11. $\begin{array}{r} 437 \\ + 359 \\ \hline \end{array}$	**12.** $\begin{array}{r} 419 \\ + 342 \\ \hline \end{array}$	**13.** $\begin{array}{r} 464 \\ + 283 \\ \hline \end{array}$	**14.** $\begin{array}{r} 6913 \\ + 479 \\ \hline \end{array}$	**15.** $\begin{array}{r} 3894 \\ + 1486 \\ \hline \end{array}$
16. $\begin{array}{r} 76 \\ 489 \\ + 326 \\ \hline \end{array}$	**17.** $\begin{array}{r} 278 \\ 435 \\ + 376 \\ \hline \end{array}$	**18.** $\begin{array}{r} 679 \\ 97 \\ + 168 \\ \hline \end{array}$	**19.** $\begin{array}{r} 65 \\ 79 \\ + 859 \\ \hline \end{array}$	**20.** $\begin{array}{r} 137 \\ 18 \\ + 274 \\ \hline \end{array}$

Subtract.

21. $\begin{array}{r} 64 \\ - 16 \\ \hline \end{array}$	**22.** $\begin{array}{r} 70 \\ - 34 \\ \hline \end{array}$	**23.** $\begin{array}{r} 35 \\ - 19 \\ \hline \end{array}$	**24.** $\begin{array}{r} 67 \\ - 29 \\ \hline \end{array}$	**25.** $\begin{array}{r} 80 \\ - 34 \\ \hline \end{array}$
26. $\begin{array}{r} 853 \\ - 749 \\ \hline \end{array}$	**27.** $\begin{array}{r} 800 \\ - 567 \\ \hline \end{array}$	**28.** $\begin{array}{r} 742 \\ - 637 \\ \hline \end{array}$	**29.** $\begin{array}{r} 4737 \\ - 2389 \\ \hline \end{array}$	**30.** $\begin{array}{r} 6885 \\ - 3457 \\ \hline \end{array}$

Brush Up

Add or subtract.

1. $5 + 6$ 2. $13 - 5$ 3. $9 + 9$ 4. $8 + 7$

5. $14 - 5$ 6. $8 + 4$ 7. $14 - 7$ 8. $15 - 7$

9. $5 + 8$ 10. $14 - 8$ 11. $7 + 2$ 12. $5 + 9$

13. $17 - 8$ 14. $6 + 6$ 15. $16 - 8$ 16. $13 - 7$

17. $4 + 7$ 18. $18 - 9$ 19. $17 - 9$ 20. $16 - 7$

21.
$$\begin{array}{r} 23 \\ + 81 \\ \hline \end{array}$$
22.
$$\begin{array}{r} 45 \\ + 17 \\ \hline \end{array}$$
23.
$$\begin{array}{r} 88 \\ + 61 \\ \hline \end{array}$$
24.
$$\begin{array}{r} 72 \\ + 89 \\ \hline \end{array}$$
25.
$$\begin{array}{r} 91 \\ + 13 \\ \hline \end{array}$$

26.
$$\begin{array}{r} 65 \\ - 32 \\ \hline \end{array}$$
27.
$$\begin{array}{r} 93 \\ - 16 \\ \hline \end{array}$$
28.
$$\begin{array}{r} 44 \\ - 27 \\ \hline \end{array}$$
29.
$$\begin{array}{r} 27 \\ - 15 \\ \hline \end{array}$$
30.
$$\begin{array}{r} 81 \\ - 28 \\ \hline \end{array}$$

31.
$$\begin{array}{r} 65 \\ 31 \\ + 14 \\ \hline \end{array}$$
32.
$$\begin{array}{r} 14 \\ 61 \\ + 23 \\ \hline \end{array}$$
33.
$$\begin{array}{r} 23 \\ 14 \\ + 9 \\ \hline \end{array}$$
34.
$$\begin{array}{r} 82 \\ 8 \\ + 72 \\ \hline \end{array}$$
35.
$$\begin{array}{r} 61 \\ 56 \\ + 43 \\ \hline \end{array}$$

36.
$$\begin{array}{r} 307 \\ + 116 \\ \hline \end{array}$$
37.
$$\begin{array}{r} 421 \\ + 153 \\ \hline \end{array}$$
38.
$$\begin{array}{r} 683 \\ + 135 \\ \hline \end{array}$$
39.
$$\begin{array}{r} 492 \\ + 166 \\ \hline \end{array}$$
40.
$$\begin{array}{r} 881 \\ + 229 \\ \hline \end{array}$$

41.
$$\begin{array}{r} 734 \\ - 602 \\ \hline \end{array}$$
42.
$$\begin{array}{r} 567 \\ - 138 \\ \hline \end{array}$$
43.
$$\begin{array}{r} 921 \\ - 290 \\ \hline \end{array}$$
44.
$$\begin{array}{r} 885 \\ - 198 \\ \hline \end{array}$$
45.
$$\begin{array}{r} 306 \\ - 57 \\ \hline \end{array}$$

46.
$$\begin{array}{r} 4718 \\ - 1129 \\ \hline \end{array}$$
47.
$$\begin{array}{r} 5613 \\ - 1943 \\ \hline \end{array}$$
48.
$$\begin{array}{r} 4182 \\ - 1016 \\ \hline \end{array}$$
49.
$$\begin{array}{r} 9713 \\ - 2081 \\ \hline \end{array}$$
50.
$$\begin{array}{r} 8460 \\ - 7580 \\ \hline \end{array}$$

CHAPTER 3

Multiplication

Using Multiplication at Work

Gail Mayes owns a nursery. She often uses
multiplication when filling orders. This customer
wants 4 plants. Each plant costs $7. Gail multiplies
4 times $7 to find the total cost. The total cost of
the plants is $28.

Adding and Multiplying

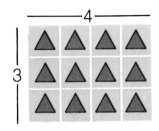

——4——

3

addition problem	multiplication fact

```
      4
      4          4  factor
    + 4        × 3  factor
    ────       ────
     12         12   product
```

**Write an addition problem and a multiplication fact
for each drawing.**

1. ——2——

4

```
    2
    2
    2      2
  + 2    × 4
  ───    ───
    8      8
```

2. ———————9———————

3

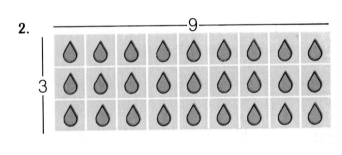

3. ——————5——————

5

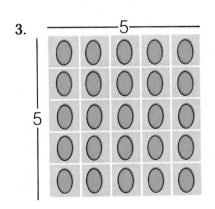

4. ——4——

6

5. —2—

2

6. ——3——

2

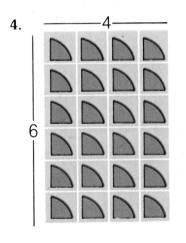

Picture Problems

On a piece of paper, copy and complete each drawing.
Write a multiplication fact.

1. Draw 4 apples in each row.
   Make 3 rows of apples.

$$\begin{array}{r} 4 \\ \times\ 3 \\ \hline 12 \end{array}$$

2. Draw 2 boxes.
   Put 6 hearts in each box.

3. Draw 8 stars in each row.
   Make 3 rows of stars.

4. Draw 3 boxes.
   Put 5 flowers in each box.

5. Draw 5 rings.
   Put 4 fish in each ring.

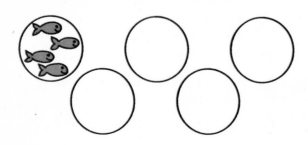

6. Draw 2 moons
   in each row.
   Make 7 rows
   of moons.

Deciding When to Multiply

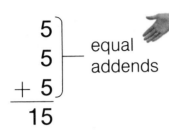

Equal addends may become multiplication facts.

$$
\begin{array}{r}
5 \\
5 \\
+\ 5 \\
\hline
15
\end{array}
\left.\vphantom{\begin{array}{c}5\\5\\5\end{array}}\right\}
\begin{array}{l}\text{equal}\\\text{addends}\end{array}
$$

$$
\begin{array}{r}
5 \\
\times\ 3 \\
\hline
15
\end{array}
$$

You cannot make a multiplication fact if addends are not equal.

$$
\begin{array}{r}
7 \\
6 \\
+\ 4 \\
\hline
17
\end{array}
\left.\vphantom{\begin{array}{c}7\\6\\4\end{array}}\right\}
\begin{array}{l}\text{not equal}\\\text{addends}\end{array}
$$

Find the sums.
Write a multiplication fact if you can.

1.
$$
\begin{array}{r}
4 \\
4 \\
+\ 4 \\
\hline
12
\end{array}
\qquad
\begin{array}{r}
4 \\
\times\ 3 \\
\hline
12
\end{array}
$$

2.
$$
\begin{array}{r}
5 \\
3 \\
+\ 4 \\
\hline
\end{array}
$$

3.
$$
\begin{array}{r}
6 \\
6 \\
6 \\
+\ 6 \\
\hline
\end{array}
$$

4.
$$
\begin{array}{r}
7 \\
8 \\
+\ 2 \\
\hline
\end{array}
$$

5.
$$
\begin{array}{r}
2 \\
2 \\
2 \\
2 \\
+\ 2 \\
\hline
\end{array}
$$

6.
$$
\begin{array}{r}
6 \\
3 \\
+\ 9 \\
\hline
\end{array}
$$

7.
$$
\begin{array}{r}
5 \\
5 \\
5 \\
+\ 5 \\
\hline
\end{array}
$$

8.
$$
\begin{array}{r}
7 \\
7 \\
7 \\
+\ 7 \\
\hline
\end{array}
$$

9.
$$
\begin{array}{r}
8 \\
3 \\
+\ 7 \\
\hline
\end{array}
$$

10.
$$
\begin{array}{r}
0 \\
0 \\
0 \\
0 \\
0 \\
+\ 0 \\
\hline
\end{array}
$$

11.
$$
\begin{array}{r}
4 \\
3 \\
5 \\
+\ 2 \\
\hline
\end{array}
$$

12. $8 + 2 + 4 + 4$

13. $3 + 3 + 3 + 3$

14. $5 + 5 + 1$

15. $8 + 8 + 8$

16. $9 + 9 + 1 + 9$

17. $1 + 1 + 1 + 1 + 1$

Multiplication Facts for 2 and 5

You can write two facts for each drawing.

———3———

$2 \times 3 = 6$
$3 \times 2 = 6$

———5———

$2 \times 5 = 10$
$5 \times 2 = 10$

Write two multiplication facts for each drawing.

1. ———6———

$2 \times 6 = 12, \quad 6 \times 2 = 12$

2. ———9———

3. ———5———

Multiply. Make drawings if you need help.

4.	5.	6.	7.	8.	9.	10.
5	2	2	5	2	5	8
$\times 4$	$\times 7$	$\times 5$	$\times 6$	$\times 9$	$\times 8$	$\times 2$
20						

11. 2×3 12. 5×9 13. 4×2 14. 7×5 15. 9×5

16. 5×5 17. 6×2 18. 5×3 19. 5×8 20. 7×2

Multiplying by 2 and 5

Write a multiplication fact for each product.
Use 2 or 5 as one of the factors.

1. 18 $2 \times 9 = 18$ 2. 2   3. 30   4. 8   5. 40

6. 45   7. 14   8. 10   9. 16   10. 35   11. 12

12. 20   13. 6   14. 15   15. 25   16. 4   17. 5

Multiply to find the answers.

18. There are 5 bananas in a bunch.
How many bananas in 2 bunches?

19. There are 5 peaches in each can.
How many peaches in 5 cans?

20. There are 7 apples in a pie.
How many apples in 2 pies?

21. Oranges come 8 in a bag.
How many oranges in 5 bags?

 Calculate

Make a guess and check it.

22. Is the product of $5 \times 5 \times 5 \times 5 \times 5 \times 5$
about 1000, about 10,000, or about 100,000?
How close was your guess?

Multiplication Facts for 3 and 4

Write two multiplication facts for each drawing.

1. ──────4──────

2 | [diamond shapes in 2 rows of 4]

$2 \times 4 = 8$
$4 \times 2 = 8$

2. ──────3──────

5 |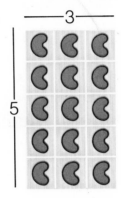

3. ──────4──────

5 |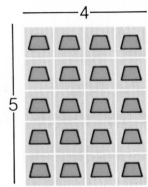

Multiply. Make drawings if you need help.

4.	5.	6.	7.	8.	9.	10.
3	4	3	4	3	3	4
$\times 6$	$\times 3$	$\times 7$	$\times 8$	$\times 8$	$\times 9$	$\times 1$
18						

11.	12.	13.	14.	15.	16.	17.
4	3	1	3	4	3	4
$\times 9$	$\times 2$	$\times 3$	$\times 5$	$\times 7$	$\times 6$	$\times 4$

18. 5×4 19. 6×4 20. 4×2 21. 8×3 22. 3×8

23. 3×9 24. 3×3 25. 3×6 26. 4×5 27. 7×3

 Challenge

Complete the facts.

28. $3 \times ? = 18$ 29. $4 \times ? = 32$ 30. $4 \times ? = 24$ 31. $3 \times ? = 24$

32. $? \times 3 = 27$ 33. $? \times 4 = 20$ 34. $? \times 4 = 36$ 35. $? \times 3 = 15$

Multiplying by 3, 4, and 5

Write a multiplication fact for each product.
Use 3, 4, or 5 as one of the factors.

1. 24 $8 \times 3 = 24$ 2. 6   3. 3   4. 20   5. 36

6. 21   7. 8   8. 27   9. 15   10. 28   11. 40

12. 9   13. 4   14. 18   15. 24   16. 12   17. 32

Write your answers.

18. Count by 4 from 8 to 36.   8, 12, 16, 20, 24, 28, 32, 36

19. Count by 2 from 4 to 18.   20. Count by 3 from 6 to 27.

 Review   (pp. 67–73)

1. 2   2. 5   3. 3   4. 8   5. 3   6. 9   7. 6
   $\times 8$ $\times 6$ $\times 7$ $\times 4$ $\times 9$ $\times 2$ $\times 3$

8. 9   9. 2   10. 3   11. 9   12. 8   13. 4   14. 5
   $\times 4$ $\times 7$ $\times 8$ $\times 3$ $\times 5$ $\times 7$ $\times 9$

1 and 0 as Factors

If one factor is 1, the product
is the same as the other factor.

$$\begin{array}{r} 1 \\ \times\ 9 \\ \hline 9 \end{array} \qquad \begin{array}{r} 26 \\ \times\ 1 \\ \hline 26 \end{array}$$

If zero is a factor,
the product is zero.

$$\begin{array}{r} 0 \\ \times\ 2 \\ \hline 0 \end{array} \qquad \begin{array}{r} 54 \\ \times\ 0 \\ \hline 0 \end{array}$$

Multiply.

1. $\begin{array}{r} 7 \\ \times\ 1 \\ \hline 7 \end{array}$
2. $\begin{array}{r} 0 \\ \times\ 4 \\ \hline \end{array}$
3. $\begin{array}{r} 45 \\ \times\ 1 \\ \hline \end{array}$
4. $\begin{array}{r} 27 \\ \times\ 0 \\ \hline \end{array}$
5. $\begin{array}{r} 23 \\ \times\ 1 \\ \hline \end{array}$

6. $\begin{array}{r} 60 \\ \times\ 0 \\ \hline \end{array}$
7. $\begin{array}{r} 34 \\ \times\ 0 \\ \hline \end{array}$
8. $\begin{array}{r} 75 \\ \times\ 0 \\ \hline \end{array}$
9. $\begin{array}{r} 99 \\ \times\ 1 \\ \hline \end{array}$
10. $\begin{array}{r} 81 \\ \times\ 0 \\ \hline \end{array}$

11. 8×1
12. 5×0
13. 40×1
14. 7×0
15. 8×1

16. 9×0
17. 4×1
18. 13×1
19. 6×0
20. 90×1

21. There are 3 packages. There are 0 seeds in
    each package. How many seeds in all?

Using 10 as a Factor

1 ten	2 tens	3 tens	4 tens	5 tens	6 tens	7 tens	8 tens	9 tens
10	20	30	40	50	60	70	80	90

3 tens equal **30**.

$3 \times 10 = 30$

Write a multiplication fact for each.

1. 7 tens $7 \times 10 = 70$ **2.** 3 tens   **3.** 9 tens   **4.** 1 ten

5. 2 tens   **6.** 8 tens   **7.** 4 tens   **8.** 6 tens   **9.** 5 tens

Multiply.

10.   1 $\times\ 10$

11.   10 $\times\ 3$

12.   10 $\times\ 7$

13.   10 $\times\ 8$

14.   10 $\times\ 5$

15.   10 $\times\ 6$

16.   10 $\times\ 2$

17.   10 $\times\ 9$

18.   10 $\times\ 4$

19.   10 $\times\ 0$

20. 6×10 **21.** 9×10 **22.** 10×4 **23.** 8×10 **24.** 0×10

25. 5×10 **26.** 3×10 **27.** 2×10 **28.** 4×10 **29.** 7×10

Sports Problems

1. There are 9 players on a baseball team. How many players on 3 teams? 27

2. There are 5 players on a basketball team. How many players on 7 teams?

3. There are 8 people on each swim team at the East Side Pool. How many people on 4 teams?

4. The baseball team plays 3 games each week. How many games do they play in 4 weeks?

5. A football team gets 6 points for each touchdown. How many points for 3 touchdowns?

6. A basketball team gets 2 points for each basket. How many points for 5 baskets?

7. The volleyball team practices 4 hours a week. How many hours do they practice in 9 weeks?

8. The soccer team plays 2 games each week. How many games do they play in 9 weeks?

9. Hockey sticks costs $4 each. How much for 7 hockey sticks?

10. There are 5 swimmers on each swim team. How many swimmers on 6 teams?

11. It takes 3 minutes to run around the track. How many minutes does it take to run around the track 7 times?

12. The tennis team practices 5 hours a week. How many hours do they practice in 8 weeks?

Switching Factors

The factors are 2 and 6.
The product is 12.

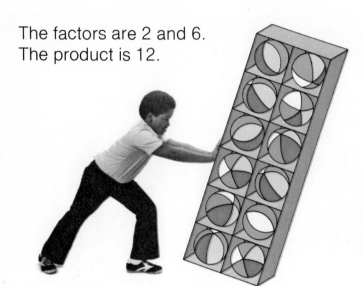

$6 \times 2 = 12$

$2 \times 6 = 12$

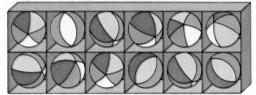

Write two facts for each drawing.

1.

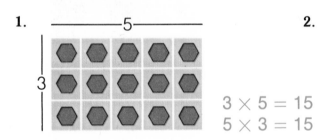

$3 \times 5 = 15$
$5 \times 3 = 15$

2.

3.

Write two facts for each pair of factors.

4. 5, 6 $6 \times 5 = 30$
        $5 \times 6 = 30$

5. 3, 7

6. 4, 8

7. 4, 6

8. 4, 9

9. 2, 9

10. 3, 8

11. 4, 7

12. 3, 4

13. 1, 5

14. 2, 6

15. 5, 9

16. 2, 4

17. 5, 7

Multiplying by 6

Put the edge of a ruler along each dotted line. Complete a multiplication fact for the drawing above the ruler.

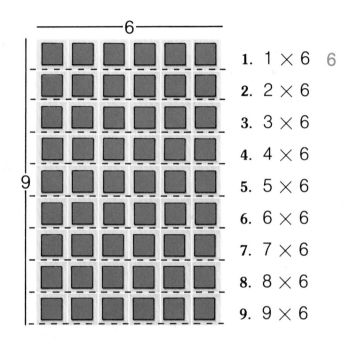

1. 1 × 6   6
2. 2 × 6
3. 3 × 6
4. 4 × 6
5. 5 × 6
6. 6 × 6
7. 7 × 6
8. 8 × 6
9. 9 × 6

1 × 6 = 6

Find the products.

10.	11.	12.	13.	14.	15.	16.
6	6	3	6	6	6	6
× 3	× 7	× 6	× 1	× 4	× 9	× 0
18						

17.	18.	19.	20.	21.	22.	23.
6	4	6	5	6	6	7
× 5	× 6	× 8	× 6	× 2	× 6	× 6

24. 7 × 6   25. 8 × 6   26. 9 × 6   27. 6 × 3   28. 5 × 6

29. 0 × 6   30. 6 × 4   31. 6 × 7   32. 2 × 6   33. 6 × 6

Multiplying by 7

Put the edge of a ruler along each dotted line. Complete a fact for the drawing above the ruler.

$1 \times 7 = 7$

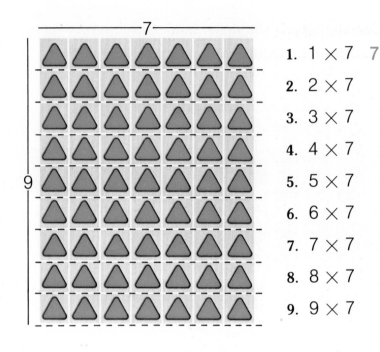

1. 1×7 7
2. 2×7
3. 3×7
4. 4×7
5. 5×7
6. 6×7
7. 7×7
8. 8×7
9. 9×7

Find the products.

10.	11.	12.	13.	14.	15.	16.
7 $\times 3$ 21	7 $\times 7$	4 $\times 7$	7 $\times 1$	7 $\times 4$	7 $\times 9$	8 $\times 7$

17.	18.	19.	20.	21.	22.	23.
7 $\times 5$	0 $\times 7$	7 $\times 8$	6 $\times 7$	7 $\times 2$	3 $\times 7$	5 $\times 7$

 Challenge

24. Joanne buys 3 chemistry kits. Each chemistry kit has 7 test tubes. How many test tubes in all?

25. Richard needs 5 liters of water for each experiment. How many liters does he need for 7 experiments?

Multiplying by 8

Complete each multiplication fact.

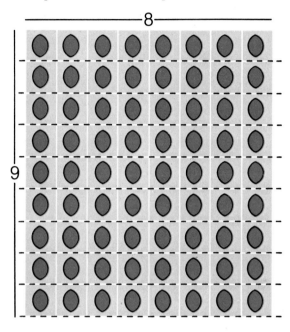

$1 \times 8 = 8$

1. 1×8 8
2. 2×8
3. 3×8
4. 4×8
5. 5×8
6. 6×8
7. 7×8
8. 8×8
9. 9×8

Find the products.

10. $\begin{array}{r} 8 \\ \times 5 \\ \hline 40 \end{array}$
11. $\begin{array}{r} 4 \\ \times 8 \\ \hline \end{array}$
12. $\begin{array}{r} 0 \\ \times 8 \\ \hline \end{array}$
13. $\begin{array}{r} 8 \\ \times 6 \\ \hline \end{array}$
14. $\begin{array}{r} 2 \\ \times 8 \\ \hline \end{array}$
15. $\begin{array}{r} 8 \\ \times 9 \\ \hline \end{array}$
16. $\begin{array}{r} 7 \\ \times 8 \\ \hline \end{array}$

17. $\begin{array}{r} 8 \\ \times 1 \\ \hline \end{array}$
18. $\begin{array}{r} 8 \\ \times 2 \\ \hline \end{array}$
19. $\begin{array}{r} 5 \\ \times 8 \\ \hline \end{array}$
20. $\begin{array}{r} 8 \\ \times 7 \\ \hline \end{array}$
21. $\begin{array}{r} 8 \\ \times 8 \\ \hline \end{array}$
22. $\begin{array}{r} 8 \\ \times 4 \\ \hline \end{array}$
23. $\begin{array}{r} 8 \\ \times 3 \\ \hline \end{array}$

24. 7×8 25. 5×8 26. 2×8 27. 4×8 28. 9×8

Write your answers.

29. Count by 7 from 14 to 63.   30. Count by 8 from 8 to 64.

Multiplying by 9

Complete each fact.
Use the drawing
if you need help.

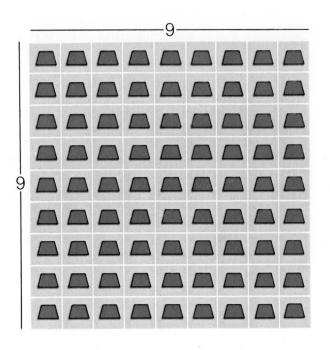

1. 1×9 9

2. 2×9 3. 3×9

4. 4×9 5. 5×9

6. 6×9 7. 7×9

8. 8×9 9. 9×9

Find the products.

10. $\begin{array}{r} 9 \\ \times 3 \\ \hline 27 \end{array}$
11. $\begin{array}{r} 9 \\ \times 7 \\ \hline \end{array}$
12. $\begin{array}{r} 9 \\ \times 1 \\ \hline \end{array}$
13. $\begin{array}{r} 6 \\ \times 9 \\ \hline \end{array}$
14. $\begin{array}{r} 9 \\ \times 0 \\ \hline \end{array}$
15. $\begin{array}{r} 9 \\ \times 9 \\ \hline \end{array}$
16. $\begin{array}{r} 9 \\ \times 4 \\ \hline \end{array}$

17. $\begin{array}{r} 9 \\ \times 5 \\ \hline \end{array}$
18. $\begin{array}{r} 9 \\ \times 8 \\ \hline \end{array}$
19. $\begin{array}{r} 4 \\ \times 9 \\ \hline \end{array}$
20. $\begin{array}{r} 5 \\ \times 9 \\ \hline \end{array}$
21. $\begin{array}{r} 9 \\ \times 2 \\ \hline \end{array}$
22. $\begin{array}{r} 9 \\ \times 6 \\ \hline \end{array}$
23. $\begin{array}{r} 7 \\ \times 9 \\ \hline \end{array}$

24. 8×9 25. 9×5 26. 9×9 27. 7×9 28. 6×9

Review   (pp. 67–82)

1. $\begin{array}{r} 6 \\ \times 7 \\ \hline \end{array}$
2. $\begin{array}{r} 8 \\ \times 9 \\ \hline \end{array}$
3. $\begin{array}{r} 4 \\ \times 6 \\ \hline \end{array}$
4. $\begin{array}{r} 7 \\ \times 8 \\ \hline \end{array}$
5. $\begin{array}{r} 3 \\ \times 9 \\ \hline \end{array}$
6. $\begin{array}{r} 5 \\ \times 7 \\ \hline \end{array}$
7. $\begin{array}{r} 9 \\ \times 6 \\ \hline \end{array}$

Practicing Multiplication

× 6	
2	**12**
6	**36**
8	**48**
9	**54**

The rule is multiply by 6.

$2 \times 6 = 12$

$6 \times 6 = 36$

$8 \times 6 = 48$

$9 \times 6 = 54$

Multiply. Write the missing numbers.

1.

× 7	
2	14
3	
4	
6	
7	
9	

2.

× 6	
3	
5	
6	
7	
8	
9	

3.

× 8	
1	
2	
4	
5	
6	
8	

4.

× 9	
0	
3	
4	
7	
8	
9	

 Calculate

Add and then multiply.

Remember ( ) mean **Do me first.**

5. $4 \times (5 + 3)$

6. $7 \times (2 + 7)$

7. $5 \times (4 + 2)$

8. $(6 + 3) \times 8$

9. $(2 + 3) \times 9$

10. $(3 + 5) \times 6$

Using Addition Patterns

5 × 7 is the sum of
2 × 7 and 3 × 7.

2 sevens	14	2 × 7 = 14
+ 3 sevens	+ 21	3 × 7 = 21
5 sevens	35	5 × 7 = 35

Find these products.

1. 3 × 5 15   2. 3 × 6   3. 3 × 7   4. 3 × 8   5. 3 × 9

6. 4 × 5   7. 4 × 6   8. 4 × 7   9. 4 × 8   10. 4 × 9

11. 5 × 5   12. 5 × 6   13. 5 × 7   14. 5 × 8   15. 5 × 9

Write the answers to these.

16a.	3 sixes	16b.	18		17a.	3 eights	17b.	24
	+ 3 sixes		+ 18			+ 3 eights		+ 24
	6 sixes							

18a.	3 sevens	18b.	21		19a.	3 nines	19b.	27
	+ 4 sevens		+ 28			+ 4 nines		+ 36

20a.	3 fives	20b.	15		21a.	2 sixes	21b.	12
	+ 5 fives		+ 25			+ 7 sixes		+ 42

22a.	6 nines	22b.	54		23a.	4 sevens	23b.	28
	+ 3 nines		+ 27			+ 4 sevens		+ 28

Spaghetti Dinner

1. Each guest eats 3 meatballs. How many meatballs will 9 guests eat? 27

2. One can of tomato sauce is enough for 5 people. How many people will 7 cans serve?

3. One package of noodles serves 2 people. How many people will 4 packages serve?

4. There are 8 mushrooms in each serving. How many mushrooms are needed for 8 servings?

5. 9 pats of butter are needed for one large loaf of bread. How many pats are needed for 4 loaves?

6. There are 7 olives in each salad. How many olives in 7 salads?

7. Each guest eats 4 dinner rolls. How many dinner rolls will 5 guests eat?

 Challenge

8. It takes 3 minutes to grate enough cheese for 4 people. How many minutes would it take to grate enough cheese for 12 people?

Using a Multiplication Table

×	0	1	2	3	4	5	6	7	8	9	10
0	0										
1	0	1									
2	0	2	4								
3	0	3	6	9							
4	0	4	8	12	16						
5	0	5	10	15	20	25					
6	0	6	12	18	24	30	36				
7	0	7	14	21	28	35	42	49			
8	0	8	16	24	32	40	48	56	64		
9	0	9	18	27	36	45	54	63	72	81	
10	0	10	20	30	40	50	60	70	80	90	100

Write as many different facts as you can for each product.

1. 36 $6 \times 6 = 36$, $9 \times 4 = 36$ 2. 12   3. 24   4. 18

5. 49   6. 64   7. 81   8. 27   9. 20   10. 56   11. 35

12. 18   13. 40   14. 28   15. 54   16. 72   17. 60   18. 56

 Challenge

19. Copy and complete the table above. Can you find a pattern?

RING THE FACTORS

A game for one player.

Get ready:
Copy the products and factors boards below.

To play:
Make a ring around a pair of factors for each product. The factors must be next to each other like this ⬛⬛, this 🄳, or this ⬛. Cross out each product when you ring its factors. You may ring a factor twice.

Products: 9, 49, 56, 18

Factors:

8	7	3
7	4	3
3	7	6

Products: 0, 32, 12, 24

Factors:

2	4	0
8	3	6
5	4	3

Products: 27, 18, 5, 54

Factors:

1	5	3
2	9	6
3	4	2

Products: 14, 35, 24, 63

Factors:

7	9	7
2	5	6
3	8	3

Chapter Review

Find the missing numbers.   (ex. 1, 2: p. 68)

1a. $7 + 7 + 7 + 7 = \boxed{?}$
  b. $4 \times 7 = \boxed{?}$

2. Draw 9 circles in a row.
   Make 7 rows.
   $7 \times 9 = \boxed{?}$

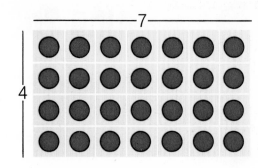

Multiply.   (ex. 3–9: p. 70), (ex. 10–16: p. 72),
(ex. 17–19: p. 74), (ex. 20, 21: p. 75)

3. $\begin{array}{r} 2 \\ \times\,8 \\ \hline \end{array}$ **4.** $\begin{array}{r} 9 \\ \times\,2 \\ \hline \end{array}$ **5.** $\begin{array}{r} 2 \\ \times\,7 \\ \hline \end{array}$ **6.** $\begin{array}{r} 3 \\ \times\,5 \\ \hline \end{array}$ **7.** $\begin{array}{r} 7 \\ \times\,5 \\ \hline \end{array}$ **8.** $\begin{array}{r} 5 \\ \times\,9 \\ \hline \end{array}$ **9.** $\begin{array}{r} 5 \\ \times\,5 \\ \hline \end{array}$

10. $\begin{array}{r} 3 \\ \times\,6 \\ \hline \end{array}$ **11.** $\begin{array}{r} 4 \\ \times\,4 \\ \hline \end{array}$ **12.** $\begin{array}{r} 4 \\ \times\,8 \\ \hline \end{array}$ **13.** $\begin{array}{r} 7 \\ \times\,3 \\ \hline \end{array}$ **14.** $\begin{array}{r} 4 \\ \times\,7 \\ \hline \end{array}$ **15.** $\begin{array}{r} 3 \\ \times\,8 \\ \hline \end{array}$ **16.** $\begin{array}{r} 4 \\ \times\,9 \\ \hline \end{array}$

17. 0×7 **18.** 1×35 **19.** 0×1 **20.** 4×10 **21.** 9×10

Multiply.   (ex. 22–25: p. 79), (ex. 26–30: p. 80),
(ex. 31–35: p. 81), (ex. 36–40: p. 82)

22. $\begin{array}{r} 6 \\ \times\,3 \\ \hline \end{array}$ **23.** $\begin{array}{r} 6 \\ \times\,5 \\ \hline \end{array}$ **24.** $\begin{array}{r} 7 \\ \times\,6 \\ \hline \end{array}$ **25.** $\begin{array}{r} 6 \\ \times\,8 \\ \hline \end{array}$ **26.** $\begin{array}{r} 7 \\ \times\,5 \\ \hline \end{array}$ **27.** $\begin{array}{r} 4 \\ \times\,7 \\ \hline \end{array}$ **28.** $\begin{array}{r} 7 \\ \times\,8 \\ \hline \end{array}$

29. $\begin{array}{r} 7 \\ \times\,3 \\ \hline \end{array}$ **30.** $\begin{array}{r} 9 \\ \times\,7 \\ \hline \end{array}$ **31.** $\begin{array}{r} 8 \\ \times\,8 \\ \hline \end{array}$ **32.** $\begin{array}{r} 8 \\ \times\,4 \\ \hline \end{array}$ **33.** $\begin{array}{r} 8 \\ \times\,5 \\ \hline \end{array}$ **34.** $\begin{array}{r} 9 \\ \times\,8 \\ \hline \end{array}$ **35.** $\begin{array}{r} 3 \\ \times\,8 \\ \hline \end{array}$

36. 6×9 **37.** 9×3 **38.** 0×9 **39.** 9×9 **40.** 3×9

Chapter Test

Find the missing numbers.

1a. $6 + 6 + 6 + 6 + 6 = $ ▢
  b. $5 \times 6 = $ ▢

2. Draw 7 circles in a row.
Make 8 rows.
$8 \times 7 = $ ▢

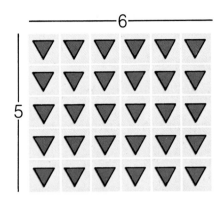

Multiply.

3. $\begin{array}{r} 5 \\ \times\, 8 \\ \hline \end{array}$	**4.** $\begin{array}{r} 9 \\ \times\, 3 \\ \hline \end{array}$	**5.** $\begin{array}{r} 8 \\ \times\, 4 \\ \hline \end{array}$	**6.** $\begin{array}{r} 0 \\ \times\, 3 \\ \hline \end{array}$	**7.** $\begin{array}{r} 7 \\ \times\, 4 \\ \hline \end{array}$	**8.** $\begin{array}{r} 5 \\ \times\, 3 \\ \hline \end{array}$	**9.** $\begin{array}{r} 6 \\ \times\, 9 \\ \hline \end{array}$

10. $\begin{array}{r} 6 \\ \times\, 6 \\ \hline \end{array}$	**11.** $\begin{array}{r} 4 \\ \times\, 9 \\ \hline \end{array}$	**12.** $\begin{array}{r} 5 \\ \times\, 7 \\ \hline \end{array}$	**13.** $\begin{array}{r} 8 \\ \times\, 8 \\ \hline \end{array}$	**14.** $\begin{array}{r} 3 \\ \times\, 8 \\ \hline \end{array}$	**15.** $\begin{array}{r} 7 \\ \times\, 3 \\ \hline \end{array}$	**16.** $\begin{array}{r} 4 \\ \times\, 6 \\ \hline \end{array}$

17. $\begin{array}{r} 9 \\ \times\, 7 \\ \hline \end{array}$	**18.** $\begin{array}{r} 6 \\ \times\, 8 \\ \hline \end{array}$	**19.** $\begin{array}{r} 8 \\ \times\, 9 \\ \hline \end{array}$	**20.** $\begin{array}{r} 0 \\ \times\, 7 \\ \hline \end{array}$	**21.** $\begin{array}{r} 9 \\ \times\, 1 \\ \hline \end{array}$	**22.** $\begin{array}{r} 10 \\ \times\, 4 \\ \hline \end{array}$	**23.** $\begin{array}{r} 10 \\ \times\, 9 \\ \hline \end{array}$

Find the products.

24. 2×7　　**25.** 0×6　　**26.** 3×10　　**27.** 6×9　　**28.** 7×8

29. 1×10　　**30.** 7×7　　**31.** 4×3　　**32.** 9×2　　**33.** 1×43

34. 2×8　　**35.** 5×3　　**36.** 6×7　　**37.** 0×1　　**38.** 5×5

Brush Up

Add or subtract.

1.   67
  + 232

2.   789
  − 432

3.   5439
  +   79

4.   903
  − 607

5.   856
  + 197

6.   642
  − 340

7.   9768
  + 1345

8.   829
  − 476

9.   1007
  + 8448

10.   800
  − 247

11.   813
  − 537

12.   732
    74
  + 5831

13.   6324
  − 5480

14.   723
  460
  + 186

15.   5882
  − 479

Write the numbers.

16. Write a number that is 200 more than 3242.

17. Order these numbers from least to greatest. 876, 768, 786, 687, 867, 678.

18. Count from 1997 to 2002.

Multiply.

19. 3×8

20. 4×7

21. 5×3

22. 9×2

23. 6×4

24. 4×9

25. 8×8

26. 9×7

27. 6×8

28. 4×4

29. 0×10

30. 3×9

31. 7×2

32. 5×6

33. 8×5

34. 8×9

35. 7×8

36. 6×10

37. 1×30

38. 9×9

CHAPTER 4

Measurement

Using Measurement at Work

Kate Foster is a carpenter. She is building a house.
One room measures 4 meters long and 3 meters
wide. She multiplies 4 meters times 3 meters to find
how much wood she needs to cover the floor. She
needs 12 square meters of wood to cover the floor.

Measuring to the Nearest Centimeter

The line is 1 **centimeter** long.
You can write **cm** for centimeter.

1 cm

The button is about 1 cm wide.

These scissors are about 9 cm long.

| cm | 1 | 2 | 3 | 4 | 5 | 6 | 7 | 8 | 9 | 10 | 11 | 12 | 13 | 14 | 15 | 16 |

Make a careful guess. Then measure each strip to the nearest centimeter.

1.　　　　　　　　　　　　　　　　　　　12 cm

2.

3.　　　　　4.　　　　　5.

Measure these. Write the lengths in centimeters.

6.　　　　　7.　　　　　8.

9.

Measuring to the Nearest Meter

There are 100 cm in 1 **meter**.
You can write **m** for meter.

nearer to 3 m

1 m

nearer to 2 m

Write the answers.

1. 2 m = ▢ cm   200

2. 5 m = ▢ cm

3. 4 m = ▢ cm

4. 200 cm = ▢ m

5. 900 cm = ▢ m

6. 7 m = ▢ cm

1 m

nearer to 1 m

1 m

Use a meter stick or cut a piece of string 1 m long. Answer these.

7. Are you nearer to 1 m or 2 m tall?

8. About how far is the doorknob from the bottom of the door?

9. About how many meters are there between your desk and the desk next to yours?

10. Start at the wall and take 4 steps. About how many meters did you walk?

Practice with Centimeters and Meters

Measure these. Write the length of each path in centimeters.

1.

2.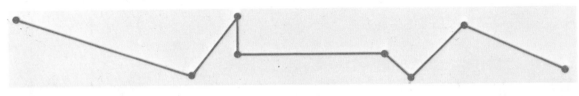

3.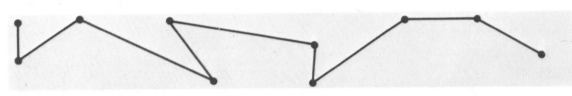

Use a centimeter ruler to draw lines with these lengths.

4. 5 cm **5.** 3 cm **6.** 8 cm **7.** 10 cm **8.** 15 cm **9.** 7 cm

Copy and complete.

10. 3 m = ▢ cm   **11.** 400 cm = ▢ m   **12.** 2 m = ▢ cm

13. 600 cm = ▢ m   **14.** 5 m = ▢ cm   **15.** 7 m = ▢ cm

16. 2 m + 1 m = ▢ cm   **17.** 100 cm + 15 cm = ▢ cm

18. 100 cm + 100 cm = ▢ m   **19.** 200 cm + 300 cm = ▢ m

20. 3 m + 40 cm = ▢ cm   **21.** 5 m + 95 cm = ▢ cm

Kilometers

Long distances are measured in **kilometers**.
You can write **km** for kilometer.
There are 1000 m in 1 km.

On this map, the distance
between two dots is 1 km.

Dave Meyer can walk 1 km
in about 10 minutes.

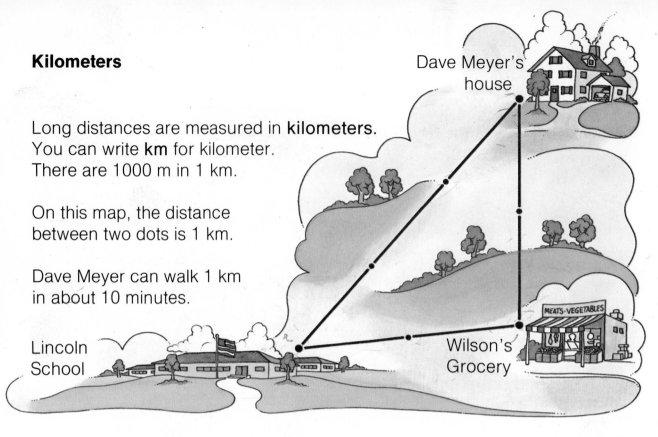

Dave Meyer's house

Lincoln School

Wilson's Grocery

Use the map to find the answers.

1. How many meters from the school to the grocery?   2000 m

2. How many kilometers from the school to the grocery?

3. About how long would it take Dave to walk from his house to the school?

4. How many meters in a trip from Dave's house to the school, to the grocery, then back to the house?

 Challenge

Would you use centimeters, meters, or kilometers to measure these?

5. length of a car

6. distance between two cities

7. width of a stamp

8. length of your bedroom

Using a Map Drawn to Scale

In a scale drawing, one unit is used to stand for another unit.

On this map, 1 centimeter stands for 5 kilometers.

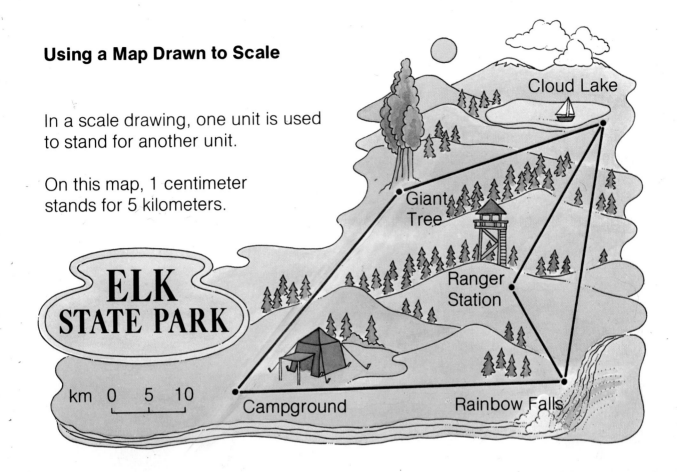

Measure the length in centimeters between places on the map. To find each distance, multiply the number of centimeters by 5.

		centimeters	kilometers
1.	Campground to Rainbow Falls	9	45
2.	Giant Tree to Cloud Lake		
3.	Rainbow Falls to Cloud Lake		
4.	Ranger Station to Rainbow Falls		
5.	Cloud Lake to Ranger Station		
6.	Campground to Giant Tree		

Perimeter

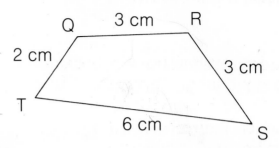

The **perimeter** of a shape is the distance around it. To find the perimeter of a shape, add the lengths of its sides.

$$3 \text{ cm} + 3 \text{ cm} + 6 \text{ cm} + 2 \text{ cm} = 14 \text{ cm}$$

The perimeter is 14 cm.

Measure the length of each side to the nearest centimeter. Add to find the perimeter.

1.

1a. A to B   5 cm
  b. B to C
  c. C to D
  d. A to D
  e. perimeter

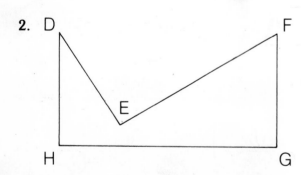

2.

2a. D to E
  b. E to F
  c. F to G
  d. G to H
  e. H to D
  f. perimeter

 Challenge
Draw a shape for each perimeter.   *use graph paper.*

3. 24 cm   **4.** 16 cm   **5.** 12 cm   **6.** 40 cm   **7.** 25 cm

Counting to Find Area

Area is the measure of surface. Surface is measured in square units. One kind of square unit is a **square centimeter** or **square cm**.

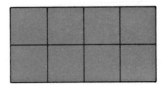 1 square centimeter

 The area is 8 square cm.

Find the area of each surface in square centimeters.

1.

   12 square cm

2.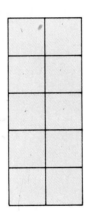

3.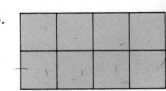

5.

4.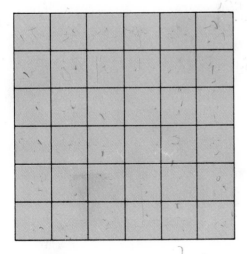

6.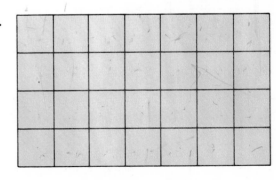

Multiplying to Find Area

To find area, multiply length times width.

6 cm

3 cm

$$\begin{array}{r} 6\text{ cm} \\ \times\ 3\text{ cm} \\ \hline 18\text{ square cm} \end{array}$$

Find the area.
The objects are shown smaller than actual size.

1.   6 cm

9 cm

54 square cm

2.   9 cm

5 cm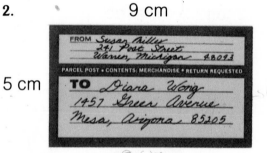

9 cm

3.   2 cm

6 cm

4.   7 cm

4 cm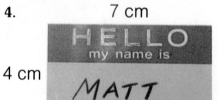

5.   4 cm

3 cm

⭐ Challenge

6. Why are square units better than round units for measuring area?

Perimeter and Area

Find the perimeter and area of each rectangle.
Rectangles are drawn smaller than actual size.

1. 6 m

2 m

Perimeter is 16 m.
Area is 12 square m.

$P = 16\,m.$
$A = 12\,m^2$

2. 5 m

3 m

3. 4 m

4 m

4a. Look at the perimeters for
rectangles 1, 2, and 3. What do
you notice?

b. Compare the areas for
rectangles 1, 2, and 3. Which
shape has the largest area?

5a. Draw three different rectangles
you could make with 20 m of
wire fence.

b. Which rectangle with a
perimeter of 20 m has the
largest area?

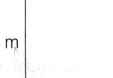

Review (pp. 93–101) *See page 94!*

Find the answers.

1a. 2 m = ▢ cm
b. 400 cm = ▢ m
c. 500 cm = ▢ m
d. 3 m = ▢ cm

2. Find the area.

3 m

3 m

Measuring Volume

This is a **cubic centimeter** or **cubic cm**.
You can use it to measure **volume**.

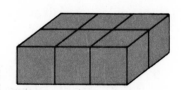

The volume is 6 cubic cm.

How many cubic centimeters?

1. 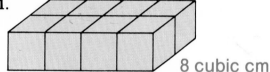 8 cubic cm

2.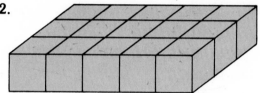

3.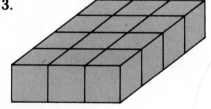

4.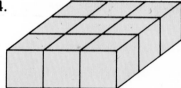

5.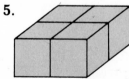

6.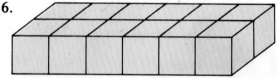

 Calculate

7. A small box has a volume of 729 cubic cm.
How many cubic centimeters in 10 boxes?

Volume

Write the answers.

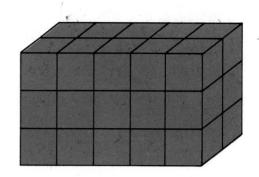

1a. How many cubic centimeters
  in one layer?   10
b. How many layers?
c. How many cubic centimeters?
d. The volume of the box is
  ▢ cubic cm.

Find each volume.

2.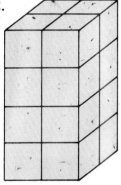

3.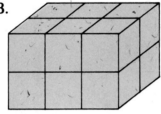

4.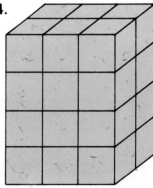

5.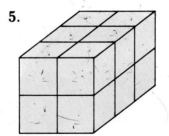

 **Challenge**

6. What is the volume of this box?

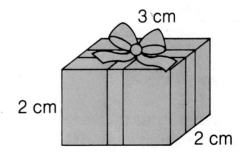

3 cm

2 cm

2 cm

Minutes and Hours

The hour hand is after 5.
The minute hand points to 2.
The time is 5:10.

There are 60 **minutes** in 1 **hour**.

Write the times.

1.    11:17

2.

3.

4.

5.

6.

 Calculate

7. A small clock costs $9.89. How much will 26 clocks cost?

8. A wristwatch costs $38.79. How much for 8 wristwatches?

Telling Time

You can say the time is **four forty-five** or **quarter to five** (4:45).

15 minutes ago the time was **half past four** or **four-thirty** (4:30).

In half an hour the time will be **five-fifteen** or **quarter after five** (5:15).

Write the times in numbers.
Draw a clock if you need help.

1a. three-thirty 3:30
 b. twenty to three
 c. three forty-five

2a. twelve-fifteen
 b. twelve twenty-five
 c. quarter to twelve

3a. five to seven
 b. quarter after seven
 c. seven-thirty

4a. five after nine
 b. twenty after nine
 c. quarter to nine

Digital clocks show time in the pictures below.
Write the answers.

5a. What time will the clock show in 15 minutes?
 b. What time will the clock show in 30 minutes?

6a. What time will the clock show in half an hour?
 b. What time will the clock show in an hour?

Seconds

A stopwatch shows **seconds**.
There are 60 seconds in 1 minute.
The red hand shows seconds.
The black hand shows minutes.

Time: 6 minutes 17 seconds
or 6 **min** 17 **s**.

Write the times shown on these stopwatches.

1.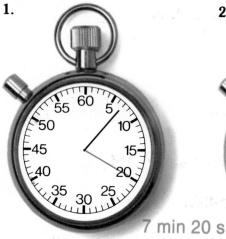

2.

3.

7 min 20 s

Change these to minutes and seconds.

4. 75 s = ⬚ min ⬚ s

5. 83 s = ⬚ min ⬚ s

6. 100 s = ⬚ min ⬚ s

7. 90 s = ⬚ min ⬚ s

8. 120 s = ⬚ min ⬚ s

9. 135 s = ⬚ min ⬚ s

10. 110 s = ⬚ min ⬚ s

11. 70 s = ⬚ min ⬚ s

12. 180 s = ⬚ min ⬚ s

A.M. and P.M.

A.M. means the time between midnight and noon.

6 A.M.

P.M. means the time between noon and midnight.

6 P.M.

midnight   noon   midnight
12 1 2 3 4 5 6 7 8 9 10 11 12 1 2 3 4 5 6 7 8 9 10 11 12

Write the times in numbers. Use A.M. or P.M.

1. ten after six at night   6:10 P.M.

2. one o'clock in the morning

3. eight o'clock at night

4. one o'clock in the afternoon

5. quarter after seven at night

6. five-thirty in the morning

7. quarter to ten in the morning

8. three o'clock in the afternoon

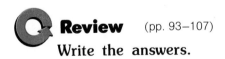

Review (pp. 93–107)

Write the answers.

1. 200 cm + 100 cm = ⬚ cm

2. 7 km = ⬚ m

3. 5000 m = ⬚ km

4. 83 seconds = ⬚ minutes ⬚ seconds

5. 1 hour = ⬚ minutes

Time Problems

This circle graph shows how Roberta spent one day. The graph shows hours and half hours.

Use the circle graph to answer these questions.

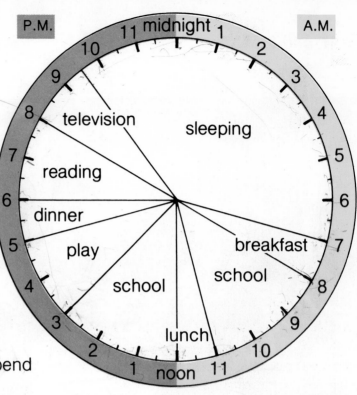

1. How many hours did Roberta spend reading? 2

2. How many hours did she spend sleeping?

3. How many hours did she spend at school?

4. How many hours did she spend playing?

5. How many hours did she spend watching television?

6. How many hours did she spend playing and reading?

7. How many hours did she spend having dinner?

8. How many hours altogether did she spend eating?

9. How many hours did she spend reading and watching television?

10. How many hours did she spend in all from breakfast to bedtime?

Time Relationships

60 seconds (s) in 1 minute (min)	28 to 31 days in 1 month
60 minutes in 1 hour	12 months in 1 year
24 hours in 1 day	365 days in 1 year
7 days in 1 week	52 weeks in 1 year

Write the missing numbers.

1. 180 seconds = ▢ minutes   3

2. 2 hours = ▢ minutes

3. 48 hours = ▢ days

4. 4 weeks = ▢ days

5. 24 months = ▢ years

6. 3 days = ▢ hours

7. 14 days = ▢ weeks

8. 1 year = ▢ weeks

Time Problems

Monroe to Skokie Bus Schedule

Leave Monroe	Arrive Skokie	
6:45 A.M.	7:15 A.M.	Daily except Saturday and Sunday
7:15 A.M.	7:50 A.M.	Daily except Sunday
8:05 A.M.	8:40 A.M.	Daily except Saturday and Sunday
9:10 A.M.	9:40 A.M.	Daily
10:55 A.M.	11:27 A.M.	Saturday only
3:47 P.M.	4:15 P.M.	Daily except Saturday and Sunday
6:05 P.M.	6:41 P.M.	Daily except Saturday and Sunday
8:16 P.M.	8:48 P.M.	Daily

Use the schedule to answer the questions.

1. On Monday morning Karen wants to arrive in Skokie by 10:00 A.M. How many buses can she take? 4

2. On Saturday afternoon Mark wants to arrive in Skokie by 9 P.M. How many buses can he take?

3. Jason takes the 7:15 A.M. bus to Skokie. How long is the trip?

4. Luisa takes the 10:55 A.M. bus to Skokie. How long is the trip?

5. Of all the buses, which bus takes the longest time?

6. How many buses go from Monroe to Skokie on Sunday?

Travel Problems

Solve each problem.

1. Tim and Vicky arrive at the train station at 1:15 P.M. Their train leaves at 1:27 P.M. How long do they have to wait?   12 min

2. The Flying Fin airline has a plane that leaves Chicago at 8:15 P.M. and arrives in New Orleans at 11:58 P.M. How long is the flying time?

3. It takes 45 minutes to get to the airport. Amanda wants to be there by 12:25 P.M. What time does she have to leave her house?

4. At 8:30 A.M. Ann and Tina start off on their trip. They arrive at 6:10 P.M. the same day. How long is the trip?

5. Bob takes a taxi from the airport at 2:45 P.M. and arrives home at 3:17 P.M. How long was the taxi trip?

6. Miguel wants to take the 7:05 P.M. train. He arrives at the station 26 minutes early. What time does he arrive?

Chapter Review

Measure the lengths in centimeters.   (ex. 1, 2: p. 93)

1. ████████████████████████████████████   2. ████████

Write the answers.   (ex. 3, 4: p. 94),   (ex. 5, 6: p. 95),   (ex. 7, 8: p. 96)

3. $2 \text{ m} = \boxed{?} \text{ cm}$

4. $400 \text{ cm} = \boxed{?} \text{ m}$

5. $300 \text{ cm} + 200 \text{ cm} = \boxed{?} \text{ m}$

6. $600 \text{ cm} = \boxed{?} \text{ m}$

7. $2 \text{ km} = \boxed{?} \text{ m}$

8. $1 \text{ km} + 3 \text{ km} = \boxed{?} \text{ m}$

Find the answers.   (ex. 9, 10: p. 101)

9. Find the perimeter of the shape.

10. Find the area of the shape.

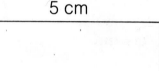

5 cm

4 cm

Write the times in numbers.   (ex. 11: p. 105),   (ex. 12, 13: p. 107)

11. quarter to eight in the morning

12. six-thirty at night

13. What time will the clock show in 30 minutes?

9:45

Chapter Test

Measure the lengths in centimeters.

1.

2.

Write the answers.

3. 1 m = ▢ cm

4. 200 cm = ▢ m

5. 4 km = ▢ m

6. 3000 m = ▢ km

7. 1 m + 5 m = ▢ cm

8. 900 cm = ▢ m

Find the answers.

9a. Find the perimeter of the shape.
 b. Find the area of the shape.

4 cm

4 cm

Write the times in numbers.

10a. What time will the clock show in 30 minutes?
 b. What time will the clock show in 60 minutes?

2:00

11. quarter past ten in the morning

12. twenty past midnight

Brush Up

Add.

1. 71 + 80	2. 52 + 93	3. 82 + 41	4. 68 + 75	5. 94 + 42
6. 123 + 248	7. 284 + 615	8. 431 + 343	9. 173 + 814	10. 262 + 326

Subtract.

11. 58 − 19	12. 93 − 21	13. 72 − 56	14. 65 − 42	15. 73 − 8
16. 848 − 621	17. 772 − 461	18. 943 − 718	19. 488 − 376	20. 973 − 801
21. 4318 − 1031	22. 6724 − 4028	23. 5893 − 387	24. 4672 − 299	25. 6944 − 3878

Multiply.

26. 7 × 9	27. 6 × 4	28. 5 × 8	29. 2 × 9	30. 3 × 9	31. 7 × 8	32. 9 × 9
33. 4 × 9	34. 5 × 7	35. 3 × 6	36. 5 × 4	37. 1 × 8	38. 4 × 4	39. 0 × 1

CHAPTER 5

Division

Using Division at Work

Bill Kido owns a house painting business. He can paint 3 doors with one can of paint. To find the number of cans of paint he will need for 18 doors, he divides 18 by 3. He will need 6 cans of paint for 18 doors.

Finding the Number of Groups

You have 12 shells. You want to put a group of
4 shells in each box. How many boxes do you need?

12 shells   Groups of 4   How many   Division fact
                                         groups?

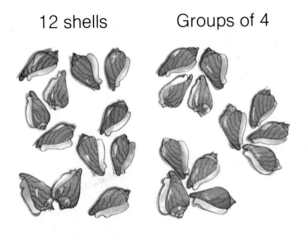

                                         3   3 quotient
                                              divisor 4) 12

                                         You need 3 boxes.

**Find the answers. Use markers or slips of paper
if you need help.**

1. 10 shells in groups of 2.
   a. How many groups?   5
   b. 2) 10

2. 12 shells in groups of 3.
   a. How many groups?   b. 3) 12

3. 8 shells in groups of 4.
   a. How many groups?   b. 4) 8

4. 15 shells in groups of 3.
   a. How many groups?   b. 3) 15

5. 16 shells in groups of 8.
   a. How many groups?   b. 8) 16

6. 16 shells in groups of 2.
   a. How many groups?   b. 2) 16

7. 14 shells in groups of 7.
   a. How many groups?   b. 7) 14

8. 18 shells in groups of 2.
   a. How many groups?   b. 2) 18

9. 9 shells in groups of 4.
   a. How many groups?
   b. How many left?

10. 17 shells in groups of 5.
    a. How many groups?
    b. How many left?

Finding the Number in Each Group

You have 12 shells. You have 3 friends. You want
to divide the shells into 3 fair shares. How many
shells in each fair share?

12 shells	Make 3 fair shares.	How many in each fair share?	Division fact

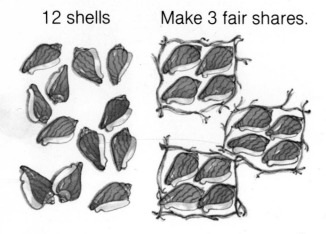

4

$$3\overline{)12}^{\,4}$$

Each friend
gets 4 shells.

**Find the answers. Use markers or slips of paper
if you need help.**

1. 20 shells, 4 fair shares
   a. How many in each fair share? 5
   b. $4\overline{)20}$

2. 6 shells, 2 fair shares
   a. How many in each fair share?
   b. $2\overline{)6}$

3. 16 shells, 4 fair shares
   a. How many in each fair share?
   b. $4\overline{)16}$

4. 12 shells, 3 fair shares
   a. How many in each fair share?
   b. $3\overline{)12}$

5. 15 shells, 5 fair shares
   a. How many in each fair share?
   b. Write a division fact.

6. 14 shells, 2 fair shares
   a. How many in each fair share?
   b. Write a division fact.

7. 11 shells, 3 fair shares
   a. How many in each fair share?
   b. How many left?

8. 23 shells, 4 fair shares
   a. How many in each fair share?
   b. How many left?

Adding to Divide

$3\overline{)12}$

Put the same number in each box.

$\boxed{4} + \boxed{4} + \boxed{4} = 12$

Division fact: $3\overline{)12}^{\,4}$

Use counters if you need help. Find the number that goes in the box. Complete the division fact.

1a. $\boxed{?} + \boxed{?} + \boxed{?} + \boxed{?} = 12$ 3

b. $4\overline{)12}^{\,3}$

2a. $\boxed{?} + \boxed{?} + \boxed{?} + \boxed{?} + \boxed{?} = 15$

b. $5\overline{)15}$

3a. $\boxed{?} + \boxed{?} + \boxed{?} = 18$

b. $3\overline{)18}$

4a. $\boxed{?} + \boxed{?} + \boxed{?} + \boxed{?} = 20$

b. $4\overline{)20}$

5a. $\boxed{?} + \boxed{?} + \boxed{?} + \boxed{?} = 28$

b. $4\overline{)28}$

6a. $\boxed{?} + \boxed{?} + \boxed{?} = 24$

b. $3\overline{)24}$

7a. $\boxed{?} + \boxed{?} + \boxed{?} + \boxed{?} = 24$

b. $4\overline{)24}$

8a. $\boxed{?} + \boxed{?} + \boxed{?} = 21$

b. $3\overline{)21}$

9a. $\boxed{?} + \boxed{?} + \boxed{?} + \boxed{?} + \boxed{?} = 20$

b. $5\overline{)20}$

10a. $\boxed{?} + \boxed{?} + \boxed{?} + \boxed{?} = 16$

b. $4\overline{)16}$

Dividing by 2 and 3

$\overline{)}$ and ÷ both mean divide.

──2──

$4 \times 2 = 8$

$$2\overline{)8}^{\,4}$$

──3──

$4 \times 3 = 12$

$12 \div 3 = 4$

Complete these facts.

1a. $4 \times \square = 12$ 3
 b. $12 \div 3 = \square$ 4

2a. $3 \times \square = 15$
 b. $15 \div 3 = \square$

3a. $2 \times \square = 10$
 b. $10 \div 2 = \square$

4a. $3 \times \square = 18$
 b. $18 \div 3 = \square$

5a. $3 \times \square = 9$
 b. $9 \div 3 = \square$

6a. $2 \times \square = 14$
 b. $14 \div 2 = \square$

7a. $3 \times \square = 27$
 b. $27 \div 3 = \square$

8a. $2 \times \square = 16$
 b. $16 \div 2 = \square$

9. $2\overline{)12}$

10. $2\overline{)18}$

11. $3\overline{)24}$

12. $2\overline{)8}$

13. $3\overline{)21}$

14. $2\overline{)6}$

15. $3\overline{)27}$

16. $3\overline{)18}$

17. $2\overline{)16}$

18. You have 8 kittens. You want to put 2 in each basket. How many baskets do you need?

19. Your cat eats 3 cans of cat food each week. How many weeks will 27 cans last?

Dividing by 2, 3, 4, and 5

$6 \times 4 = 24$
$24 \div 4 = 6$

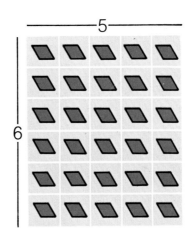

$6 \times 5 = 30$
$30 \div 5 = 6$

Complete these facts.

1a. $5 \times \boxed{?} = 35$ 7   **2a.** $4 \times \boxed{?} = 16$ **3a.** $2 \times \boxed{?} = 14$ **4a.** $3 \times \boxed{?} = 24$
b. $35 \div 5 = \boxed{?}$ 7   **b.** $16 \div 4 = \boxed{?}$ **b.** $14 \div 2 = \boxed{?}$ **b.** $24 \div 3 = \boxed{?}$

Divide.

5. $6 \div 2$ **6.** $20 \div 4$ **7.** $12 \div 3$ **8.** $25 \div 5$ **9.** $3 \div 3$

10. $15 \div 3$ **11.** $14 \div 2$ **12.** $28 \div 4$ **13.** $20 \div 5$ **14.** $12 \div 4$

15. $5\overline{)30}$ **16.** $3\overline{)27}$ **17.** $2\overline{)8}$ **18.** $4\overline{)36}$ **19.** $3\overline{)18}$

20. $2\overline{)12}$ **21.** $4\overline{)28}$ **22.** $5\overline{)40}$ **23.** $4\overline{)8}$ **24.** $5\overline{)10}$

25. $4\overline{)24}$ **26.** $5\overline{)45}$ **27.** $2\overline{)16}$ **28.** $4\overline{)32}$ **29.** $5\overline{)15}$

Dividing by 6 and 7

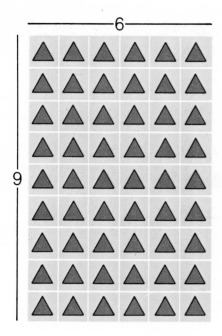

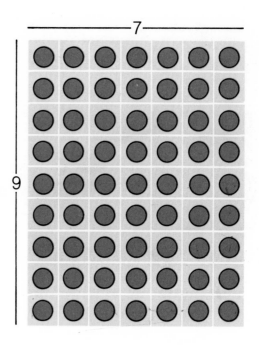

$$9 \times 6 = 54$$
$$54 \div 6 = 9$$

$$9 \times 7 = 63$$
$$63 \div 7 = 9$$

Complete these facts.

1a. $6 \times \boxed{?} = 12$ 2   **2a.** $7 \times \boxed{?} = 35$ **3a.** $7 \times \boxed{?} = 21$ **4a.** $6 \times \boxed{?} = 42$
b. $12 \div 6 = \boxed{?}$ 2   **b.** $35 \div 7 = \boxed{?}$ **b.** $21 \div 7 = \boxed{?}$ **b.** $42 \div 6 = \boxed{?}$

Divide.

5. $21 \div 7$ **6.** $42 \div 7$ **7.** $12 \div 6$ **8.** $7 \div 7$ **9.** $18 \div 6$

10. $7\overline{)14}$ **11.** $6\overline{)36}$ **12.** $6\overline{)54}$ **13.** $7\overline{)28}$ **14.** $7\overline{)56}$

15. $6\overline{)30}$ **16.** $7\overline{)49}$ **17.** $6\overline{)48}$ **18.** $7\overline{)63}$ **19.** $6\overline{)24}$

Dividing by 7 and 8

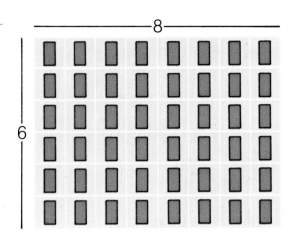

$$6 \times 8 = 48$$
$$48 \div 8 = 6$$

Sometimes a drawing can help.

6 × 8 = 48

Divide.

1. $24 \div 8$ 3
2. $42 \div 7$
3. $32 \div 8$
4. $56 \div 8$
5. $8 \div 8$

6. $28 \div 7$
7. $64 \div 8$
8. $48 \div 8$
9. $49 \div 7$
10. $14 \div 7$

11. $8\overline{)16}$
12. $8\overline{)24}$
13. $8\overline{)40}$
14. $7\overline{)35}$
15. $8\overline{)8}$

16. $7\overline{)7}$
17. $8\overline{)72}$
18. $7\overline{)21}$
19. $7\overline{)63}$
20. $7\overline{)56}$

 Challenge

21. It takes Matt 8 minutes to practice a new tune on the piano. How many times can he practice in 32 minutes?

22. There are 56 music students. There are 8 students in each class. How many classes of music students?

Dividing by 8 and 9

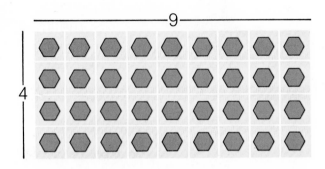

$$4 \times 9 = 36$$
$$36 \div 9 = 4$$

Divide.

1. $45 \div 9$ 5
2. $16 \div 8$
3. $56 \div 8$
4. $27 \div 9$
5. $49 \div 7$

6. $54 \div 9$
7. $24 \div 8$
8. $42 \div 7$
9. $63 \div 7$
10. $9 \div 9$

11. $7\overline{)7}$
12. $8\overline{)64}$
13. $9\overline{)18}$
14. $8\overline{)40}$
15. $7\overline{)35}$

16. $8\overline{)32}$
17. $9\overline{)81}$
18. $8\overline{)48}$
19. $7\overline{)21}$
20. $7\overline{)14}$

21. $8\overline{)8}$
22. $8\overline{)72}$
23. $7\overline{)28}$
24. $7\overline{)56}$
25. $9\overline{)63}$

 Challenge

Write the answers.

26. 36 divided by 9, plus 4

27. 54 divided by 9, plus 9

28. 72 divided by 9, plus 16.

0 and 1 in Division

If a number is divided by 1,
the quotient is the same as the number.

$6 \div 1 = 6$ $78 \div 1 = 78$

If 0 is divided by a number,
the quotient is 0.

$0 \div 6 = 0$ $0 \div 32 = 0$

You can
never divide
by 0.

Divide.

1. $7 \div 1$ 7
2. $0 \div 9$
3. $5 \div 1$
4. $0 \div 2$
5. $0 \div 14$

6. $9 \div 1$
7. $0 \div 5$
8. $0 \div 1$
9. $0 \div 3$
10. $39 \div 1$

11. $10 \div 1$
12. $0 \div 21$
13. $4 \div 1$
14. $13 \div 1$
15. $0 \div 10$

16. $23 \overline{)0}$
17. $1 \overline{)17}$
18. $14 \overline{)0}$
19. $1 \overline{)8}$
20. $1 \overline{)10}$

21. $1 \overline{)90}$
22. $1 \overline{)41}$
23. $1 \overline{)2}$
24. $12 \overline{)0}$
25. $1 \overline{)45}$

 Review   (pp. 117–125)

1. $3 \overline{)18}$
2. $4 \overline{)24}$
3. $7 \overline{)42}$
4. $8 \overline{)64}$
5. $9 \overline{)63}$

6. $9 \overline{)72}$
7. $5 \overline{)40}$
8. $6 \overline{)36}$
9. $3 \overline{)27}$
10. $7 \overline{)56}$

Checking Division

You can multiply to check division.

Divide.   Check.

$$6\overline{)24} \quad = 4$$

$$\begin{array}{r} 6 \\ \times\ 4 \\ \hline 24 \end{array}$$

Divide and check.

1. $8\overline{)32}$ $\begin{array}{r} 8 \\ \times\ 4 \\ \hline 32 \end{array}$ 2. $5\overline{)20}$

3. $9\overline{)63}$ 4. $7\overline{)42}$ 5. $6\overline{)36}$ 6. $3\overline{)24}$ 7. $9\overline{)18}$

8. $6\overline{)48}$ 9. $6\overline{)42}$ 10. $6\overline{)54}$ 11. $8\overline{)48}$ 12. $7\overline{)49}$

13. $9\overline{)54}$ 14. $9\overline{)72}$ 15. $7\overline{)56}$ 16. $7\overline{)63}$ 17. $8\overline{)40}$

18. $5\overline{)35}$ 19. $8\overline{)64}$ 20. $9\overline{)72}$ 21. $6\overline{)30}$ 22. $4\overline{)36}$

 Calculate

Find the missing number in each problem. Find the pattern.

23a. $1 + 3 + 5 = 3 \times \boxed{?}$
  b. $1 + 3 + 5 + 7 = 4 \times \boxed{?}$
  c. $1 + 3 + 5 + 7 + 9 = 5 \times \boxed{?}$
  d. Write the next problem in the pattern.

24a. $3 + 9 + 15 = 3 \times \boxed{?}$
  b. $9 + 15 + 21 = 5 \times \boxed{?}$
  c. $15 + 21 + 27 = 7 \times \boxed{?}$
  d. Write the next problem in the pattern.

Greenhouse Problems

Write a division fact for each.

1. There are 63 flowers, 7 in each pot. How many pots?
$63 \div 7 = 9$

2. There are 64 empty pots in 8 equal stacks. How many pots in each stack?

3. There are 42 daisies in 6 equal rows. How many in each row?

4. There are 48 rose bushes, 8 in each row. How many rows?

5. There are 63 ferns in 9 equal rows. How many in each row?

6. There are 54 pansy plants, 6 in each box. How many boxes?

7. There are 56 pine trees, 8 in each row. How many rows?

⭐ **Challenge**

8. There are 24 small ivy plants, 4 in each pot. There are 12 large ivy plants, 2 in each pot. How many pots of ivy are there altogether?

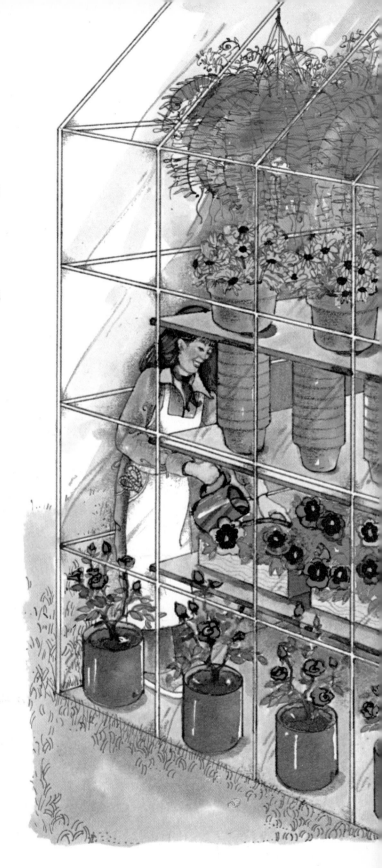

Finding Remainders

To find $3\overline{)14}$, think:

$$\overset{4}{3\overline{)12}} \text{ and } \overset{5}{3\overline{)15}},$$

so the answer to $3\overline{)14}$, must be 4 with a remainder.

×	1	2	3	4	5	6	7	8	9
2	2	4	6	8	10	12	14	16	18
3	3	6	9	12	15	18	21	24	27

First write the quotient 4.
Then multiply: $3 \times 4 = 12$.
Then subtract: $14 - 12 = 2$.
2 is the remainder.

quotient **4 r2** remainder

$$\text{divisor } 3\overline{)14}$$
$$\underline{-12} \quad {\scriptstyle 4 \times 3 = 12}$$
$$2$$

Use the multiplication table. Divide. Remember, the remainder must be less than the divisor.

1. $\overset{3 \text{ r1}}{2\overline{)7}}$

2. $2\overline{)15}$

3. $2\overline{)9}$

4. $2\overline{)5}$

5. $2\overline{)13}$

6. $2\overline{)3}$

7. $2\overline{)19}$

8. $2\overline{)11}$

9. $2\overline{)17}$

10. $3\overline{)17}$

11. $3\overline{)10}$

12. $3\overline{)25}$

13. $3\overline{)13}$

14. $3\overline{)7}$

15. $3\overline{)11}$

16. $3\overline{)8}$

17. $3\overline{)4}$

18. $3\overline{)22}$

19. $3\overline{)23}$

20. $3\overline{)19}$

21. Justina has 16 pictures. She puts 3 pictures on each page of her album. How many full pages does she have? How many pictures left over?

22. Roberto has 25 pictures. He puts 2 pictures on each page of his album. How many full pages does he have? How many pictures left over?

Division with Remainders

The remainder must be less than the divisor.

```
    3 r4
6 ) 22
  − 18
     4
```

RECYCLING CENTER

Divide.

1. 4) 27   6 r3
2. 3) 19
3. 5) 26
4. 6) 45
5. 2) 13

6. 8) 39
7. 7) 29
8. 9) 28
9. 5) 37
10. 3) 10

11. 8) 28
12. 4) 21
13. 5) 16
14. 3) 22
15. 2) 11

16. 6) 21
17. 8) 19
18. 7) 43
19. 8) 23
20. 9) 47

21. 4) 25
22. 6) 17
23. 5) 31
24. 3) 29
25. 6) 53

26. 7) 51
27. 3) 13
28. 8) 44
29. 9) 56
30. 5) 42

 **Review** (pp. 117–129)

1. 8) 64
2. 4) 32
3. 7) 27
4. 3) 26
5. 8) 31

Multiply or Divide Puzzle

To find a factor, divide. To find a product, multiply.

Factor	Factor	Product
3	6	?
?	5	35
7	?	28

$3 \times 6 = 18$

$35 \div 5 = 7$

$28 \div 7 = 4$

Find the factor or the product. Copy and complete each chart.

	Factor	Factor	Product
1.	8	9	?
2.	?	7	56
3.	7	6	?
4.	9	?	63
5.	8	?	64
6.	5	0	?

72

	Factor	Factor	Product
7.	?	8	8
8.	7	?	21
9.	?	4	36
10.	9	?	27
11.	6	?	54
12.	?	9	81

 Calculate

13. 12 sweaters cost $143.40. How much does each sweater cost?

Bus Trip Problems

Use the map and solve these problems by dividing. Remember, kilometers can be written km.

1. Jennie Foster drives a bus between Danville and Rosewood. How many trips does she make if she drives 35 km? 7

2. Jim Franklin drives a bus between Danville and Phelps. How many trips does he make if he drives 40 km?

3. Greg Powell drives a bus between Danville and Newton. If he drives 48 km, how many trips does he make?

4. Lucy Perkins drives a bus between Danville and Parker. If she drives 18 km, how many trips does she make?

 Challenge

5. It takes 7 minutes to drive from Danville to Rosewood. How many complete trips in 45 minutes?

Chapter Review

Find the answers.   (ex. 1: p. 117),   (ex. 2: p. 118)

1. 15 shells in groups of 5.
   a. How many groups?
   b. $5\overline{)15}$

2. 12 shells, 4 fair shares.
   a. How many in each fair share?
   b. Write a division fact.

Divide.   (ex. 3–6: p. 120),   (ex. 7–14: p. 121),   (ex. 15–24: p. 122)

3. $18 \div 2$
4. $27 \div 3$
5. $15 \div 3$
6. $12 \div 2$

7. $24 \div 4$
8. $20 \div 4$
9. $16 \div 4$
10. $36 \div 4$

11. $40 \div 5$
12. $15 \div 5$
13. $30 \div 5$
14. $20 \div 5$

15. $6\overline{)42}$
16. $6\overline{)30}$
17. $6\overline{)18}$
18. $6\overline{)48}$
19. $6\overline{)54}$

20. $7\overline{)35}$
21. $7\overline{)42}$
22. $7\overline{)63}$
23. $7\overline{)56}$
24. $7\overline{)28}$

Divide.   (ex. 25–32: p. 124),   (ex. 33–37: p. 125),   (ex. 38–42: p. 129)

25. $40 \div 8$
26. $16 \div 8$
27. $32 \div 8$
28. $64 \div 8$

29. $63 \div 9$
30. $45 \div 9$
31. $27 \div 9$
32. $54 \div 9$

33. $5\overline{)0}$
34. $1\overline{)4}$
35. $12\overline{)0}$
36. $1\overline{)13}$
37. $1\overline{)0}$

38. $4\overline{)27}$
39. $6\overline{)33}$
40. $5\overline{)21}$
41. $4\overline{)14}$
42. $3\overline{)29}$

Chapter Test

Find the answers.

1. 16 shells in groups of 4.
   a. How many groups?
   b. $4\overline{)16}$

2. 20 shells, 5 fair shares.
   a. How many in each fair share?
   b. Write a division fact.

Divide.

3. $15 \div 3$

4. $27 \div 3$

5. $16 \div 4$

6. $32 \div 4$

7. $25 \div 5$

8. $35 \div 5$

9. $20 \div 5$

10. $45 \div 5$

11. $12 \div 6$

12. $24 \div 6$

13. $36 \div 6$

14. $42 \div 6$

15. $28 \div 7$

16. $14 \div 7$

17. $49 \div 7$

18. $35 \div 7$

19. $8\overline{)32}$

20. $8\overline{)24}$

21. $8\overline{)40}$

22. $8\overline{)72}$

23. $8\overline{)64}$

24. $9\overline{)27}$

25. $9\overline{)36}$

26. $9\overline{)81}$

27. $9\overline{)54}$

28. $9\overline{)63}$

29. $1\overline{)9}$

30. $8\overline{)0}$

31. $1\overline{)1}$

32. $4\overline{)0}$

33. $1\overline{)5}$

Divide.

34. $4\overline{)15}$

35. $5\overline{)33}$

36. $3\overline{)17}$

37. $6\overline{)29}$

38. $4\overline{)26}$

39. $7\overline{)25}$

40. $6\overline{)39}$

41. $4\overline{)21}$

42. $3\overline{)11}$

43. $2\overline{)15}$

Brush Up

Add or subtract.

1. 486
   + 197

2. 396
   + 637

3. 43
   − 27

4. 60
   − 38

5. 481
   + 237

6. $631
   + 197

7. $705
   − 431

8. $8.91
   + 0.47

9. $6.00
   − 2.78

10. $4.73
    + 2.49

11. 431
    282
    + 190

12. 623
    − 108

13. 561
    43
    + 272

14. 784
    − 438

15. 24
    35
    + 870

16. $3005 - 840$

17. $4976 + 27$

18. $8608 - 959$

Multiply or divide.

19. 4
    × 6

20. 5
    × 9

21. 3
    × 7

22. 8
    × 9

23. 5
    × 3

24. 7
    × 8

25. 7
    × 6

26. 8
    × 6

27. 9
    × 5

28. 8
    × 4

29. 4
    × 3

30. 7
    × 7

31. 3
    × 4

32. 8
    × 2

33. 9
    × 9

34. 4
    × 8

35. 5
    × 6

36. 6
    × 9

37. $4\overline{)16}$

38. $9\overline{)36}$

39. $7\overline{)56}$

40. $3\overline{)27}$

41. $5\overline{)40}$

42. $64 \div 8$

43. $35 \div 5$

44. $45 \div 9$

45. $72 \div 9$

46. $54 \div 6$

CHAPTER 6

Problem Solving

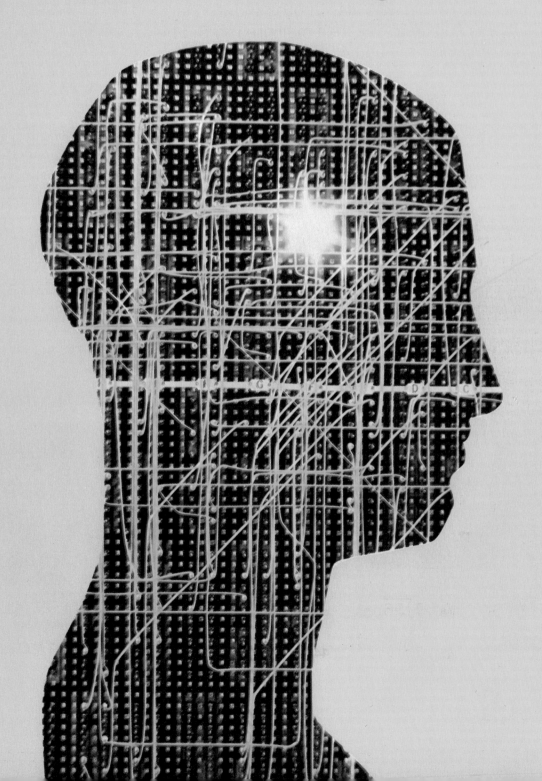

Using Problem Solving at Work

Josephine Malinski is a doctor. Each day she spends
6 hours working at her office and 3 hours working
at the hospital. To find how many hours she works
in 5 days, she adds 6 and 3, then multiplies by 5. She
works 9 hours each day and 45 hours in 5 days.

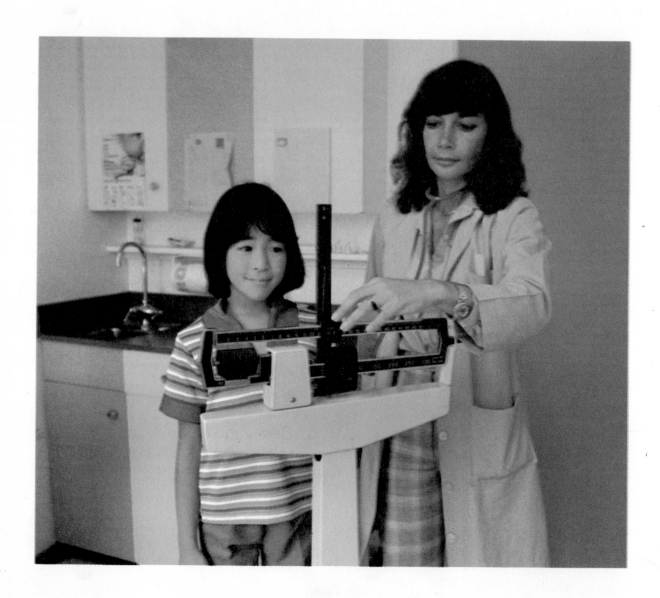

Reading Problems

When you read a problem, look for the important information:

- What is the question?
- What are the important facts?

Read each problem, then answer the questions about it.

1. Movie film costs $9 a package. How much do 8 packages cost?
   a. What is the question?
      How much do 8 packages of film cost?
   b. What are the important facts?
      Each package costs $9. There are 8 packages.

2. It took 56 hours to make 7 clown costumes. How many hours did it take to make each costume?
   a. What is the question?
   b. What are the important facts?

3. 900 actors were in the tornado scene. 358 actors were in the party scene. How many more were in the tornado scene?
   a. What is the question?
   b. What are the important facts?

4. Janna, a stuntwoman, did a stunt 15 times one day. She did it 28 times the next day. How many times did she do the stunt in all?
   a. What is the question?
   b. What are the important facts?

5. Casey the cat was paid $2470 to be in the movie. Penny the parrot was paid $250 more than that amount. How much was Penny paid?
   a. What is the question?
   b. What are the important facts?

Choosing the Operation

- To solve problems, think about whether
  to add, subtract, multiply, or divide.

**Choose the correct way to solve
each problem, then solve it.**

1. Beth buys a mask for 79¢
   and a hat for 47¢. How much
   does she spend?

   79¢ + 47¢ or 79¢ − 47¢

   79¢ + 47¢ = 126¢ or $1.26

2. Paul uses 2 slices of bread
   to make each sandwich. How
   many sandwiches can he make
   with 10 slices?

   10×2 or $10 \div 2$

3. Jeanette rakes leaves for 3
   hours. She earns $2 an hour.
   How much money does she
   earn in all?

   $2 \div 3$ or 2×3

4. Alma pays $18 for 6 piano
   lessons. What is the cost of
   each lesson?

   $18 \div 6$ or 18×6

5. Milk costs 35¢, juice costs 49¢.
   How much more does juice
   cost than milk?

   35¢ + 49¢ or 49¢ − 35¢

6. Marcia plans a 681-kilometer
   bicycle trip. The first day she
   travels 96 kilometers. How far
   does she have left to travel?

   681 + 96 or 681 − 96

7. Michael uses 4 cans of water to
   make one liter of lemonade.
   How many cans of water does
   he need to make 6 liters of
   lemonade?

   6×4 or $6 + 4$

Choosing the Operation

In these problems, triangles and squares take the place of numbers. You cannot solve the problem, but you can decide to add, subtract, multiply, or divide.

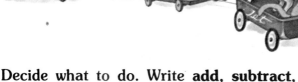

Decide what to do. Write **add, subtract, multiply,** or **divide** for each problem.

1. There are ■ large dogs and ▲ small dogs in the pet parade. How many dogs in all?   add

2. ■ small turtles cost $ ▲ How much does each turtle cost?

3. Susan buys ■ goldfish for ▲ ¢ each. How much does she pay?

4. The pet shop has ■ rabbits and ▲ hamsters. How many more rabbits than hamsters?

5. Jose had ■ hamsters. One of the hamsters had ▲ babies. How many hamsters did Jose have then?

 Challenge
Tell how you would solve this problem.

6. The pet shop has ■ dogs, ▲ cats, ● fish, and ◆ birds. How many more dogs and cats than fish and birds?

Choosing the Operation

Decide what to do. Write **add, subtract, multiply,** or **divide** for each problem.

1. Jane is ■ centimeters tall. Ted is ▲ centimeters tall. How much taller is Jane? subtract

2. Miguel gave the clerk $ ■ and received ▲ ¢ in change. How much did the groceries cost?

3. Peter drove ■ kilometers in ▲ hours. How far did he drive each hour?

4. Anne is ■ years old. Her grandfather is ▲ years older. How old is he?

5. Suzy bought ■ apples at ▲ ¢ apiece. What was the total cost?

6. There are ■ children in school. ▲ are boys. How many are girls?

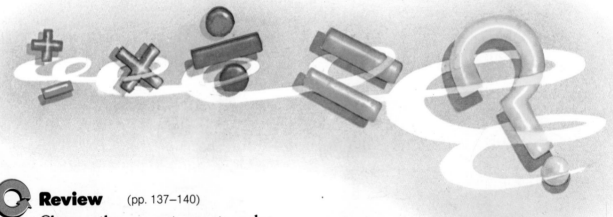

Review   (pp. 137–140)

Choose the correct way to solve each problem, then solve it.

1. Cathy bought 5 tickets for the circus. Altogether she paid $15. How much did each ticket cost?

   5 × $15 or $15 ÷ 5

2. Jack needs $7.98 to buy a shirt. He has $4.75. How much more does he need?

   $7.98 + $4.75 or $7.98 − $4.75

Too Much Information

- Look for the important facts. Sometimes you might have too much information.

Read each problem, then answer the questions about it.

1. About 2300 people visit Lakeside Park each day. The park is open 6 days a week. How many days is it open in 4 weeks?
   a. What is the question?
      How many days is the park open in 4 weeks?
   b. Will you add, subtract, multiply, or divide?
   c. What numbers do you need?
   d. What number is not needed?
   e. Solve the problem.

2. There are 15 little restaurants at the park. Helga's Hamburgers sells 498 hamburgers. Sammy's Sandwiches sells 639 sandwiches. How many more sandwiches than hamburgers?
   a. What is the question?
   b. Will you add, subtract, multiply, or divide?
   c. What numbers do you need?
   d. What number is not needed?
   e. Solve the problem.

3. For 10 years Lakeside Park has had a Pumpkin Party. This year $27 was spent on pumpkins to give away as prizes. Each pumpkin cost $3. How many pumpkins were given as prizes?
   a. What is the question?
   b. Will you add, subtract, multiply, or divide?
   c. What numbers do you need?
   d. What number is not needed?
   e. Solve the problem.

Too Much Information

Each problem has too much information. Look for the important facts, choose the operation, then solve the problem.

1. Susan Alwood's orchard has 8049 apple trees, 2347 peach trees, and 3706 plum trees. How many more apple trees than plum trees? 4343

2. The Espinoza ranch sells 467 cows at $1455 each and 25 horses at $2075 each. How many more cows are sold than horses?

3. In one field there are 328 rows of corn with 96 plants in each row. In another field there are 450 rows of corn with 76 plants in each row. How many rows of corn in all?

4. Alan planted 9 tomato plants in each row, with 45 plants in all. Each row produces 3 baskets of tomatoes. How many rows of tomato plants?

Calculate

5. Jane pays $1280 to rent a tractor for 4 months and $1020 to rent a truck for 6 months. What is the cost of renting the tractor for 1 month?

Too Little Information

- Sometimes you have too little information to solve a problem. You have to decide what facts you need.

Something is missing. What do you need to know before you can solve each problem?

1. Katy made 3 posters for a contest. How long did it take her to make them?

   You need to know how much time she spent on each poster.

2. Katy paid $1.57 for paper and paint. How much did the paper cost?

3. Ricardo used 5 more colors than Katy. How many colors did Ricardo use?

4. Each art class at Lincoln School entered 2 posters in the contest. How many posters did Lincoln School enter?

5. There were three prizes. First prize was $25. Second prize was $12. How much prize money in all?

 Challenge

What information is missing?

6. David bought 8 sheets of poster board and gave the clerk $10. What was David's change?

Solving Two-Step Problems

Sometimes you must do two steps to solve a problem. Remember:

- What is the question?
- What are the important facts?
- Decide which step you will do first.

Linda, Tim, and Mary Carlson are going to the beach for a vacation. Solve these problems.

1. Linda buys 3 beach towels. Each one costs $6. She gives the clerk $20. How much change does she get?

   Step 1
   $6
   × 3
   $18

   Step 2
   $20
   − 18
   $2 change

2. Mary can take 36 pictures with one roll of film. She takes 6 pictures on Monday and 17 pictures on Tuesday. How many pictures left on the roll?

3. Linda and Tim cook dinner. Each day they spend $2.50 for meat and $1.75 for fruit and vegetables. How much do they spend for 3 dinners?

4. Before vacation Tim had 152 shells in his collection. On vacation he finds 38 shells and gives 17 of them away. How many shells does he have now?

5. Linda brings a 256-page book to read on the beach. She reads 30 pages on Monday and 42 pages on Tuesday. How many does she have left to read?

6. Mary buys a roll of black-and-white film for $2 and 3 rolls of color film for $3 each. How much does she spend altogether?

7. Tim buys 3 bottles of suntan lotion. He gives the clerk $10 and receives $4 change. What is the cost of each bottle of suntan lotion?

8. Linda, Tim, Mary, and 6 friends have a picnic. The total cost for food is $36. They share the costs equally. How much does each one owe?

9. Mary buys 6 postcards for 8¢ each and a magazine for 95¢. How much does she pay in all?

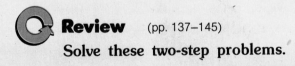 **Review**   (pp. 137–145)

Solve these two-step problems.

1. Sandra buys a camera bag for $8.98 and a battery for $1.29. She gives the clerk $11.00. How much change does she get?

2. Jacob buys 8 rolls of film. He gives the clerk $20 and gets $4 change. What was the cost of each roll of film?

Estimating Answers

You can round to the nearest ten cents to estimate answers.

Less than 5 cents rounds down:
21¢, 22¢, 23¢, 24¢ all round to 20¢.

More than 5¢ rounds up:
25¢, 26¢, 27¢, 28¢, 29¢ all round to 30¢.

Round each price to the nearest ten cents. Add to find about how much the total cost will be.

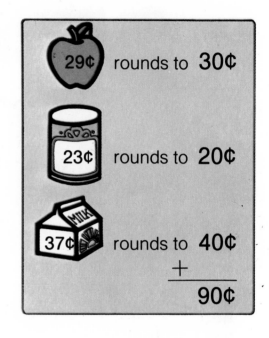

29¢ rounds to **30¢**

23¢ rounds to **20¢**

37¢ rounds to **40¢**
$+$
90¢

1. tea   37¢   40¢
   peas   28¢   30¢
   carrots   22¢ + 20¢
                   90¢

2. peaches   39¢
   tomatoes   15¢
   rolls   24¢

3. ketchup   54¢
   bananas   20¢
   onions   19¢

4. soup   34¢
   lettuce   29¢
   pears   27¢

5. mustard   24¢
   grapes   43¢
   bread   57¢

6. corn   41¢
   juice   39¢
   potatoes   24¢

7. crackers   45¢
   oranges   34¢
   cereal   50¢

⭐ Challenge

8. You have $3.00. A jar of peanut butter costs $0.69. A loaf of bread costs $0.78. Can you buy 2 jars of peanut butter and 2 loaves of bread?

9. You have $5.00. Apple juice costs $1.54. Cheese costs $1.85. Eggs cost $1.20. Beans cost $0.50. Can you buy all of these?

Writing Problems

Writing problems will help you solve problems.

Write a question about each. Answer the question.

1. Janet sells 19 pickles. Then she sells 16 more. How many pickles does she sell? 35

2. Janet orders 8 boxes of bread. There are 6 loaves of bread in each box.

3. Sarah cuts up 342 carrot sticks and 271 celery sticks.

4. Leo had 50 cartons of milk. He sold 38 of them.

5. There are 8 bags of hard rolls. There are 96 hard rolls altogether.

6. Leo sells 17 roast beef sandwiches on white bread and 23 on rye bread.

7. There are 45 slices of ham in each package. There are 5 slices of ham in each sandwich.

8. Monday there were 452 customers. Tuesday there were 509 customers.

Calculate

Find the answer.

9. Leo works 4 hours a day at the Sandwich Shop. He earns $5 an hour. How many days does he need to work to earn $100?

Chapter Review

Read each problem. Answer the questions.   (ex. 1: p. 137),   (ex. 2: p. 139),
(ex. 3, 4: p. 141),   (ex. 5, 6: p. 143)

1. You have $10.00. You buy shoes for $8.95. How much do you have left?
   a. What is the question?
   b. What are the important facts?

2. You work ■ hours and earn $ ▲. How much do you earn each hour?
   a. Will you add, subtract, multiply, or divide?

3. You have 39 stamps. Each one costs 10¢. You buy 12 more stamps. How many stamps do you have now?
   a. What numbers do you need?
   b. What number is not needed?
   c. Solve the problem.

4. Mark buys a pen for 39¢, an eraser for 15¢, and a box of pencils for 89¢. How much more does he spend for pencils than for pens?
   a. What numbers do you need?
   b. What number is not needed?
   c. Solve the problem.

5. Books cost $3 each. How many books can you buy?
   a. What do you need to know before you can solve the problem?

6. Linda buys 4 pens at $2 each. How much change does she get?
   a. What do you need to know before you can solve the problem?

Solve these two-step problems.   (ex. 7, 8: p. 144)

7. Jeff buys a pair of shoes for $12 and 3 pairs of socks at $2 for each pair. How much does he spend?

8. Jane has $20 to spend on gifts. She buys gifts that cost $2, $3, and $5. How much does she have left to spend?

Chapter Test

Read each problem. Answer the questions.

1. Jill bicycles 8 kilometers each hour. How far does she bicycle in 3 hours?
   a. What is the question?
   b. What are the important facts?

2. You have $ ■ . You spend $ ▲ . How much money do you have left?
   a. Will you add, subtract, multiply, or divide?

3. You have 8 model airplanes. You buy 1 more for $1.59. How many do you have now?
   a. What numbers do you need?
   b. What number is not needed?
   c. Solve the problem.

4. Mina has 35 model airplanes. She gives 4 to her brother and 3 to a friend. How many does she give away?
   a. What numbers do you need?
   b. What number is not needed?
   c. Solve the problem.

5. Leo collected $16 for roast beef sandwiches. What was the cost of each one?
   a. What do you need to know before you can solve the problem?

6. Laura sold 5 more cameras on Tuesday than she did on Monday. How many cameras did she sell on Tuesday?
   a. What do you need to know before you can solve the problem?

Solve these two-step problems.

7. Peter buys a book for $2.98 and a record for $5.00. He gives the clerk $10.00. How much change does he get?

8. Joan buys 7 brushes. She gives the clerk $15 and gets $1 change. What is the cost of each brush?

Brush Up

Add.

1. 34
+ 82

2. 58
+ 19

3. 72
+ 37

4. 88
+ 46

5. 63
+ 89

6. 493
+ 25

7. 215
+ 87

8. 849
+ 134

9. 632
+ 204

10. 718
+ 165

Subtract.

11. 41
− 17

12. 62
− 9

13. 35
− 18

14. 59
− 28

15. 82
− 37

16. 407
− 42

17. 831
− 178

18. 967
− 318

19. 828
− 193

20. 675
− 426

Multiply.

21. 3×5

22. 2×6

23. 4×7

24. 5×8

25. 9×3

26. 6×9

27. 4×4

28. 6×7

29. 6×3

30. 8×7

31. 5×7

32. 3×8

33. 9×4

34. 8×9

35. 7×7

Divide.

36. $21 \div 7$

37. $20 \div 4$

38. $32 \div 4$

39. $56 \div 7$

40. $48 \div 6$

41. $63 \div 9$

42. $36 \div 6$

43. $54 \div 9$

44. $30 \div 6$

45. $81 \div 9$

CHAPTER 7

Geometry

Using Geometry at Work

Sara Whitehawk is an architect. She has designed a museum and plans to build a path around the perimeter. The building is a rectangle 150 meters long and 100 meters wide. To find the perimeter, she adds the lengths of the sides: 150 + 150 + 100 + 100. The perimeter of the museum is 500 meters.

Testing for Right Angles

Step 1
Fold a piece of paper.

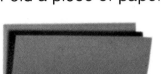

Step 2
Fold again.

Mark this corner.
This is a right angle.

Use your right angle.
How many right angles in each?

1.
Square

4

2.
Triangle

3.
Rectangle

4.
Circle

5.

6.

7. Draw a shape that has one right angle.

8. Draw a shape that has four right angles.

Comparing Angles

An angle is made of two **rays**.
Some angles are less than a right angle.
Some angles are greater than a right angle.

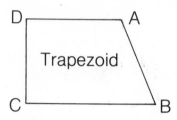

Trapezoid

Use your right angle.
The angle at A is
greater than a right angle.

The angle at B is
less than a right angle.

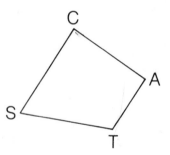

Use your right angle.
Write letters to answer the questions.

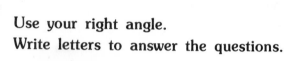
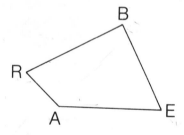

1a. Which angle is a
right angle?   B

b. Which angles are less than
a right angle?

c. Which angle is greater than
a right angle?

2a. Which angles are right
angles?

b. Which angle is less than
a right angle?

c. Which angle is greater than
a right angle?

 Challenge

3. Draw a triangle that has no right angles.

More Comparing Angles

Right angle

Less than a right angle
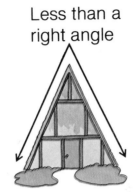

Greater than a right angle

Write **right angle**, **less**, or **greater** for each angle.

1. 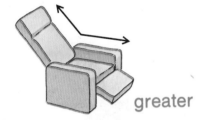 greater

2.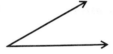

3.

4.

5.

6.

7.

8.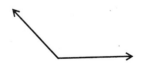

9.

Squares

 Square

A **square** has four right angles and four equal sides.

Is each shape a square? Write yes or no.

1. no

2.

3.

4.

5.

6.

7.

8.

9.

⭐ **Challenge**

10. Make a list of five squares, five circles, and five triangles in your classroom.

Rectangles

A **rectangle** has four right angles. Opposite sides of a rectangle are the same length.

Rectangle

Is each shape a rectangle? Write yes or no.

1. no

2.

3.

4.

5.

6.

7.

8.

9.

10.

11. Is every square a rectangle?

12. Is every rectangle a square?

Parallel Lines

Parallel lines never meet.

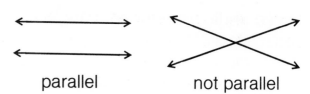

parallel   not parallel

Are the lines parallel? Write yes or no.

1.

yes

2.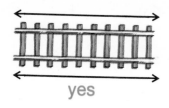

3.

4.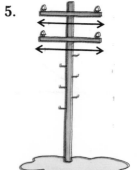

5.

6.

7.

8.

9.

Intersecting Lines

Intersecting lines meet or cross.

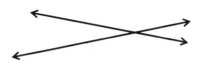

Intersecting lines that form a right angle
are **perpendicular**.

Look at the lines. Write **parallel, perpendicular,**
or **intersecting.** Some problems have more than one answer.

1.
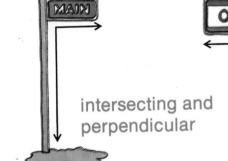
intersecting and
perpendicular

2.

ONE WAY

3.

SAFETY ZONE

4.

5.
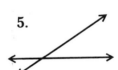

6.
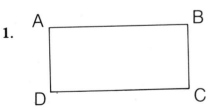

Review (pp. 153–159)

1.

A   B

D   C

1a. Which angles are right angles?
b. Is this shape a rectangle?
c. Is this shape a square?

2. Are the lines parallel?
Write **yes** or **no.**

2a.

2b.

2c.

Coordinate Graphing

You can name the corner where a street
and an avenue intersect. The grocery store
is at the corner of **Zero Street** and **Fourth Avenue**.

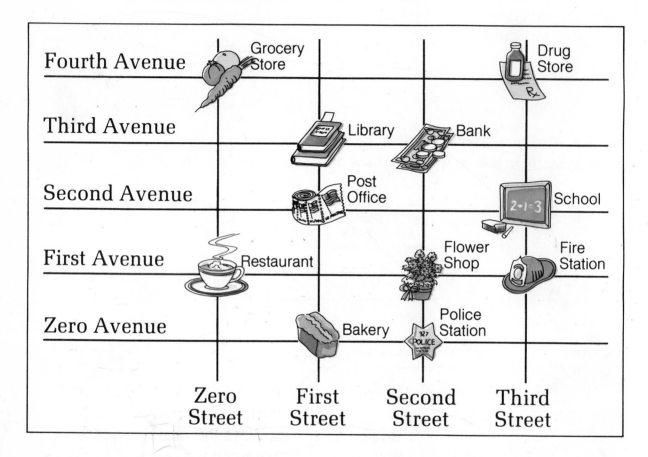

Write the avenue and the street to name the corner.

1. Bank   Second Street and Third Avenue

2. Drug Store

3. Police Station

4. Restaurant

5. Post Office

6. Grocery Store

7. Library

8. Flower Shop

9. Fire Station

10. Bakery

11. School

Ordered Pairs

Ordered pairs can name positions. **Point A** is at
ordered pair **(4, 2)**. To find point A, go from 0 to 4
on the **horizontal** line, then move up 2 on the
vertical line.

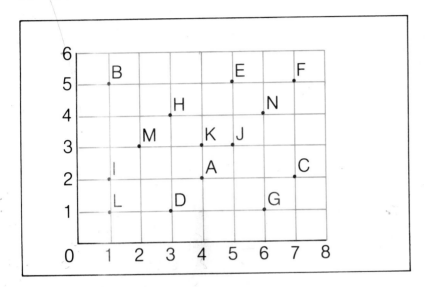

Use the graph to find the answers.

1. Put your finger on 4 on the
   horizontal line. Move up 3.
   a. On what letter do you land?   K
   b. Write the ordered pair that
      names the place.

2. Put your finger on 6 on the
   horizontal line. Move up 4.
   a. Write the ordered pair that
      names the place.
   b. Does (6, 4) name a different
      place than (4, 6)?

Write the ordered pairs for the location of these letters.

3. F (7, 5)   4. L   5. H   6. B   7. D   8. J

9. M   10. N   11. G   12. C   13. E   14. I

Lines of Symmetry

Make a square.
All sides are the same length.
All the angles are right angles.

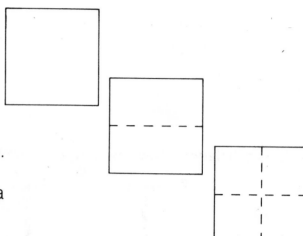

Fold the square in half. Unfold.
The fold line is a **line of symmetry**.
Each half is the same size and shape.

Fold across. Unfold. This fold line is a
line of symmetry too.

Use the same square. Make these folds too.

1. How many new lines of
   symmetry have you made? 2

2. Are there any other lines of
   symmetry in the square?

3. How many lines of symmetry
   does the square have in all?

4. Do all lines of symmetry
   pass through the center?

5. Are the lines of symmetry
   parallel or intersecting?

6. Make a rectangle that is not a square.
   How many lines of symmetry can you find?

Symmetry in Letters and Words

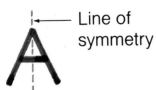 — Line of symmetry

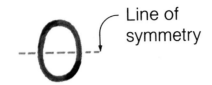 — Line of symmetry

Copy each letter. Draw the line of symmetry.

1. H   2. T   3. M   4. C   5. V

The line of symmetry divides each word in half. Write the word.

6.

7.

8.

9.

 Challenge

10. Which capital letters of the alphabet can have a line of symmetry?

11. Use capital letters. Write two words that have a line of symmetry.

Congruence

Figures that have the same size and shape are **congruent**.

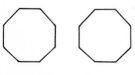

congruent

not congruent

Are these shapes congruent? Write yes or no.

1.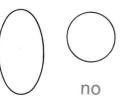

no

2.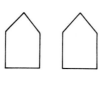

3.

4.

5.

6.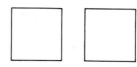

7. Write the letters of the triangles which are congruent.

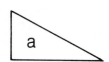 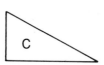

Similarity

Figures that have the same shape are **similar**.

similar   not similar

Are these shapes similar? Write yes or no.

1. 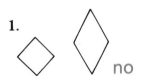 no

2.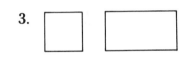

3.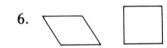

4.

5.

6.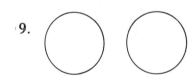

7.

8.

9.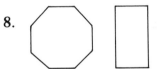

 Calculate

10. This shape has 52 sides.
    Each side is 2 meters long.
    Find the perimeter and the
    area of the shape.

Congruence and Similarity

Are these shapes congruent? Write yes or no.

1. no

2.

3.

Are these shapes similar? Write yes or no.

4.

5.

6.

7.

8.

9.

 Review (pp. 153–166)

Write the answers.

e   f   g

1a. Which lines are parallel?
 b. Which lines are intersecting?
 c. Which lines are perpendicular?

2. Are these shapes congruent?
 Write **yes** or **no**.

3. Are these shapes similar?
 Write **yes** or **no**.

2a.   2b.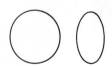

3a.   3b.

Drawing Solid Shapes

Squares are flat.

Cubes are solid.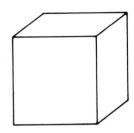

Follow these steps to draw a cube.

1a. Draw a square.

1b. Draw another square the same size.

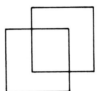

1c. Connect the corners.

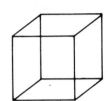

This solid is called a **triangular prism**.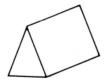

Follow these steps to draw a triangular prism.

2a. Draw a triangle.

2b. Draw another triangle the same size.

2c. Connect the corners.

More Solid Shapes

Each flat surface of a solid is a **face**.

Two faces intersect in an **edge**.

Three edges intersect in a **corner**.

A cube has 6 faces, 12 edges, and 8 corners.

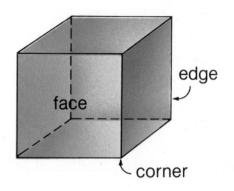

Count the number of edges, faces, and corners for each figure.

1a. ⬚ edges   9
 b. ⬚ faces
 c. ⬚ corners

2a. ⬚ edges
 b. ⬚ faces
 c. ⬚ corners

3a. ⬚ edges
 b. ⬚ faces
 c. ⬚ corners

 Calculate

4. This solid has six faces. Find the area of each face. Then add to find the total surface area of the solid.

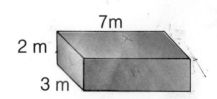

7m
2 m
3 m

Matching Solids with Flat Shapes

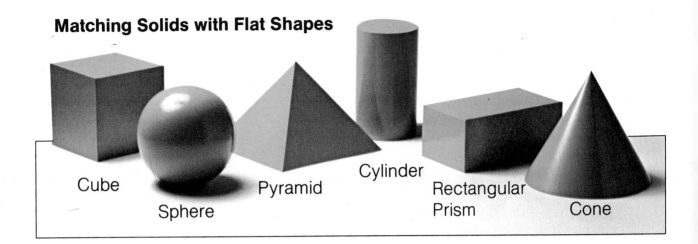

Cube

Sphere

Pyramid

Cylinder

Rectangular
Prism

Cone

Some solids above were made from these flat shapes. Match them.

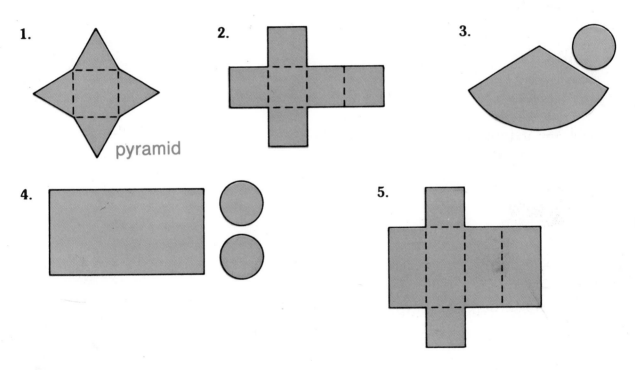

1.

pyramid

2.

3.

4.

5.

⭐ **Challenge**

6. In what two ways is the sphere different from the other five solids?

Chapter Review

Write the letters of the angles. (ex. 1: p. 154)

1a. Which are the right angles?
 b. Which angle is less than a
    right angle?
 c. Which angle is greater than
    a right angle?

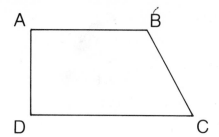

Write the letters of the figures. (ex. 2: p. 156), (ex. 3: p. 157)

2. Which shape is a square?

3. Which shapes are rectangles?

**Write intersecting or parallel for
each pair of lines.** (ex. 4–7: pp. 158, 159)

4.   5.   6.   7.

Write the answers. (ex. 8: p. 163), (ex. 9: p. 164), (ex. 10: p. 165)

8. Draw three capital letters of the alphabet which
   have a line of symmetry.

9. Is each pair congruent?   10. Is each pair similar?
   Write **yes** or **no**.   Write **yes** or **no**.

9a.   9b.   10a.   10b.

Chapter Test

Write the letters of the angles.

1a. Which are the right angles?
b. Which angles are less than right angles?
c. Which angles are greater than right angles?

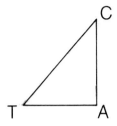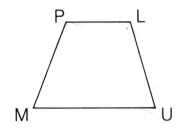

Write the letters of the figures.

2. Which shapes are rectangles?

3. Which shape is a square?

Write the answers.

4. Write **intersecting** or **parallel** for each pair of lines.

4a.   **4b.**    **4c.**   **4d.**

5. Which shapes have a line of symmetry?

a   b   c ...

d

6. Is each pair congruent? Write **yes** or **no**.

7. Is each pair similar? Write **yes** or **no**.

6a.   **6b.**   **7a.**   **7b.**

Brush Up

Add or subtract.

1.	2.	3.	4.	5.
29 + 87	78 + 96	496 + 37	712 + 34	7139 + 1478

6.	7.	8.	9.	10.
89 − 52	5448 + 2173	76 − 12	47 − 13	8650 + 2491

11.	12.	13.	14.	15.
647 − 258	723 − 456	3074 − 1826	419 − 199	2654 − 839

Multiply or divide.

16. 5×8 **17.** 6×4 **18.** 9×7 **19.** 0×4 **20.** 9×9

21. 8×7 **22.** 3×9 **23.** 6×7 **24.** 4×4 **25.** 10×5

26. $63 \div 7$ **27.** $54 \div 6$ **28.** $48 \div 8$ **29.** $36 \div 9$ **30.** $27 \div 3$

31. $35 \div 5$ **32.** $28 \div 4$ **33.** $81 \div 9$ **34.** $32 \div 4$ **35.** $56 \div 8$

Write the answers.

36.

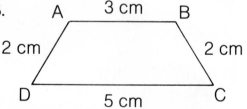

36a. Find the perimeter of shape ABCD.

b. Which angles in shape ABCD are greater than a right angle?

37. Are the lines parallel? Write **yes** or **no**.

37a.   **37b.**    **37c.**

CHAPTER 8

Fractions and Decimals

Using Fractions at Work

Dennis Crawford is a chef. In the morning he had $5\frac{3}{4}$ sacks of flour in his kitchen. During the day he used $2\frac{1}{4}$ sacks of flour to bake bread and muffins. He subtracts $2\frac{1}{4}$ from $5\frac{3}{4}$ to find how many sacks of flour he has left. He has $3\frac{2}{4}$ sacks of flour left.

Naming Parts of Shapes

You can divide a whole into equal parts.
Equal parts have the same size and the same shape.

Here are some names for equal parts of a whole.

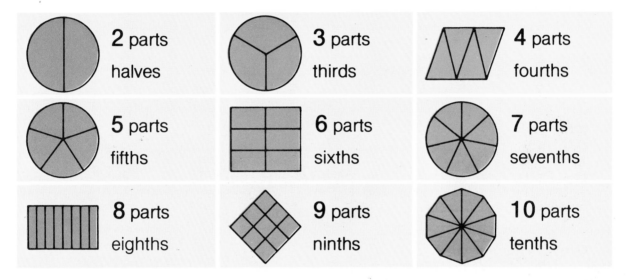

2 parts halves	3 parts thirds	4 parts fourths
5 parts fifths	6 parts sixths	7 parts sevenths
8 parts eighths	9 parts ninths	10 parts tenths

Give the number of parts. Name the kind of parts.

1.   4, fourths

2.

3.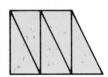

4.

5.

6.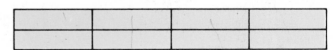

7.

8.

9.

10.

Naming Parts of Groups

The whole group has 5 parts.
Each part is called a fifth.

Total number of parts: 5
Kind of parts: fifths

Give the number of parts. Name the kind of parts.

1.

3, thirds

2.

3.

4.

5.

6.

7.

8.

Fractions

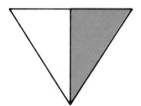

One-half of the triangle is red.
You can write one-half as a **fraction**.

$\frac{1}{2}$ **numerator** (number of red parts)
denominator (total number of parts)

What part of the group is apples?
2 out of 3 are apples.
Two-thirds are apples.

Fraction: $\frac{2}{3}$

Write the fraction.

1. Yellow: $\frac{3}{6}$

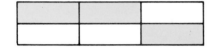

2. Cherries:

3. You have 4 oranges. You give 2 away. What part of the group have you given away?

4. You cut an apple into 4 equal pieces. You eat 1 piece. What part have you eaten?

5. You have 5 berries. 3 are strawberries. What part of the group is strawberries?

6. You have 8 vegetables. 4 are carrots. What part of the group is carrots?

7. You have 6 potatoes. You bake 2 of them. What part of the group have you baked?

8. You cut a melon into 8 equal pieces. You eat 3 pieces. What part have you eaten?

Fraction Strips

The fraction strip is divided into 6 equal parts.

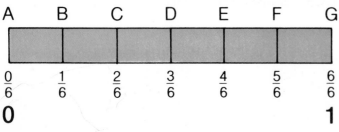

$$\frac{0}{6} \quad \frac{1}{6} \quad \frac{2}{6} \quad \frac{3}{6} \quad \frac{4}{6} \quad \frac{5}{6} \quad \frac{6}{6}$$

0   **1**

A to C is $\frac{2}{6}$ of the fraction strip.

Use the fraction strip. Write the answers.

1. A to B is ▢. $\frac{1}{6}$ 2. A to C is ▢.   3. A to F is ▢.

4. A to D is ▢.   5. A to E is ▢.   6. A to G is ▢.

If the numerator and denominator are the same, the fraction is equal to 1. Write the fractions that are equal to 1.

7a. $\frac{4}{4}$ b. $\frac{7}{8}$ c. $\frac{9}{9}$ d. $\frac{10}{10}$ e. $\frac{6}{8}$ f. $\frac{7}{7}$

If the numerator is 0, the fraction is equal to 0. Write the fractions that are equal to 0.

8a. $\frac{5}{7}$ b. $\frac{0}{7}$ c. $\frac{4}{5}$ d. $\frac{0}{12}$ e. $\frac{6}{14}$ f. $\frac{0}{8}$

Fraction Problems

These are gas gauges. They show how much gas there is in a car's gas tank. Use the gas gauges to answer the questions.

a b c d

1. Each gas gauge is divided into ⬜ parts.   4

2. How full is tank **a**? Write a fraction.

3. How full is tank **b**? Write a fraction.

4. How full is tank **c**? Write a fraction.

5. Tank **d** is empty. Show this with a fraction.

6. Write the fraction for a full gas tank.

Use the measuring cup. Write a fraction to show what part of the cup is filled if milk is poured to each mark.

7. h   8. g   9. e

10. d   11. b   12. a

13. Milk is poured to mark **h**. To make a cake, you need the amount of milk shown by mark **g**. How much more milk do you need?

Ordering Like Fractions

Both circles have the same number
of equal parts. Compare shaded parts.
Which fraction is greater?

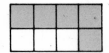

$\frac{4}{6}$ is greater than $\frac{2}{6}$.

Look at the rectangles. Which fraction is greater?

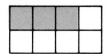 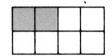 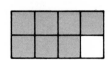

1. $\frac{5}{8}$ or $\frac{2}{8}$ $\frac{5}{8}$ 2. $\frac{2}{8}$ or $\frac{3}{8}$ 3. $\frac{5}{8}$ or $\frac{3}{8}$ 4. $\frac{5}{8}$ or $\frac{7}{8}$ 5. $\frac{6}{8}$ or $\frac{4}{8}$

Which fraction is greater?

6. $\frac{2}{3}$ or $\frac{1}{3}$ 7. $\frac{5}{9}$ or $\frac{7}{9}$ 8. $\frac{9}{10}$ or $\frac{6}{10}$ 9. $\frac{5}{12}$ or $\frac{6}{12}$ 10. $\frac{7}{5}$ or $\frac{5}{5}$

11. $\frac{7}{4}$ or $\frac{5}{4}$ 12. $\frac{9}{8}$ or $\frac{11}{8}$ 13. $\frac{5}{2}$ or $\frac{3}{2}$ 14. $\frac{13}{12}$ or $\frac{15}{12}$ 15. $\frac{8}{3}$ or $\frac{4}{3}$

 Calculate

Divide to change each fraction to a whole number.

16. $\frac{57}{3}$ $57 \div 3 = 19$ 17. $\frac{234}{9}$ 18. $\frac{126}{7}$ 19. $\frac{325}{5}$ 20. $\frac{387}{9}$

Ordering Unlike Fractions

$\frac{1}{2}$

$\frac{1}{3}$

$\frac{1}{4}$

$\frac{1}{5}$

Each part of circle **a** is larger than each part of circle **b**. $\frac{1}{2}$ is greater than $\frac{1}{3}$.

Each part of circle **c** is smaller than each part of circle **b**. $\frac{1}{4}$ is smaller than $\frac{1}{3}$.

Look at the circles. Which fraction is greater?

1. $\frac{1}{3}$ or $\frac{1}{5}$ $\frac{1}{3}$

2. $\frac{1}{4}$ or $\frac{1}{3}$

3. $\frac{1}{2}$ or $\frac{1}{3}$

4. $\frac{1}{5}$ or $\frac{1}{2}$

5. $\frac{1}{10}$ or $\frac{1}{4}$

Which fraction is greater?

6. $\frac{1}{4}$ or $\frac{1}{5}$

7. $\frac{1}{8}$ or $\frac{1}{6}$

8. $\frac{1}{9}$ or $\frac{1}{10}$

9. $\frac{1}{8}$ or $\frac{1}{10}$

10. $\frac{1}{10}$ or $\frac{1}{2}$

11. $\frac{1}{6}$ or $\frac{1}{9}$

12. $\frac{1}{7}$ or $\frac{1}{4}$

13. $\frac{1}{8}$ or $\frac{1}{3}$

14. $\frac{1}{15}$ or $\frac{1}{20}$

15. $\frac{1}{9}$ or $\frac{1}{19}$

16. $\frac{1}{5}$ or $\frac{1}{10}$

17. $\frac{1}{2}$ or $\frac{1}{8}$

18. $\frac{1}{4}$ or $\frac{1}{12}$

19. $\frac{1}{9}$ or $\frac{1}{5}$

20. $\frac{1}{6}$ or $\frac{1}{12}$

⭐ Challenge

Which fraction is greater?

21. $\frac{1}{3}$ or $\frac{2}{5}$

22. $\frac{2}{3}$ or $\frac{2}{5}$

23. $\frac{1}{6}$ or $\frac{1}{4}$

24. $\frac{3}{6}$ or $\frac{3}{4}$

25. $\frac{4}{5}$ or $\frac{4}{8}$

Adding Like Fractions

Like fractions have
the same denominators.

$\frac{3}{10}$ and $\frac{4}{10}$ are like fractions.

You can add like fractions
by adding numerators.

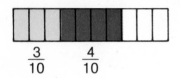

$$\frac{3}{10} \qquad \frac{4}{10}$$

$$\frac{3}{10} + \frac{4}{10} = \frac{7}{10}$$

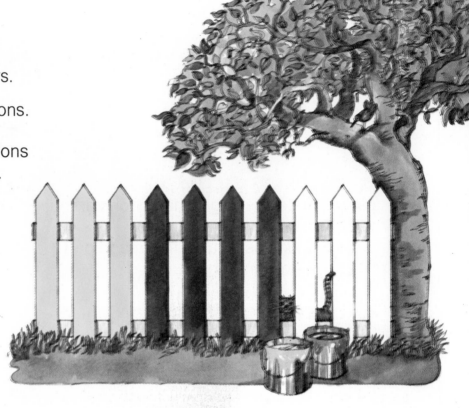

Add.

1. $\frac{1}{5} + \frac{3}{5}$ $\frac{4}{5}$

2. $\frac{1}{4} + \frac{2}{4}$

3. $\frac{1}{3} + \frac{1}{3}$

4. $\frac{1}{6} + \frac{1}{6}$

5. $\frac{1}{2} + \frac{1}{2}$

6. $\frac{2}{5} + \frac{1}{5}$

7. $\frac{3}{6} + \frac{2}{6}$

8. $\frac{2}{8} + \frac{2}{8}$

9. $\frac{2}{7} + \frac{3}{7}$

10. $\frac{1}{10} + \frac{3}{10}$

11. $\frac{1}{4} + \frac{1}{4}$

12. $\frac{5}{7} + \frac{1}{7}$

13. $\frac{4}{8} + \frac{2}{8}$

14. $\frac{5}{12} + \frac{4}{12}$

15. $\frac{4}{9} + \frac{3}{9}$

16. $\frac{1}{3} + \frac{1}{3}$

17. $\frac{1}{6} + \frac{4}{6}$

18. $\frac{3}{8} + \frac{2}{8}$

19. $\frac{3}{10} + \frac{2}{10}$

20. $\frac{4}{12} + \frac{7}{12}$

21. Raymond plants corn in $\frac{1}{4}$ of his garden and tomatoes in $\frac{2}{4}$ of his garden. How much of his garden is planted in corn and tomatoes?

22. Lucy plants beans in $\frac{3}{8}$ of her garden and lettuce in $\frac{2}{8}$ of her garden. How much of the garden is planted in beans and lettuce?

Subtracting Like Fractions

You can subtract like fractions.
Subtract numerators.

$$\frac{7}{10} - \frac{3}{10} = \frac{4}{10}$$

The denominators
are the same.

Subtract.

1. $\frac{3}{4} - \frac{1}{4}$ $\frac{2}{4}$ 2. $\frac{9}{10} - \frac{6}{10}$ 3. $\frac{7}{8} - \frac{4}{8}$ 4. $\frac{5}{6} - \frac{2}{6}$ 5. $\frac{7}{12} - \frac{1}{12}$

6. $\frac{5}{7} - \frac{3}{7}$ 7. $\frac{8}{10} - \frac{5}{10}$ 8. $\frac{10}{12} - \frac{8}{12}$ 9. $\frac{3}{4} - \frac{2}{4}$ 10. $\frac{4}{4} - \frac{2}{4}$

11. $\begin{array}{r} \frac{5}{8} \\ -\frac{2}{8} \\ \hline \end{array}$ 12. $\begin{array}{r} \frac{4}{5} \\ -\frac{2}{5} \\ \hline \end{array}$ 13. $\begin{array}{r} \frac{7}{8} \\ -\frac{6}{8} \\ \hline \end{array}$ 14. $\begin{array}{r} \frac{6}{7} \\ -\frac{2}{7} \\ \hline \end{array}$ 15. $\begin{array}{r} \frac{11}{12} \\ -\frac{2}{12} \\ \hline \end{array}$ 16. $\begin{array}{r} \frac{7}{9} \\ -\frac{5}{9} \\ \hline \end{array}$

17. $\begin{array}{r} \frac{10}{12} \\ -\frac{3}{12} \\ \hline \end{array}$ 18. $\begin{array}{r} \frac{7}{9} \\ -\frac{2}{9} \\ \hline \end{array}$ 19. $\begin{array}{r} \frac{8}{8} \\ -\frac{1}{8} \\ \hline \end{array}$ 20. $\begin{array}{r} \frac{9}{10} \\ -\frac{1}{10} \\ \hline \end{array}$ 21. $\begin{array}{r} \frac{4}{5} \\ -\frac{3}{5} \\ \hline \end{array}$ 22. $\begin{array}{r} \frac{3}{7} \\ -\frac{3}{7} \\ \hline \end{array}$

23. Ann and Adam have $\frac{8}{10}$ kilogram of hamburger. They use $\frac{3}{10}$ kilogram to make lunch. How much do they have left?

24. Ann spends $\frac{1}{4}$ hour making lunch. Adam spends $\frac{2}{4}$ hour making dinner. How much more time does it take to make dinner than lunch?

Budget Problems

Think about the important facts. Decide to add or subtract. Find each answer.

1. Every month Dave's family spends $\frac{4}{10}$ of their money to pay for their house. They spend $\frac{3}{10}$ of their money to buy food. What part of their money do they spend for these together? $\frac{7}{10}$

2. Lena's family spends $\frac{1}{6}$ of their money on a new car and $\frac{1}{6}$ of their money to add a garage to their house. What part of their money do they spend for these together?

3. Erica spends $\frac{4}{12}$ of her time working and $\frac{1}{12}$ of her time reading. How much more time does she spend working than reading?

4. John spends $\frac{2}{8}$ of his time at school and $\frac{1}{8}$ of his time building a boat. How much of his time does he spend on both?

5. Luisa puts $\frac{1}{10}$ of her money into savings. She pays $\frac{3}{10}$ of her money for rent. How much more for rent than savings?

Adding and Subtracting Like Fractions

Add or subtract.

1. $\frac{4}{5}$
$-\frac{2}{5}$
$\frac{2}{5}$

2. $\frac{9}{10}$
$-\frac{1}{10}$

3. $\frac{3}{6}$
$+\frac{2}{6}$

4. $\frac{4}{6}$
$-\frac{1}{6}$

5. $\frac{3}{5}$
$-\frac{2}{5}$

6. $\frac{8}{10}$
$-\frac{3}{10}$

7. $\frac{6}{10}$
$+\frac{2}{10}$

8. $\frac{7}{8}$
$-\frac{4}{8}$

9. $\frac{4}{7}$
$+\frac{1}{7}$

10. $\frac{7}{12}$
$+\frac{2}{12}$

11. $\frac{6}{7}$
$-\frac{3}{7}$

12. $\frac{1}{8}$
$+\frac{2}{8}$

13. $\frac{3}{4}$
$-\frac{1}{4}$

14. $\frac{5}{12}$
$+\frac{2}{12}$

15. $\frac{8}{9}$
$-\frac{4}{9}$

16. $\frac{5}{7}$
$-\frac{2}{7}$

17. $\frac{3}{3}$
$-\frac{1}{3}$

18. $\frac{7}{9}$
$-\frac{2}{9}$

19. $\frac{4}{5}$
$+\frac{1}{5}$

20. $\frac{7}{10}$
$-\frac{3}{10}$

21. $\frac{3}{7}$
$+\frac{2}{7}$

22. $\frac{5}{10}$
$+\frac{4}{10}$

23. $\frac{11}{12}$
$-\frac{7}{12}$

24. $\frac{3}{8}$
$+\frac{1}{8}$

25. $\frac{7}{12}$
$+\frac{3}{12}$

26. $\frac{8}{8}$
$-\frac{4}{8}$

27. $\frac{8}{10}$
$+\frac{1}{10}$

28. $\frac{4}{6}$
$+\frac{2}{6}$

29. $\frac{6}{7}$
$-\frac{5}{7}$

30. $\frac{9}{10}$
$-\frac{5}{10}$

 Review (pp. 175–185)

1. $\frac{2}{3}$
$-\frac{1}{3}$

2. $\frac{5}{6}$
$-\frac{3}{6}$

3. $\frac{4}{8}$
$+\frac{3}{8}$

4. $\frac{4}{5}$
$-\frac{2}{5}$

5. $\frac{3}{7}$
$+\frac{1}{7}$

6. $\frac{7}{12}$
$+\frac{4}{12}$

Mixed Numbers

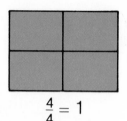

$\frac{4}{4} = 1$ $\frac{2}{4}$

$\dfrac{4}{4} + \dfrac{2}{4} = \dfrac{6}{4}$

$\frac{6}{4} = 1$ whole and $\frac{2}{4}$ of a whole

$\frac{6}{4} = 1\frac{2}{4}$ Read this:
one and two fourths

$1\frac{2}{4}$ is a **mixed number**.

$1\frac{1}{3}$, $2\frac{5}{6}$, $4\frac{3}{8}$, and numbers like them are mixed numbers.

Write a fraction and a mixed number for the shaded parts.

1. $\frac{5}{3}$, $1\frac{2}{3}$

2.

3.

4.

How many wholes can you make from these fractions? Make drawings if you need help.

5. $\frac{6}{3}$ 2   6. $\frac{2}{2}$ 7. $\frac{4}{2}$ 8. $\frac{6}{2}$ 9. $\frac{4}{4}$ 10. $\frac{8}{4}$ 11. $\frac{3}{3}$

12. $\frac{9}{3}$ 13. $\frac{5}{5}$ 14. $\frac{10}{5}$ 15. $\frac{8}{8}$ 16. $\frac{6}{6}$ 17. $\frac{12}{6}$ 18. $\frac{20}{4}$

Changing Mixed Numbers to Fractions

A mixed number is the sum of
a whole number and a fraction.

$$2\frac{1}{3} = 2 + \frac{1}{3}$$

Change $2\frac{1}{3}$ to a fraction.

Step 1
Change the whole
number to a fraction.

$$2\frac{1}{3} = \frac{6}{3} + \frac{1}{3}$$

$$2 = \frac{6}{3}$$

Step 2
Add.

$$\frac{6}{3} + \frac{1}{3} = \frac{7}{3}$$

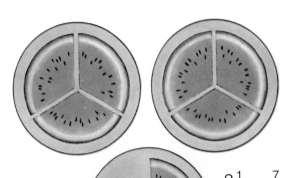

$$2\frac{1}{3} = \frac{7}{3}$$

Complete the fraction. Make drawings if you need help.

1. $1\frac{3}{4} = \frac{?}{4}$ $\frac{7}{4}$ 2. $1\frac{2}{3} = \frac{?}{3}$ 3. $1\frac{3}{5} = \frac{?}{5}$ 4. $1\frac{1}{2} = \frac{?}{2}$ 5. $1\frac{5}{7} = \frac{?}{7}$

6. $2\frac{1}{4} = \frac{?}{4}$ 7. $2\frac{2}{6} = \frac{?}{6}$ 8. $2\frac{1}{2} = \frac{?}{2}$ 9. $5\frac{2}{4} = \frac{?}{4}$ 10. $4\frac{3}{5} = \frac{?}{5}$

Change these mixed numbers to fractions.

11. $1\frac{2}{3}$ 12. $1\frac{3}{8}$ 13. $1\frac{1}{5}$ 14. $1\frac{2}{6}$ 15. $1\frac{3}{4}$ 16. $1\frac{5}{7}$

17. $2\frac{2}{4}$ 18. $4\frac{1}{8}$ 19. $3\frac{2}{3}$ 20. $2\frac{2}{5}$ 21. $5\frac{1}{6}$ 22. $2\frac{2}{9}$

Changing Fractions to Mixed Numbers

Change $\frac{9}{4}$ to a mixed number.

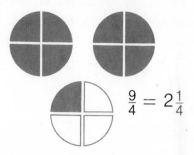

Step 1
Make as many wholes as you can.

$$\frac{9}{4} = \frac{8}{4} + \frac{1}{4}$$

$\frac{8}{4}$ = 2 wholes

Step 2
Add the wholes and the leftover fraction.

$$2 + \frac{1}{4} = 2\frac{1}{4}$$

$\frac{9}{4} = 2\frac{1}{4}$

Complete these mixed numbers.
Make drawings if you need help.

1. $\frac{7}{3} = ?\frac{1}{3}$ $2\frac{1}{3}$
2. $\frac{5}{4} = ?\frac{1}{4}$
3. $\frac{7}{2} = ?\frac{1}{2}$
4. $\frac{7}{6} = ?\frac{1}{6}$
5. $\frac{9}{7} = ?\frac{2}{7}$

6. $\frac{7}{4} = ?\frac{3}{4}$
7. $\frac{10}{4} = ?\frac{?}{4}$
8. $\frac{8}{5} = ?\frac{?}{5}$
9. $\frac{5}{2} = ?\frac{?}{2}$
10. $\frac{8}{3} = ?\frac{?}{3}$

Change the fractions to mixed numbers.

11. $\frac{4}{3}$
12. $\frac{7}{5}$
13. $\frac{9}{4}$
14. $\frac{5}{3}$
15. $\frac{6}{4}$
16. $\frac{9}{2}$

17. $\frac{7}{4}$
18. $\frac{11}{4}$
19. $\frac{3}{2}$
20. $\frac{6}{5}$
21. $\frac{9}{8}$
22. $\frac{7}{3}$

Adding and Subtracting Mixed Numbers

You can add and subtract mixed numbers. Just be sure the fractions have the same denominators.

Add the fractions.
Add the numbers.

$$1\frac{2}{4}$$
$$+\ 3\frac{1}{4}$$
$$\overline{4\frac{3}{4}}$$

Add or subtract.

1. $1\frac{1}{3}$
   $+\ 2\frac{1}{3}$
   $\overline{\ \ 3\frac{2}{3}}$

2. $2\frac{2}{5}$
   $+\ 3\frac{1}{5}$

3. $3\frac{1}{4}$
   $+\ 4\frac{2}{4}$

4. $5\frac{3}{4}$
   $-\ 1\frac{2}{4}$

5. $4\frac{7}{8}$
   $-\ 3\frac{2}{8}$

6. $1\frac{2}{5}$
   $-\ 1\frac{1}{5}$

7. $9\frac{1}{8}$
   $-\ 2\frac{1}{8}$

8. $5\frac{4}{6}$
   $+\ 1\frac{1}{6}$

9. $7\frac{1}{3}$
   $+\ 1\frac{1}{3}$

10. $4\frac{1}{2}$
    $-\ 2\frac{1}{2}$

11. $3\frac{5}{6}$
    $-\ \ \frac{4}{6}$

12. $2\frac{2}{4}$
    $-\ 1\frac{1}{4}$

13. $12\frac{4}{6}$
    $-\ 8\frac{2}{6}$

14. $10\frac{8}{10}$
    $+\ 3\frac{1}{10}$

15. $6\frac{1}{5}$
    $+\ 4\frac{1}{5}$

16. $9\frac{6}{8}$
    $-\ 3\frac{3}{8}$

17. $2\frac{4}{10}$
    $+\ 3\frac{2}{10}$

18. $6\frac{3}{5}$
    $-\ 2\frac{2}{5}$

 Challenge

Remember, $\frac{8}{8} = 1$, 1 is a whole.

19. Michael eats $\frac{3}{8}$ of his apple and gives away $\frac{3}{8}$ of his apple. What part of the apple does he have left?

20. Avelina uses $\frac{2}{8}$ of all the apples to make applesauce and $\frac{1}{8}$ of all the apples to make a pie. What part of all the apples is left?

Equal Fractions

Equal fractions name the same amount.

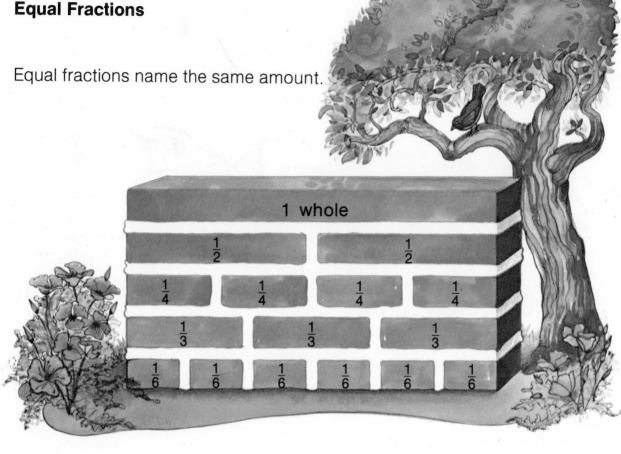

Use the fraction fence. Copy and complete.

1. $\frac{1}{2} = \frac{?}{4}$ $\frac{1}{2} = \frac{2}{4}$ 2. $\frac{3}{6} = \frac{?}{2}$ 3. $\frac{2}{4} = \frac{?}{2}$ 4. $0 = \frac{?}{6}$ 5. $\frac{1}{2} = \frac{?}{6}$

6. $\frac{1}{3} = \frac{?}{6}$ 7. $\frac{2}{3} = \frac{?}{6}$ 8. $\frac{3}{3} = \frac{?}{6}$ 9. $1 = \frac{?}{2}$ 10. $1 = \frac{?}{4}$

11. $\frac{2}{6} = \frac{?}{3}$ 12. $\frac{2}{4} = \frac{?}{6}$ 13. $1 = \frac{?}{3}$ 14. $0 = \frac{?}{2}$ 15. $\frac{6}{6} = \frac{?}{4}$

16. $\frac{2}{2} = \frac{?}{3}$ 17. $0 = \frac{?}{4}$ 18. $1 = \frac{?}{6}$ 19. $\frac{3}{3} = \frac{?}{2}$ 20. $\frac{2}{2} = \frac{?}{4}$

21. May has $\frac{2}{3}$ of an apple. How many sixths is that?

22. Tom has 1 melon. How many fourths can he make?

Finding Equal Fractions

To get equal fractions, multiply the numerator and the denominator by the same number.

$\dfrac{1}{3} = \dfrac{?}{6}$ There are **2** three's in 6, so multiply the 1 by **2**.

$\dfrac{1}{3} = \dfrac{2}{6}$

Find equal fractions. Copy and complete.

1. $\dfrac{1}{3} = \dfrac{?}{9}$ $\dfrac{1}{3} = \dfrac{3}{9}$ 2. $\dfrac{3}{4} = \dfrac{?}{8}$ 3. $\dfrac{1}{3} = \dfrac{?}{6}$ 4. $\dfrac{5}{6} = \dfrac{?}{12}$ 5. $\dfrac{1}{2} = \dfrac{?}{8}$

6. $\dfrac{4}{5} = \dfrac{?}{10}$ 7. $\dfrac{1}{2} = \dfrac{?}{10}$ 8. $\dfrac{1}{4} = \dfrac{?}{8}$ 9. $\dfrac{3}{7} = \dfrac{?}{14}$ 10. $\dfrac{2}{3} = \dfrac{?}{6}$

11. $\dfrac{3}{5} = \dfrac{?}{15}$ 12. $\dfrac{1}{6} = \dfrac{?}{18}$ 13. $\dfrac{2}{3} = \dfrac{?}{12}$ 14. $\dfrac{2}{5} = \dfrac{?}{10}$ 15. $\dfrac{1}{4} = \dfrac{?}{12}$

 Challenge
Find equal fractions. Copy and complete.

16. $\dfrac{6}{15} = \dfrac{?}{5}$ 17. $\dfrac{6}{10} = \dfrac{?}{5}$ 18. $\dfrac{3}{9} = \dfrac{?}{3}$ 19. $\dfrac{7}{14} = \dfrac{?}{2}$ 20. $\dfrac{3}{18} = \dfrac{?}{6}$

Adding Unlike Fractions

Like fractions have a **common denominator.**
You must have like fractions before
you can add or subtract.

Find an equal fraction,
then add.

$$\frac{3}{4} = \frac{6}{8}$$

$$+ \frac{1}{8} = + \frac{1}{8}$$

$$\frac{7}{8}$$

8 is the
common
denominator.

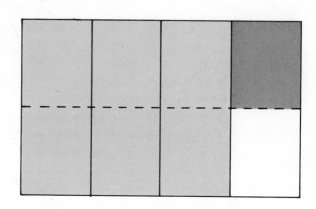

Add. Use 12 as the common denominator.

1. $\frac{5}{12}$ $\frac{5}{12}$
$+ \frac{1}{6}$ $+ \frac{2}{12}$
        $\frac{7}{12}$

2. $\frac{5}{12}$
$+ \frac{1}{3}$

3. $\frac{3}{12}$
$+ \frac{2}{6}$

4. $\frac{2}{12}$
$+ \frac{3}{4}$

5. $\frac{7}{12}$
$+ \frac{1}{3}$

Find a common denominator. Add.

6. $\frac{1}{2}$
$+ \frac{3}{10}$

7. $\frac{3}{4}$
$+ \frac{3}{8}$

8. $\frac{2}{3}$
$+ \frac{1}{6}$

9. $\frac{1}{4}$
$+ \frac{1}{8}$

10. $\frac{2}{3}$
$+ \frac{2}{6}$

11. $\frac{1}{5}$
$+ \frac{2}{10}$

12. $\frac{1}{4} + \frac{3}{8}$

13. $\frac{2}{5} + \frac{1}{10}$

14. $\frac{2}{12} + \frac{1}{2}$

15. $\frac{1}{2} + \frac{1}{8}$

16. $\frac{3}{6} + \frac{2}{12}$

Subtracting Unlike Fractions

You must have like fractions
before you can subtract.

$$\begin{array}{ccc} \dfrac{3}{10} & = & \dfrac{3}{10} \\[6pt] -\dfrac{1}{5} & = & -\dfrac{2}{10} \\[6pt] & & \dfrac{1}{10} \end{array}$$

10 is the
common
denominator.

$\dfrac{3}{10}$ numerator
denominator

Subtract. Use 12 as the common denominator.

1. $\dfrac{8}{12}$ $\dfrac{8}{12}$
    $-\dfrac{2}{6}$ $-\dfrac{4}{12}$
    _____
                      $\dfrac{4}{12}$

2. $\dfrac{1}{3}$
    $-\dfrac{3}{12}$

3. $\dfrac{1}{3}$
    $-\dfrac{1}{12}$

4. $\dfrac{3}{4}$
    $-\dfrac{5}{12}$

5. $\dfrac{10}{12}$
    $-\dfrac{1}{3}$

Find a common denominator. Subtract.

6. $\dfrac{1}{2}$
    $-\dfrac{2}{10}$

7. $\dfrac{7}{8}$
    $-\dfrac{2}{4}$

8. $\dfrac{6}{9}$
    $-\dfrac{1}{3}$

9. $\dfrac{5}{8}$
    $-\dfrac{1}{2}$

10. $\dfrac{3}{4}$
    $-\dfrac{4}{12}$

11. $\dfrac{8}{10}$
    $-\dfrac{2}{5}$

12. $\dfrac{9}{10} - \dfrac{1}{2}$

13. $\dfrac{8}{12} - \dfrac{1}{4}$

14. $\dfrac{1}{2} - \dfrac{1}{6}$

15. $\dfrac{3}{8} - \dfrac{1}{4}$

16. $\dfrac{2}{3} - \dfrac{2}{6}$

17. Miguel spends $\dfrac{1}{2}$ of his allowance on a present
for his sister. He spends $\dfrac{1}{4}$ of his allowance on
a book for himself. How much more for the gift
than the book?

Practicing Addition and Subtraction

Use common denominators. Add or subtract.

1. $\frac{3}{8}$ $\frac{3}{8}$
   $+\frac{1}{2}$ $+\frac{4}{8}$
   $\frac{7}{8}$

2. $\frac{4}{5}$
   $-\frac{1}{10}$

3. $\frac{1}{3}$
   $-\frac{1}{6}$

4. $\frac{1}{4}$
   $-\frac{1}{8}$

5. $\frac{6}{12}$
   $-\frac{1}{3}$

6. $\frac{9}{10}$
   $-\frac{4}{5}$

7. $\frac{1}{2}$
   $+\frac{1}{4}$

8. $\frac{4}{10}$
   $+\frac{1}{2}$

9. $\frac{4}{12}$
   $-\frac{1}{4}$

10. $\frac{3}{8}$
    $-\frac{1}{4}$

11. $\frac{6}{8}$
    $-\frac{1}{2}$

12. $\frac{2}{6}$
    $+\frac{1}{3}$

13. $\frac{5}{6}$
    $-\frac{1}{2}$

14. $\frac{4}{8}$
    $+\frac{1}{4}$

15. $\frac{5}{6}$
    $+\frac{2}{12}$

16. $\frac{7}{10}$
    $-\frac{3}{5}$

17. $\frac{1}{4}$
    $+\frac{3}{8}$

18. $\frac{1}{4}$
    $+\frac{3}{12}$

19. $\frac{7}{8}$
    $-\frac{2}{4}$

20. $\frac{5}{10}$
    $-\frac{1}{5}$

21. $\frac{2}{6}$
    $-\frac{1}{12}$

22. $\frac{3}{8}$
    $-\frac{1}{4}$

23. $\frac{1}{10}$
    $+\frac{4}{5}$

24. $\frac{7}{8}$
    $-\frac{3}{4}$

25. $\frac{7}{12}$
    $+\frac{1}{3}$

26. $\frac{1}{2}$
    $+\frac{3}{10}$

27. $\frac{3}{4}$
    $-\frac{5}{12}$

28. $\frac{1}{8}$
    $+\frac{2}{4}$

29. $\frac{7}{10}$
    $-\frac{1}{2}$

 Challenge

30. The City Museum spends $\frac{3}{10}$ of its money to buy new art. $\frac{3}{10}$ of the money pays for all other costs. How much of the money is spent in all?

31. $\frac{2}{3}$ of the art at the City Museum is painting. $\frac{1}{6}$ is sculpture. How much more painting than sculpture?

Park Problems

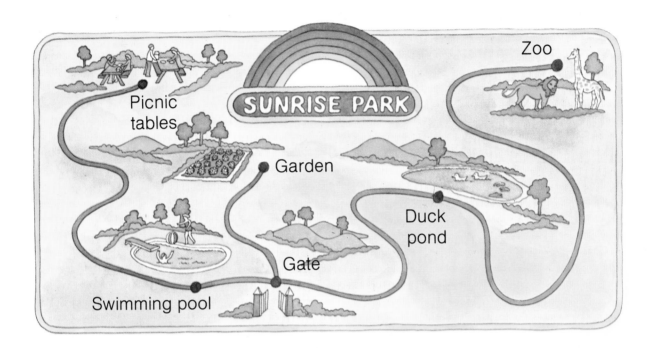

Add to find each answer.

1. At Sunrise Park the garden is $\frac{2}{10}$ kilometer from the gate. The duck pond is $\frac{2}{5}$ kilometer from the gate. How far is the garden from the duck pond?
$\frac{6}{10}$ kilometer

2. The distance from the gate to the swimming pool is $\frac{1}{10}$ kilometer. The distance from the pool to the picnic tables is $\frac{1}{2}$ kilometer. How far is that altogether?

3. The distance from the zoo to the duck pond is $\frac{7}{10}$ kilometer. The pond is $\frac{2}{5}$ kilometer from the gate. What is the distance from the zoo to the gate?

4. The zoo has black and brown bears. $\frac{1}{12}$ of all the animals are black bears. $\frac{1}{6}$ of all the animals are brown bears. What part of all the animals are bears?

Getting Ready to Multiply Fractions

This group of 12 jacks is divided into fourths.

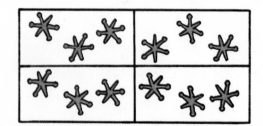

$\frac{1}{4}$ of 12 is **3**.

$\frac{3}{4}$ of 12 is **9**.

$\frac{4}{4}$ of 12 is **12**.

Use the pictures to answer the questions.

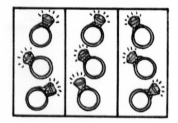

1a. $\frac{1}{3}$ of 9 is ▢.　3

b. $\frac{2}{3}$ of 9 is ▢.

c. $\frac{3}{3}$ of 9 is ▢.

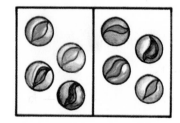

2a. $\frac{1}{2}$ of 8 is ▢.

b. $\frac{2}{2}$ of 8 is ▢.

c. $\frac{0}{2}$ of 8 is ▢.

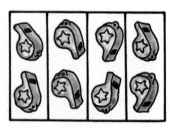

3a. $\frac{1}{4}$ of 8 is ▢.

b. $\frac{2}{4}$ of 8 is ▢.

c. $\frac{3}{4}$ of 8 is ▢.

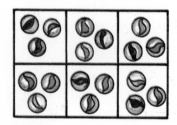

4a. $\frac{2}{6}$ of 18 is ▢.

b. $\frac{3}{6}$ of 18 is ▢.

c. $\frac{5}{6}$ of 18 is ▢.

5a. $\frac{1}{4}$ of 16 is ▢.

b. $\frac{2}{4}$ of 16 is ▢.

c. $\frac{3}{4}$ of 16 is ▢.

6a. $\frac{1}{3}$ of 6 is ▢.

b. $\frac{2}{3}$ of 6 is ▢.

c. $\frac{3}{3}$ of 6 is ▢.

Multiplying by a Fraction

$\frac{1}{4}$ of **12** means $\frac{1}{4}$ × **12.**

$\frac{1}{4}$ × **12 = 3**

Think: 12 ÷ 4 = 3

Find the answers.

1a. $\frac{1}{3}$ × 18   6   **2a.** $\frac{1}{3}$ × 12   **3a.** $\frac{1}{5}$ × 20   **4a.** $\frac{1}{2}$ × 8   **5a.** $\frac{1}{6}$ × 12

  b. 18 ÷ 3   6   **b.** 12 ÷ 3   **b.** 20 ÷ 5   **b.** 8 ÷ 2   **b.** 12 ÷ 6

6a. $\frac{1}{7}$ × 21   **7a.** $\frac{1}{4}$ × 16   **8a.** $\frac{1}{8}$ × 16   **9a.** $\frac{1}{5}$ × 40   **10a.** $\frac{1}{6}$ × 24

  b. 21 ÷ 7   **b.** 16 ÷ 4   **b.** 16 ÷ 8   **b.** 40 ÷ 5   **b.** 24 ÷ 6

11a. $\frac{1}{2}$ × 18   **12a.** $\frac{1}{6}$ × 42   **13a.** $\frac{1}{8}$ × 32   **14a.** $\frac{1}{6}$ × 36   **15a.** $\frac{1}{3}$ × 27

  b. 18 ÷ 2   **b.** 42 ÷ 6   **b.** 32 ÷ 8   **b.** 36 ÷ 6   **b.** 27 ÷ 3

16a. $\frac{1}{4}$ × 20   **17a.** $\frac{1}{5}$ × 30   **18a.** $\frac{1}{2}$ × 10   **19a.** $\frac{1}{8}$ × 56   **20a.** $\frac{1}{5}$ × 45

  b. 20 ÷ 4   **b.** 30 ÷ 5   **b.** 10 ÷ 2   **b.** 56 ÷ 8   **b.** 45 ÷ 5

21. Mariko had 16 gifts. She gave away $\frac{1}{8}$ of them. How many did she give away?

22. Dan had 10 balloons. He gave away $\frac{1}{2}$ of them. How many did he give away?

Decimals for Fractions

Tenths may be written as **decimals**.

Remember the zero and the decimal point.

$\frac{3}{10}$ is red.

0.3 is red.

zero ones ⤴ ⤴ decimal point

Write each fraction as a decimal.

1. $\frac{4}{10}$ 0.4   2. $\frac{8}{10}$ 3. $\frac{5}{10}$ 4. $\frac{9}{10}$ 5. $\frac{6}{10}$ 6. $\frac{1}{10}$ 7. $\frac{3}{10}$

Write a fraction and a decimal for each.

   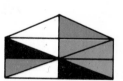

8a. What part is blue?
 b. What part is red?
 c. What part is white?
 d. What part is red **and** blue?
 e. What part is blue **and** white?

9a. What part is red?
 b. What part is blue?
 c. What part is white?
 d. What part is black?
 e. What part is white **and** red?

 Challenge

Make a drawing to show each decimal.

10. 0.3   11. 0.5   12. 0.1   13. 0.9   14. 0.2   15. 0.6

Decimals for Mixed Numbers

Mixed numbers can be written as decimals, too.

$2\frac{3}{10} = 2.3$

Write a decimal for each.

1. $1\frac{2}{10}$ 1.2   2. $1\frac{5}{10}$ 3. $1\frac{7}{10}$ 4. $1\frac{9}{10}$ 5. $1\frac{1}{10}$ 6. $1\frac{3}{10}$

7. $2\frac{3}{10}$ 8. $2\frac{6}{10}$ 9. $3\frac{8}{10}$ 10. $5\frac{4}{10}$ 11. $17\frac{5}{10}$ 12. $18\frac{2}{10}$

Write a fraction for each.

13. 1.6   14. 1.9   15. 2.4   16. 3.8   17. 4.3   18. 9.1

19. 3.2   20. 4.4   21. 7.5   22. 10.7   23. 12.8   24. 15.1

 Challenge
Write the tenths that come between these.

25. 0.2 _____ 0.5   26. 0.8 _____ 1.1   27. 1.7 _____ 2.1

28. 2.9 _____ 3.1   29. 0.0 _____ 0.3   30. 1.8 _____ 2.2

Using Decimals for Measurement

Centimeters (cm) are divided into 10 parts.
Each part is called a **millimeter (mm)**.

You can use decimals to write
metric measurements in millimeters.

10 mm = 1 cm   1 mm = 0.1 cm

```
cm 1   2   3   4   5   6   7   8   9
```

Change to centimeters. Use the ruler above.

1. 3 mm 0.3 cm   **2.** 7 mm   **3.** 9 mm   **4.** 6 mm   **5.** 1 mm

6. 2 mm   **7.** 4 mm   **8.** 5 mm   **9.** 0 mm   **10.** 3 mm

Change to millimeters.

11. 0.2 cm   **12.** 0.4 cm   **13.** 0.5 cm   **14.** 1.8 cm   **15.** 3.7 cm

16. 1.1 cm   **17.** 5.3 cm   **18.** 0.9 cm   **19.** 0.6 cm   **20.** 0.0 cm

Nora Nakamura planted seeds and measured the heights of the seedlings in millimeters. Change these measurements to centimeters.

21. daisies: 12 mm   **22.** tomatoes: 36 mm

23. pumpkins: 83 mm   **24.** squash: 29 mm

25. peas: 94 mm   **26.** sunflowers: 62 mm

Adding and Subtracting Decimals

Find an answer that makes sense.
Look at whole numbers first.

$$8.4$$ $8 + 1 = 9$
The answer
$$+ 1.2$$ has to be about 9.

$$8.4$$ $8 - 1 = 7$
The answer
$$- 1.2$$ has to be about 7.

Look at each problem. Choose the answer that makes the most sense.

1.   5.4
    + 2.1
    (70, 3, 7, or 30)   7

2.   8.4
    − 2.2
    (10, 100, 60, or 6)

3.   12.1
    − 9.0
    (3, 21, 30, or 210)

4.   24.2
    − 10.1
    (14, 340, 34, or 140)

5.   52.4
    + 21.2
    (31, 310, 730, or 73)

6.   120.3
    − 120.2
    (24, 2400, 240, or 0)

7.   80.3
    − 16.1
    (64, 640, 6, or 96)

8.   36.2
    + 12.2
    (24, 18, 480, or 48)

9.   115.4
    − 89.1
    (26, 194, 260, or 19)

 Calculate

Find the sum. Add or subtract from left to right.

10. $4.5 - 1.8 + 0.1 + 8.9$

11. $1.1 + 3.7 + 7.6 - 4.2 - 0.8 + 0.5 - 2.3$

12. $4.8 + 0.9 - 2.1 - 0.6 + 2.7 + 5.8 + 3.6 - 0.8 - 2.7 + 4.7 - 2.9$

Decimal Practice

Be sure to line up
the decimal points.

Add.

$$\begin{array}{r} 7.4 \\ + \ 2.1 \\ \hline 9.5 \end{array}$$

Subtract.

$$\begin{array}{r} 7.4 \\ - \ 2.1 \\ \hline 5.3 \end{array}$$

How much
taller?

7.4 m

2.1 m

Add or subtract.
Remember the decimal point.

1. $\begin{array}{r} 8.2 \\ + \ 1.6 \\ \hline 9.8 \end{array}$ **2.** $\begin{array}{r} 6.5 \\ - \ 3.1 \\ \hline \end{array}$ **3.** $\begin{array}{r} 12.6 \\ - \ \ 9.4 \\ \hline \end{array}$ **4.** $\begin{array}{r} 15.3 \\ + \ 21.2 \\ \hline \end{array}$ **5.** $\begin{array}{r} 19.7 \\ - \ 15.5 \\ \hline \end{array}$

6. $\begin{array}{r} 2.1 \\ + \ 4.3 \\ \hline \end{array}$ **7.** $\begin{array}{r} 59.7 \\ - \ 23.4 \\ \hline \end{array}$ **8.** $\begin{array}{r} 176.6 \\ - \ \ 92.5 \\ \hline \end{array}$ **9.** $\begin{array}{r} 23.1 \\ + \ 46.3 \\ \hline \end{array}$ **10.** $\begin{array}{r} 823.8 \\ - \ 401.2 \\ \hline \end{array}$

11. $342.5 + 281.1$ **12.** $560.4 + 120.5$ **13.** $51.7 + 2.1$

14. $103.4 + 12.3$ **15.** $59.2 + 120.5$ **16.** $30.7 + 200.2$

 **Review**   (pp. 175–202)

1. $\frac{4}{10} + \frac{3}{10}$ **2.** $\frac{7}{12} - \frac{5}{12}$ **3.** $9\frac{1}{8} + 2\frac{1}{8}$ **4.** $\frac{3}{6} - \frac{1}{3}$ **5.** $\frac{1}{4} + \frac{3}{8}$

6. $\frac{1}{3} \times 9$ **7.** $\frac{1}{4} \times 24$ **8.** $3.4 + 1.2$ **9.** $19.6 - 13.5$

Writing Hundredths

Hundredths may be written as decimals.

one-hundredth

$$\frac{1}{100} = 0.01$$

zero ones ⌡ │ └ one-hundredth
zero tenths

twenty-five hundredths

$$\frac{25}{100} = 0.25$$

Write each as a decimal. Remember to use 0 and the decimal point.

1. $\frac{3}{100}$ 0.03 2. $\frac{8}{100}$ 3. $\frac{15}{100}$ 4. $\frac{22}{100}$ 5. $\frac{63}{100}$ 6. $\frac{3}{100}$

7. $\frac{25}{100}$ 8. $\frac{40}{100}$ 9. $\frac{75}{100}$ 10. $\frac{99}{100}$ 11. $\frac{50}{100}$ 12. $\frac{9}{100}$

13. thirty-six hundredths 14. four-hundredths 15. twenty-hundredths

Each part is one-hundredth.

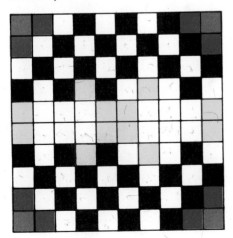

Use the square to answer the questions. Write a fraction and a decimal.

16a. How much is red? $\frac{4}{100}$, 0.04
  b. How much is white?
  c. How much is black?
  d. How much is blue?
  e. How much is yellow?
  f. How much is black and blue?
  g. How much is blue and red?

Tenths and Hundredths

1 tenth = 10 hundredths	6 tenths = 60 hundredths
$\dfrac{1}{10} = \dfrac{10}{100}$	$\dfrac{6}{10} = \dfrac{60}{100}$
0.1 = 0.10	0.6 = 0.60

Write these as hundredths.

1. 0.5 0.50
2. 0.8
3. 0.9
4. 0.7
5. 0.3

6. 0.2
7. 0.1
8. 0.4
9. 0.6
10. 0.0

Write a different decimal which has the same value.

11. 0.50 0.5
12. 0.10
13. 0.2
14. 0.3
15. 0.4

16. 0.60
17. 0.5
18. 0.1
19. 0.90
20. 0.70

21. 0.20
22. 0.40
23. 0.30
24. 0.6
25. 0.8

Write the missing hundredths.

26. 0.78, ▢, 0.80
27. 0.81, ▢, 0.83
28. 0.09, ▢, 0.11

29. ▢, 0.31, 0.32
30. 0.78, ▢, 0.80
31. 0.07, 0.08, ▢

32. 0.49, ▢, 0.51
33. 0.97, 0.98, ▢
34. 0.19, 0.20, ▢

35. 0.60, ▢, 0.62
36. ▢, 0.01, 0.02
37. 0.03, ▢, 0.05

Adding and Subtracting Decimals

Trade here, too!

Add.

$$\begin{array}{r} \overset{1\;\;1}{24.32} \\ +\;32.78 \\ \hline 57.10 \end{array}$$

Subtract.

$$\begin{array}{r} \overset{3\;\;12\;12}{\cancel{4}.\cancel{3}\cancel{2}} \\ -\;1.58 \\ \hline 2.74 \end{array}$$

Add or subtract. Remember the decimal point.

1. $\begin{array}{r} 5.82 \\ +\;7.19 \\ \hline 13.01 \end{array}$

2. $\begin{array}{r} 25.67 \\ +\;58.98 \\ \hline \end{array}$

3. $\begin{array}{r} 6.53 \\ -\;2.17 \\ \hline \end{array}$

4. $\begin{array}{r} 84.76 \\ -\;21.89 \\ \hline \end{array}$

5. $\begin{array}{r} 20.32 \\ -\;8.65 \\ \hline \end{array}$

6. $\begin{array}{r} 0.70 \\ +\;1.84 \\ \hline \end{array}$

7. $\begin{array}{r} 5.00 \\ -\;2.98 \\ \hline \end{array}$

8. $\begin{array}{r} 3.70 \\ -\;1.84 \\ \hline \end{array}$

9. $\begin{array}{r} 23.29 \\ +\;7.60 \\ \hline \end{array}$

10. $\begin{array}{r} 51.63 \\ -\;30.54 \\ \hline \end{array}$

11. $\begin{array}{r} 23.60 \\ -\;8.74 \\ \hline \end{array}$

12. $\begin{array}{r} 8.03 \\ +\;0.80 \\ \hline \end{array}$

13. $\begin{array}{r} 7.09 \\ -\;2.83 \\ \hline \end{array}$

14. $\begin{array}{r} 237.08 \\ +\;64.39 \\ \hline \end{array}$

15. $\begin{array}{r} 100.05 \\ -\;42.31 \\ \hline \end{array}$

 Challenge

16. $4.7 + 26.38 + 0.25$

17. $84.5 - 23.89$

18. $3 - 1.25$

19. $68.12 + 8.74 + 75.9$

20. $73.27 - 6.25$

21. $20 - 16.7$

Money Problems

4 dollars and 98 cents $4.98

95 cents $0.95

$$
\begin{array}{r}
\overset{1}{}\overset{1}{} \\
\$4.98 \\
+\ 0.95 \\
\hline
\$5.93
\end{array}
$$

Use $ with the first amount and with the answer.

Add or subtract.
Be sure to use . and $ in the answer.

1. $ 4.23
    + 12.82
    ———
    $17.05

2. $17.86
    − 8.42

3. $8.17
    + 2.23

4. $9.20
    − 2.30

5. $2.83
    + 1.09

6. $5.00
    − 2.89

7. $3.22
    − 0.75

8. $0.88
    + 4.37

9. $14.95
    − 3.00

10. $20.25
    + 1.95

11. $8.45
    − 3.50

12. $4.00
    − 2.35

13. $10.00
    + 7.39

14. $39.95
    + 12.50

15. $0.95
    − 0.39

16. $6.59
    − 3.85

17. $12.15
    − 9.45

18. $5.00
    + 0.93

19. $23.50
    + 39.83

20. $44.07
    − 23.82

21. You choose a shirt that costs $8.25. You give the salesperson $10.00. How much change will you get?

22. You choose a pair of shoes that cost $13.98. You give the salesperson $15.00. How much change will you get?

Hardware Store Problems

These are two-step problems. You can add
and then subtract to solve them.

1. John and Ann go to the
   hardware store and buy a
   hammer for $7.50 and nails
   for $0.49. How much change
   do they get from $10.00?

Step 1	Step 2
$7.50	$10.00
+ 0.49	− 7.99
$7.99	$2.01

2. Peter Simpson has $12.75.
   He buys a saw for $9.54 and
   glue for $1.46. How much
   money does he have left?

3. Pamela buys floor tiles for
   $13.60 and wooden shelves
   for $8.95. How much change
   does she get from $25.00?

4. Tom Gomez has $25.00. He
   buys three paint brushes
   for $9.40 and paint for
   $10.50. How much money
   does he have left?

5. Rebecca has $14.00. She
   pays $8.50 for a tool box and
   $1.45 for copper wire. How
   much money does she have
   left?

Chapter Review

Which fraction is greater? (ex. 1–3: p. 180), (ex. 4, 5: p. 181)

1. $\frac{2}{5}$ or $\frac{4}{5}$ 2. $\frac{5}{9}$ or $\frac{7}{9}$ 3. $\frac{7}{8}$ or $\frac{3}{8}$ 4. $\frac{1}{3}$ or $\frac{1}{4}$ 5. $\frac{1}{8}$ or $\frac{1}{12}$

Add or subtract. (ex. 6, 7: p. 182), (ex. 8–10: p. 183),
(ex. 11–13: p. 192), (ex. 14, 15: p. 193)

6. $\frac{5}{8} + \frac{2}{8}$ 7. $\frac{3}{7} + \frac{2}{7}$ 8. $\frac{5}{6} - \frac{4}{6}$ 9. $\frac{8}{10} - \frac{5}{10}$ 10. $\frac{7}{9} - \frac{3}{9}$

11. $\begin{array}{r} \frac{3}{12} \\ + \frac{1}{6} \\ \hline \end{array}$ 12. $\begin{array}{r} \frac{2}{4} \\ + \frac{2}{8} \\ \hline \end{array}$ 13. $\begin{array}{r} \frac{3}{4} \\ + \frac{1}{12} \\ \hline \end{array}$ 14. $\begin{array}{r} \frac{6}{8} \\ - \frac{1}{4} \\ \hline \end{array}$ 15. $\begin{array}{r} \frac{9}{10} \\ - \frac{2}{5} \\ \hline \end{array}$

Find the answers. (ex. 16–20: p. 197)

16. $\frac{1}{4} \times 8$ 17. $\frac{1}{3} \times 27$ 18. $\frac{1}{5} \times 15$ 19. $\frac{1}{8} \times 24$ 20. $\frac{1}{7} \times 35$

Write a decimal for each. (ex. 21, 22: p. 198), (ex. 23, 24: p. 199), (ex. 25, 26: p. 203)

21. $\frac{7}{10}$ 22. $\frac{9}{10}$ 23. $1\frac{5}{10}$ 24. $2\frac{4}{10}$ 25. $\frac{62}{100}$ 26. $\frac{99}{100}$

Add or subtract. (ex. 27, 28: p. 202), (ex. 29, 30: p. 205), (ex. 31: p. 206)

27. $\begin{array}{r} 7.9 \\ - 3.5 \\ \hline \end{array}$ 28. $\begin{array}{r} 15.3 \\ + 4.2 \\ \hline \end{array}$ 29. $\begin{array}{r} 12.54 \\ - 6.38 \\ \hline \end{array}$ 30. $\begin{array}{r} 8.45 \\ + 2.65 \\ \hline \end{array}$ 31. $\begin{array}{r} \$4.00 \\ - 2.65 \\ \hline \end{array}$

Chapter Test

Which fraction is greater?

1. $\frac{3}{4}$ or $\frac{2}{4}$ 2. $\frac{3}{8}$ or $\frac{4}{5}$ 3. $\frac{1}{8}$ or $\frac{1}{6}$ 4. $\frac{1}{9}$ or $\frac{1}{6}$ 5. $\frac{1}{3}$ or $\frac{1}{6}$

Add or subtract.

6. $\frac{1}{5}$ 7. $\frac{2}{8}$ 8. $\frac{3}{6}$ 9. $\frac{2}{6}$ 10. $\frac{3}{8}$ 11. $\frac{2}{5}$
   $+\frac{2}{5}$ $+\frac{3}{8}$ $-\frac{1}{6}$ $-\frac{1}{12}$ $+\frac{2}{4}$ $+\frac{3}{10}$

Find the answers.

12. $\frac{1}{2} \times 24$ 13. $\frac{1}{7} \times 28$ 14. $\frac{1}{6} \times 18$ 15. $\frac{1}{5} \times 20$ 16. $\frac{1}{4} \times 16$

Write a decimal for each.

17. $\frac{8}{10}$ 18. $\frac{6}{10}$ 19. $1\frac{2}{10}$ 20. $\frac{13}{10}$ 21. $\frac{7}{100}$ 22. $\frac{50}{100}$

Add or subtract.

23.   14.8   24.   8.0   25.   7.3   26.   8.20   27.   3.86
    $-$ 7.4 $+$ 3.2 $-$ 2.5 $-$ 3.45 $+$ 12.34

Brush Up

Add or subtract.

1. $\begin{array}{r} 23 \\ + 47 \\ \hline \end{array}$

2. $\begin{array}{r} 58 \\ + 21 \\ \hline \end{array}$

3. $\begin{array}{r} 92 \\ + 65 \\ \hline \end{array}$

4. $\begin{array}{r} 73 \\ + 38 \\ \hline \end{array}$

5. $\begin{array}{r} 48 \\ + 17 \\ \hline \end{array}$

6. $\begin{array}{r} 265 \\ + 91 \\ \hline \end{array}$

7. $\begin{array}{r} 288 \\ + 371 \\ \hline \end{array}$

8. $\begin{array}{r} 459 \\ + 293 \\ \hline \end{array}$

9. $\begin{array}{r} 371 \\ + 467 \\ \hline \end{array}$

10. $\begin{array}{r} 962 \\ + 198 \\ \hline \end{array}$

11. $\begin{array}{r} 485 \\ - 107 \\ \hline \end{array}$

12. $\begin{array}{r} 871 \\ - 206 \\ \hline \end{array}$

13. $\begin{array}{r} 673 \\ - 181 \\ \hline \end{array}$

14. $\begin{array}{r} 591 \\ - 219 \\ \hline \end{array}$

15. $\begin{array}{r} 437 \\ - 388 \\ \hline \end{array}$

Multiply or divide.

16. 3×8

17. 4×6

18. $27 \div 9$

19. 3×9

20. $63 \div 9$

21. 7×9

22. $32 \div 4$

23. 4×7

24. 5×9

25. 6×8

26. $48 \div 6$

27. $24 \div 3$

28. 7×5

29. $56 \div 7$

30. 8×7

31. $64 \div 8$

32. 8×8

33. $36 \div 6$

34. $18 \div 3$

35. $45 \div 5$

Add or subtract.

36. $\frac{2}{9} + \frac{5}{9}$

37. $\frac{8}{9} - \frac{1}{9}$

38. $\frac{3}{4} + \frac{1}{8}$

39. $\frac{2}{3} + \frac{4}{9}$

40. $\frac{7}{12} - \frac{4}{12}$

41. $\frac{11}{4} - \frac{1}{4}$

42. $\frac{7}{6} + \frac{4}{6}$

43. $\frac{3}{4} - \frac{3}{8}$

44. $\frac{5}{6} - \frac{1}{3}$

45. $\frac{4}{10} + \frac{1}{5}$

46. $\begin{array}{r} 0.4 \\ + 0.8 \\ \hline \end{array}$

47. $\begin{array}{r} 2.9 \\ - 1.6 \\ \hline \end{array}$

48. $\begin{array}{r} 4.13 \\ + 0.60 \\ \hline \end{array}$

49. $\begin{array}{r} 5.09 \\ - 0.31 \\ \hline \end{array}$

50. $\begin{array}{r} 8.60 \\ + 1.09 \\ \hline \end{array}$

CHAPTER 9

Numbers

Using Numbers at Work

Terry Freitas manages a state park. 32,465 people used the park in July. On her report she rounds the number of people to the nearest hundred. 32,465 rounded to the nearest hundred is 32,500. About 32,500 people visited the park in July.

Place Value and Sums

You can write an addition problem to show the total value of each digit of a number. Try 23,467.

Place Value	Digit	Value
Ten Thousands	2	20,000
Thousands	3	3 000
Hundreds	4	400
Tens	6	60
Ones	7	+ 7
		23,467

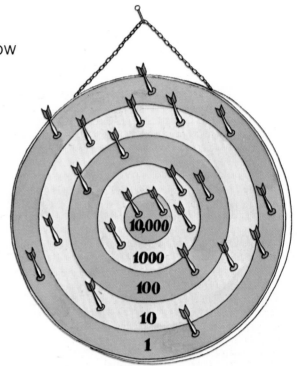

Find each sum.

1.
$$\begin{array}{r} 40,000 \\ 6\,000 \\ 10 \\ +\quad 2 \\ \hline 46,012 \end{array}$$

2.
$$\begin{array}{r} 60,000 \\ 4\,000 \\ 700 \\ 20 \\ +\quad 2 \\ \hline \end{array}$$

3.
$$\begin{array}{r} 70,000 \\ 1\,000 \\ 400 \\ +\quad 6 \\ \hline \end{array}$$

4.
$$\begin{array}{r} 10,000 \\ 8\,000 \\ 900 \\ 90 \\ +\quad 3 \\ \hline \end{array}$$

5. $2000 + 500 + 10 + 6$

6. $10{,}000 + 6000 + 400 + 60 + 5$

 Challenge
Write an addition problem to show the total value of each digit.

7. 52,784   8. 1476   9. 3,287,641   10. 3659   11. 12,816

Hundred Thousands

Number: 847,361

Hundred Thousands	Ten Thousands	Thousands	Hundreds	Tens	Ones
8	4	7	3	6	1

When you have a number larger than 9999,
count 3 places from the right-hand side and put a comma:

10,000   999,375   400,200

Copy. Put in the commas.

1. 624179   624,179   2. 80123   3. 700009   4. 90800

5. 93456   6. 126883   7. 224269   8. 29070   9. 53071

10. 60405   11. 834798   12. 643792   13. 23402   14. 105466

Write an addition problem to show the
total value of each digit.

15. 479,635   16. 746,031   17. 100,352

18. 350,425   19. 932,736   20. 205,321

21. The Ace Balloon Machine makes 100,000 balloons.
The Star Balloon Machine makes 9000 balloons.
How many balloons altogether?

Words for Numbers

Thousands Period			Ones Period		
Hundreds	Tens	Ones	Hundreds	Tens	Ones
6	2	0	3	9	6

620,396

six hundred twenty thousand, three hundred ninety-six

Use the chart to write the answers.

1. Which digit is in the one thousands place?   0

2. Which digit is in the tens place?

3. Which digit is in the ten thousands place?

Welcome to
Everett
Pop. 620,396

Write the numbers.

4. eighty-four thousand, seventeen

5. eight hundred five thousand, six hundred

6. six hundred thousand, two hundred seventy-five

7. seven hundred fifty thousand, four hundred six

8. three hundred eighty-two thousand, three hundred eighty-two

Ordering Numbers

Compare the thousands ~~periods~~ *families*.

If the thousands ~~periods~~ *families* are the same, compare the ~~ones periods~~.
simple families.

497,682   462,619

327,146   327,198

497 is greater than 462.
> means **is greater than.**
497,682 > 462,619

146 is less than 198.
< means **is less than.**
327,146 < 327,198

Order these numbers. Use > for **is greater than** and < for **is less than.**

1. 89,164 < 89,238

2. 37,817 ◯ 32,119

3. 72,814 ◯ 74,396

4. 98,817 ◯ 98,099

5. 20,304 ◯ 20,340

6. 482,111 ◯ 428,141

7. 768,128 ◯ 786,915

8. 55,430 ◯ 55,043

9. One week the distance from the earth to the moon was 384,403 kilometers. Another week the distance was 384,405 kilometers. Which distance is greater?

 Review   (pp. 213–216)

1. Write a sum for this number: 61,347.

2. Write a number: six hundred eighty-five thousand, three hundred six

GREATEST NUMBER GAME

A game for 2 or more players.

Get ready:
Each player makes
a set of digit cards
like these.
Mix up all the cards.
Put them face down.

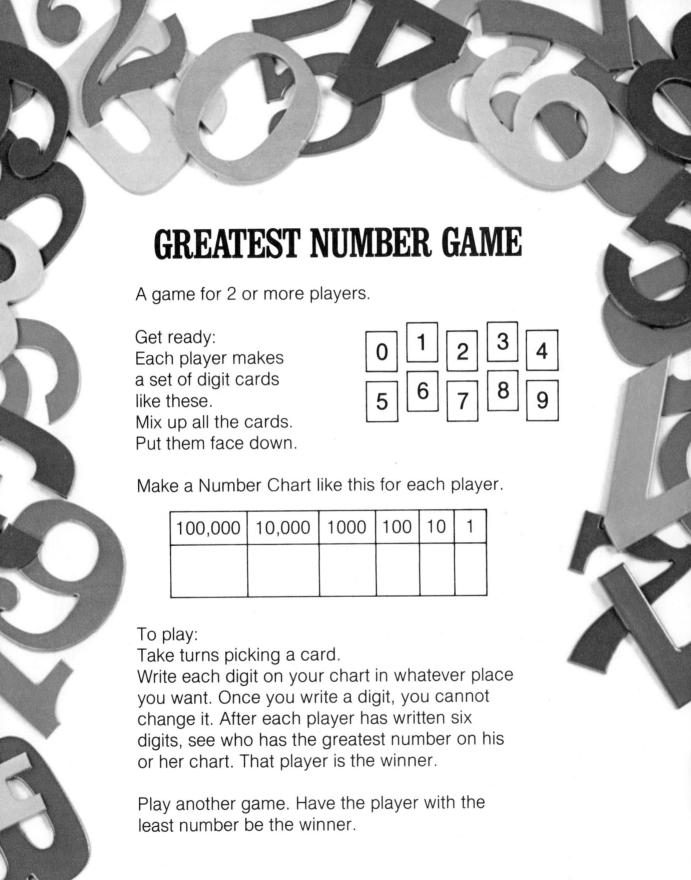

| 0 | 1 | 2 | 3 | 4 |
| 5 | 6 | 7 | 8 | 9 |

Make a Number Chart like this for each player.

100,000	10,000	1000	100	10	1

To play:
Take turns picking a card.
Write each digit on your chart in whatever place
you want. Once you write a digit, you cannot
change it. After each player has written six
digits, see who has the greatest number on his
or her chart. That player is the winner.

Play another game. Have the player with the
least number be the winner.

Millions

Family			Family			Simple Family		
Millions Period			Thousands Period			~~Ones Period~~		
Hundreds	Tens	Ones	Hundreds	Tens	Ones	Hundreds	Tens	Ones
8	2	3	4	6	5	1	0	9

823,465,109

eight hundred twenty-three million, four hundred sixty-five thousand, one hundred nine

Write the numbers.

1. seventy million, four hundred thousand
   70,400,000

2. eight million, three hundred six

3. six hundred thirty-two million

4. one million, six hundred thousand

Copy. Put commas between periods.

5. 7268042   6. 6178004   7. 9241765

 Calculate

8. 60 minutes = 1 hour. 1,000,000 divided by 60 is about 16,666. So 1,000,000 minutes is about 16,666 hours. 1,000,000 minutes is equal to about how many years?

Rounding to the Nearest Ten

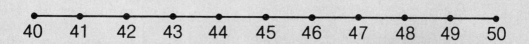

40 41 42 43 44 45 46 47 48 49 50

41 to 44 are	45 is in the middle.	46 to 49 are
nearer to 40.	It rounds to 50.	nearer to 50.
They round to 40.		They round to 50.

Think about the nearest ten. Write the answers.

1a. 49 is between 40 and ▢. 50
 b. 49 rounds to ▢.

2a. 65 is between ▢ and ▢.
 b. 65 rounds to ▢.

3a. 73 is between 70 and ▢.
 b. 73 rounds to ▢.

4a. 54 is between ▢ and ▢.
 b. 54 rounds to ▢.

5. Write the numbers between 40 and 50 that round to 40.

6. Write the numbers between 40 and 50 that round to 50.

7. Write the numbers between 20 and 30 that round to 20.

8. Write the numbers between 20 and 30 that round to 30.

Round to the nearest ten.

9. 18	**10.** 93	**11.** 15	**12.** 24	**13.** 71	**14.** 49
15. 38	**16.** 55	**17.** 74	**18.** 56	**19.** 22	**20.** 67
21. 85	**22.** 21	**23.** 11	**24.** 17	**25.** 91	**26.** 33
27. 64	**28.** 98	**29.** 12	**30.** 41	**31.** 19	**32.** 75

Rounding to the Nearest Hundred

```
 •    •    •    •    •    •    •    •    •    •    •
500  510  520  530  540  550  560  570  580  590  600
```

501 to 549 are
nearer to 500.
They round to 500.

550 is in the middle.
It rounds to 600.

551 to 599 are
nearer to 600.
They round to 600.

Think about the nearest hundred. Write the answers.

1. 501 to 549 round to ⍰.　500

2. 550 to 599 round to ⍰.

3a. 643 is between 600 and ⍰.
 b. 643 rounds to ⍰.

4a. 872 is between ⍰ and ⍰.
 b. 872 rounds to ⍰.

5a. 350 is between ⍰ and ⍰.
 b. 350 rounds to ⍰.

6a. 249 is between ⍰ and ⍰.
 b. 249 rounds to ⍰.

Round to the nearest hundred.

7. 438　　8. 911　　9. 753　　10. 542　　11. 355　　12. 208

13. 250　　14. 549　　15. 801　　16. 490　　17. 949　　18. 850

Round each number twice, once to the nearest hundred and once to the nearest ten.

19. 784 800, 780　　20. 111　　21. 649　　22. 351　　23. 521

24. 352　　25. 749　　26. 851　　27. 449　　28. 674

Rounding Large Numbers

Round to the nearest hundred.
Look at hundreds and tens.

7834

834 rounds to 800,
so 7834 rounds to 7800.

279,384

384 rounds to 400,
so 279,384 rounds to 279,400.

Round to the nearest hundred.

1. 57,123   57,100

2. 8572

3. 350

4. 7350

5. 249

6. 79,105

7. 811

8. 31,811

9. 254

10. 348,254

11. 150

12. 197,150

13. 29,186

14. 7550

15. 13,130

16. 47,910

 Challenge

17. Round 58,736 to the nearest thousand.

18. Round 478,285 to the nearest ten thousand.

19. Round 734,629 to the nearest ten thousand.

20. Round 4,872,653 to the nearest hundred thousand.

21. Round 7,143,975 to the nearest hundred thousand.

Rounding Problems

JACKSON CITY ELECTIONS

MAYOR			JUDGE	
Alan Pierce	12,150		James Grant	2009
Carol Scott	27,598		Diane Wilson	1774
Selena Young	4350		POLICE CHIEF	
SHERIFF			Frank Estrada	857
Nancy Chan	264		Helen Larson	615
Donald Hill	185		Joan Schwartz	436

Round to the nearest ten. Use the chart to answer the questions.

1. About how many votes does Nancy Chan have?   260

2. About how many votes does Donald Hill have?

3. About how many votes does Frank Estrada have?

4. About how many votes does Joan Schwartz have?

Round to the nearest hundred. Use the chart to answer the questions.

5. About how many votes does Alan Pierce have?   12,200

6. About how many votes does Carol Scott have?

7. About how many votes does Selena Young have?

8. About how many votes does James Grant have?

9. About how many votes does Diane Wilson have?

10. About how many votes does Helen Larson have?

Estimating Answers

You can use rounding
to estimate answers.

You have $2.00. A glider costs $0.45 and
a kite costs $1.79. Can you buy both?

Think: $0.45 rounds to $0.50.
$1.79 rounds to $1.80.
The sum of $0.50 and $1.80 is $2.30.
You only have $2.00, so you cannot
buy the glider and the kite.

Use rounding to answer each question. Write yes or no.

1. You have $3.00. Crayons cost
   $0.39. Watercolors cost $2.75.
   Can you buy both?   no

2. You have $5.00. A model car
   costs $3.65. A book costs
   $1.98. Can you buy both?

3. You have $8.00. A hammer
   costs $4.98 and a brush costs
   $2.44. Can you buy both?

4. You have $5.00. A record costs
   $2.98. A tape costs $1.96. Can
   you buy both?

5. You have $10.00. A dog collar
   and a leash cost $6.80. A pet
   brush costs $2.69. Can you buy
   all these items?

6. You have $20.00. A sweater
   costs $11.85. Gym shoes cost
   $7.10. Socks cost $1.25. Can
   you buy all three items?

 Calculate

   Round each amount to the nearest ten cents and add.
   Add again without rounding.

7. $0.39 + $0.71 + $1.15 + $2.76 + $0.59 + $0.30 + $1.48 + $1.82

Tenths and Hundredths

Number: 6983.52

Thousands	6	6000
Hundreds	9	900
Tens	8	80
Ones	3	3
Tenths	5	0.5
Hundredths	2	+ 0.02
		6983.52

Write the sum.

1. 30 + 4 + 0.2 + 0.01   34.21

2. 50 + 1 + 0.8 + 0.01

3. 4000 + 70 + 8 + 0.3 + 0.07   4. 60 + 9 + 0.4 + 0.08

5. 800 + 90 + 3 + 0.7 + 0.02   6. 7000 + 400 + 70 + 2 + 0.5

Write a sum to show the total value of each digit.

7. 5.23   8. 41.69   9. 3.05   10. 27.48   11. 70.18

12. 148.56   13. 234.10   14. 400.85   15. 6492.78   16. 1005.35

17. Lucy Wong finished the race in 60.05 seconds.
Maria Lopez finished in 59.26 seconds. Who won?

Decimals and Place Value

Ten Thousands	Thousands	Hundreds	Tens	Ones	Tenths	Hundredths
7	6	5	4	3 .	2	1

Use the number 76,543.21. Write the values.

1a. 4 is in the ⯑ place. tens
b. It has a value of ⯑.

2a. 2 is in the ⯑ place.
b. It has a value of ⯑.

3a. 6 is in the ⯑ place.
b. It has a value of ⯑.

4a. 7 is in the ⯑ place.
b. It has a value of ⯑.

5a. 3 is in the ⯑ place.
b. It has a value of ⯑.

6a. 5 is in the ⯑ place.
b. It has a value of ⯑.

7a. 1 is in the ⯑ place.
b. It has a value of ⯑.

8. What is the value of 2 and 1 together?

Challenge
Use the number 66,666.66. Answer these questions.

9. 6 in the thousands place is how many times greater than 6 in the tens place?

10. 6 in the ones place is how many times greater than 6 in the tenths place?

Speed Record Problems

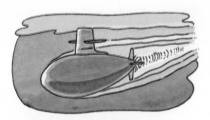

Fastest submarine:
55.2 kilometers per hour

Fastest ocean liner:
65.8 kilometers per hour

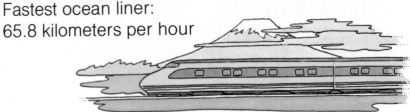

Fastest biplane:
516.8 kilometers per hour

Fastest racing car:
411.2 kilometers per hour

Fastest train: 374.7 kilometers per hour

Use the speeds given above to answer these questions.
You can order decimals the same way you order whole numbers.

1. Put the speeds of the train, submarine, and ocean liner in order from least to greatest.
   55.2 km, 65.8 km, 374.7 km

2. Put the speeds of the biplane, train, and racing car in order from least to greatest.

3. How much faster is the racing car than the submarine?

4. How much faster is the ocean liner than the submarine?

 Challenge

5. Put all the above speeds in order from the greatest to the least.

Writing Decimals

232.15
two hundred thirty-two **and** fifteen-hundredths
Say *and* for the decimal point.

Write the numbers.

1. two hundred twenty-three and eight-tenths   223.8

2. sixty-one and sixteen-hundredths

3. forty-seven and three-hundredths

4. five hundred eleven and seventy-four hundredths

5. thirty-five thousand, eight hundred ninety and four-tenths

6. sixty thousand, twenty and eight-hundredths

7. one hundred nineteen thousand and twenty-one hundredths

8. seventy-five and seventy-six hundredths

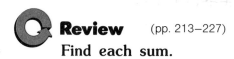 **Review**   (pp. 213–227)
        Find each sum.

1. $100 + 60 + 3 + 0.4 + 0.04$

2. $30 + 8 + 0.09$

Use the number 34,857.29 to answer these questions.

3. Which digit is in the tens place?

4. Which digit is in the hundredths place?

Egyptian Numerals

Egyptian numerals were invented
over 5000 years ago.

𓆼	𓏲	∩	I
1000	100	10	1
Thousand	Hundred	Ten	One

Egyptian numerals may be written from left to right
or right to left. But when reading the number always
start with the numeral that has the greatest value.

3911 may be written both ways.

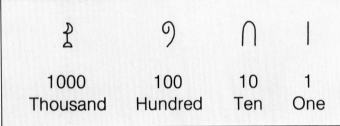

or

Write these numbers.

1. 𓏭𓏭𓏭∩∩∩𓏲
    ∩∩∩ 183

2. 𓆼𓏲𓏲∩𓏭𓏭

3. 𓏭∩∩∩𓏲𓆼

4. 𓏲𓏲𓏲𓏲∩∩∩𓏭𓏭𓏭
    𓏲𓏲𓏲𓏲 𓏭𓏭𓏭

5. ∩∩∩𓏲𓆼
    ∩∩∩𓏲

6. 𓆼𓆼∩∩∩∩∩

Write an Egyptian numeral for each.

7. 17   **8.** 324   **9.** 1216   **10.** 3074   **11.** 2609   **12.** 5006

Roman Numerals

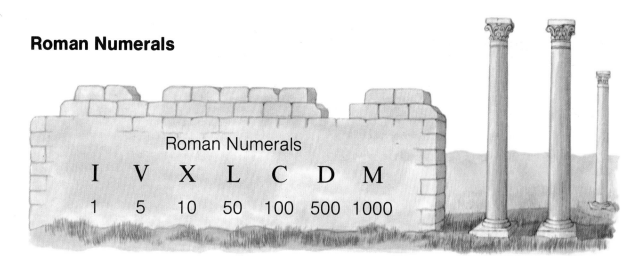

Roman Numerals

I	V	X	L	C	D	M
1	5	10	50	100	500	1000

The Romans used addition to name some numbers.

VI = 5 + 1, or 6   XXVI = 10 + 10 + 5 + 1, or 26

They used subtraction to name other numbers.

IV = 5 − 1, or 4   XL = 50 − 10, or 40

Find the number by adding.

1. VII 7   2. VIII   3. II   4. VI   5. XI

6. XXXV   7. XXIII   8. XII   9. XVI   10. XX

Find the number by subtracting.

11. XL   12. CM   13. CD   14. IX   15. IV   16. XC

MCM means 1900. Find these dates.

17. MCML   18. MCMLXXX   19. MCMXLV   20. MCMIX

Chapter Review

Find each sum.   (ex. 1, 2: p. 213),   (ex. 3, 4: p. 224)

1. 40,000 + 2000 + 500 + 60 + 9

2. 80,000 + 1000 + 700 + 20 + 1

3. 20 + 0.9 + 0.01

4. 800 + 40 + 0.9 + 0.01

Write the numbers.   (ex. 5, 6: p. 215)

5. six hundred twenty-eight thousand, four hundred thirty-seven

6. four hundred fifty thousand, two hundred three

Order these numbers. Use > for **is greater than** and
< for **is less than.**   (ex. 7–12: p. 216)

7. 23,417 ◯ 22,920

8. 38,712 ◯ 38,099

9. 768,945 ◯ 786,202

10. 654,723 ◯ 645,724

11. 345,729 ◯ 345,279

12. 245,678 ◯ 254,000

Round each number to the nearest ten.   (ex. 13–18: p. 219)

13. 42   14. 94   15. 35   16. 57   17. 13   18. 35

Round each number to the nearest hundred.   (ex. 19–24: p. 220)

19. 543   20. 901   21. 627   22. 350   23. 749   24. 209

Chapter Test

Find each sum.

1. $40,000 + 9000 + 200 + 40 + 5$ 2. $70,000 + 3000 + 100 + 3$

3. $10 + 2 + 0.01$ 4. $40 + 6 + 0.7 + 0.05$

Write the numbers.

5. fifty-four thousand, six hundred twelve

6. four hundred thirty-five thousand, three hundred eight

**Order these numbers. Use > for is greater than and
< for is less than.**

7. $13,405 \bigcirc 13,450$ 8. $60,922 \bigcirc 61,100$

9. $435,292 \bigcirc 435,792$ 10. $683,417 \bigcirc 638,417$

11. $445,002 \bigcirc 449,002$ 12. $349,345 \bigcirc 394,245$

Round each number to the nearest ten.

13. 78   14. 26   15. 49   16. 14   17. 92   18. 65

Round each number to the nearest hundred.

19. 693   20. 349   21. 870   22. 750   23. 690   24. 203

Brush Up

Multiply.

1. 7×5 2. 8×7 3. 6×5 4. 8×5 5. 9×7

6. 9×6 7. 6×6 8. 9×8 9. 5×3 10. 7×7

11. 4×7 12. 8×8 13. 9×9 14. 4×9 15. 5×9

Add.

16. $18 + 3$ 17. $45 + 2$ 18. $63 + 5$ 19. $27 + 4$ 20. $59 + 7$

21. $54 + 6$ 22. $28 + 3$ 23. $49 + 4$ 24. $35 + 3$ 25. $21 + 9$

26. $42 + 5$ 27. $15 + 2$ 28. $36 + 5$ 29. $72 + 3$ 30. $47 + 6$

31. $\begin{array}{r} 132 \\ + 330 \\ \hline \end{array}$
32. $\begin{array}{r} 204 \\ + 340 \\ \hline \end{array}$
33. $\begin{array}{r} 336 \\ + 840 \\ \hline \end{array}$
34. $\begin{array}{r} 576 \\ + 720 \\ \hline \end{array}$
35. $\begin{array}{r} 489 \\ + 621 \\ \hline \end{array}$

36. $\begin{array}{r} 456 \\ + 1140 \\ \hline \end{array}$
37. $\begin{array}{r} 322 \\ + 1380 \\ \hline \end{array}$
38. $\begin{array}{r} 344 \\ + 4300 \\ \hline \end{array}$
39. $\begin{array}{r} 541 \\ + 2820 \\ \hline \end{array}$
40. $\begin{array}{r} 847 \\ + 3670 \\ \hline \end{array}$

41. $\begin{array}{r} 256 \\ + 640 \\ \hline \end{array}$
42. $\begin{array}{r} 185 \\ + 2960 \\ \hline \end{array}$
43. $\begin{array}{r} 252 \\ + 1680 \\ \hline \end{array}$
44. $\begin{array}{r} 102 \\ + 1530 \\ \hline \end{array}$
45. $\begin{array}{r} 465 \\ + 3290 \\ \hline \end{array}$

Write the number.

46. thirty   47. six hundred   48. eight thousand

49. five hundred   50. ninety   51. four thousand

CHAPTER 10

Multiplication

Using Multiplication at Work

Tony Fields owns a sporting goods store.
He orders 6 sleeping bags at $80 each.
He multiplies 6 times $80 to find the total cost.
6 sleeping bags cost a total of $480.

Adding to Multiply Tens

If you can add, then you can multiply.

Step 1
Add ones.

$$\begin{array}{r} 72 \\ 72 \\ +\ 72 \\ \hline 6 \end{array}$$

Step 2
Add tens.

$$\begin{array}{r} 72 \\ 72 \\ +\ 72 \\ \hline 216 \end{array}$$

Step 1
Multiply ones.

$$\begin{array}{r} 72 \\ \times\ \ 3 \\ \hline 6 \end{array}$$

Step 2
Multiply tens.

$$\begin{array}{r} 72 \\ \times\ \ 3 \\ \hline 216 \end{array}$$

Multiply. Check by adding.

1.
$$\begin{array}{r} 42 \\ \times\ 2 \\ \hline 84 \end{array} \qquad \begin{array}{r} 42 \\ +\ 42 \\ \hline 84 \end{array}$$

2.
$$\begin{array}{r} 21 \\ \times\ 4 \\ \hline \end{array}$$

3.
$$\begin{array}{r} 40 \\ \times\ 3 \\ \hline \end{array}$$

4.
$$\begin{array}{r} 33 \\ \times\ 2 \\ \hline \end{array}$$

5.
$$\begin{array}{r} 32 \\ \times\ 3 \\ \hline \end{array}$$

Find the products.

6.
$$\begin{array}{r} 22 \\ \times\ 4 \\ \hline \end{array}$$

7.
$$\begin{array}{r} 10 \\ \times\ 5 \\ \hline \end{array}$$

8.
$$\begin{array}{r} 31 \\ \times\ 4 \\ \hline \end{array}$$

9.
$$\begin{array}{r} 30 \\ \times\ 3 \\ \hline \end{array}$$

10.
$$\begin{array}{r} 24 \\ \times\ 2 \\ \hline \end{array}$$

11.
$$\begin{array}{r} 44 \\ \times\ 2 \\ \hline \end{array}$$

12.
$$\begin{array}{r} 50 \\ \times\ 3 \\ \hline \end{array}$$

13.
$$\begin{array}{r} 21 \\ \times\ 3 \\ \hline \end{array}$$

14.
$$\begin{array}{r} 32 \\ \times\ 4 \\ \hline \end{array}$$

15.
$$\begin{array}{r} 11 \\ \times\ 7 \\ \hline \end{array}$$

16.
$$\begin{array}{r} 21 \\ \times\ 6 \\ \hline \end{array}$$

17.
$$\begin{array}{r} 20 \\ \times\ 5 \\ \hline \end{array}$$

18.
$$\begin{array}{r} 32 \\ \times\ 3 \\ \hline \end{array}$$

19.
$$\begin{array}{r} 60 \\ \times\ 4 \\ \hline \end{array}$$

20.
$$\begin{array}{r} 51 \\ \times\ 3 \\ \hline \end{array}$$

21.
$$\begin{array}{r} 23 \\ \times\ 3 \\ \hline \end{array}$$

22.
$$\begin{array}{r} 70 \\ \times\ 3 \\ \hline \end{array}$$

23.
$$\begin{array}{r} 63 \\ \times\ 3 \\ \hline \end{array}$$

Multiply and Add

6 times 3, plus 2 = ▢

	× 3	+ 2
6	18	20

$6 \times 3 = 18,\ 18 + 2 = 20$

Copy the charts. Multiply and add to complete.

1.

	× 4	+ 3
6	24	27
7		
9		

2.

	× 5	+ 2
8		
4		
7		

3.

	× 3	+ 4
7		
9		
6		

4.

	× 6	+ 5
4		
6		
8		

5.

	× 7	+ 3
5		
9		
7		

6.

	× 9	+ 1
7		
8		
6		

7.

	× 8	+ 2
5		
6		
9		

8.

	× 4	+ 7
6		
7		
8		

9.

	× 6	+ 3
7		
9		
5		

Trading Ones in Multiplication

Step 1
Multiply ones.
Trade 10 ones for 1 ten.

$$\begin{array}{r} \overset{1}{5}6 \\ \times\ 3 \\ \hline 8 \end{array}$$
$3 \times 6 = 18$
$18 = 1$ ten 8 ones

Step 2
Multiply tens.
Add tens from trade.

$$\begin{array}{r} \overset{1}{5}6 \\ \times\ 3 \\ \hline 168 \end{array}$$
3×5 tens $= 15$ tens
15 tens $+ 1$ ten $= 16$ tens

Multiply. Check the first row by adding.

1. $\begin{array}{r} 58 \\ \times\ 2 \\ \hline 116 \end{array}$

2. $\begin{array}{r} 47 \\ \times\ 3 \\ \hline \end{array}$

3. $\begin{array}{r} 16 \\ \times\ 4 \\ \hline \end{array}$

4. $\begin{array}{r} 27 \\ \times\ 2 \\ \hline \end{array}$

5. $\begin{array}{r} 58 \\ \times\ 3 \\ \hline \end{array}$

6. $\begin{array}{r} 35 \\ \times\ 2 \\ \hline \end{array}$

7. $\begin{array}{r} 45 \\ \times\ 3 \\ \hline \end{array}$

8. $\begin{array}{r} 28 \\ \times\ 4 \\ \hline \end{array}$

9. $\begin{array}{r} 57 \\ \times\ 4 \\ \hline \end{array}$

10. $\begin{array}{r} 16 \\ \times\ 7 \\ \hline \end{array}$

11. $\begin{array}{r} 44 \\ \times\ 5 \\ \hline \end{array}$

12. $\begin{array}{r} 48 \\ \times\ 6 \\ \hline \end{array}$

13. $\begin{array}{r} 83 \\ \times\ 7 \\ \hline \end{array}$

14. $\begin{array}{r} 56 \\ \times\ 4 \\ \hline \end{array}$

15. $\begin{array}{r} 94 \\ \times\ 6 \\ \hline \end{array}$

16. $\begin{array}{r} 63 \\ \times\ 9 \\ \hline \end{array}$

17. $\begin{array}{r} 27 \\ \times\ 8 \\ \hline \end{array}$

18. $\begin{array}{r} 24 \\ \times\ 8 \\ \hline \end{array}$

19. $\begin{array}{r} 78 \\ \times\ 5 \\ \hline \end{array}$

20. $\begin{array}{r} 87 \\ \times\ 6 \\ \hline \end{array}$

21. $\begin{array}{r} 93 \\ \times\ 4 \\ \hline \end{array}$

22. There are 24 hours in a day. How many hours in 7 days?

23. There are 7 days in a week. How many days in 52 weeks?

Marble Problems

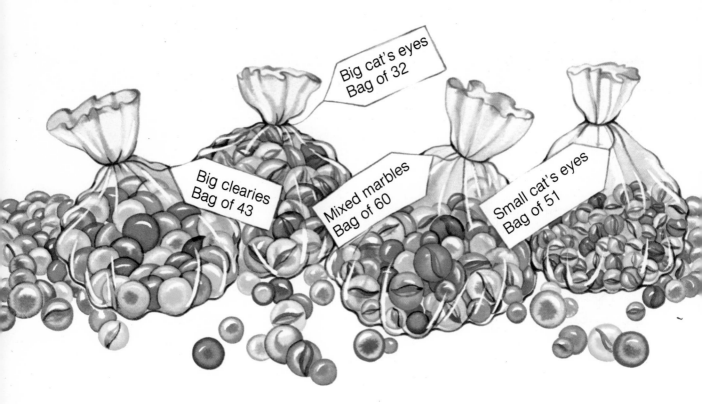

Big cat's eyes Bag of 32

Big clearies Bag of 43

Mixed marbles Bag of 60

Small cat's eyes Bag of 51

1. Frank has 4 bags of mixed marbles. How many marbles is that? 240

2. Althea has 3 bags of big clearies. How many marbles is that?

3. Rita has 4 bags of small cat's eyes. How many marbles is that?

4. Eduardo has 2 bags of big cat's eyes. How many marbles is that?

5. Dan has 4 bags of big cat's eyes. How many marbles is that?

6. Sophie has 5 bags of small cat's eyes. How many marbles is that?

7. Maria has 6 bags of mixed marbles. How many marbles is that?

8. Walt has 5 bags of big clearies. How many marbles is that?

Multiplication Code

Crack the code to find the highest point on earth.

Code	e	m	n	o	r	s	t	u	v
	192	168	415	136	114	576	376	392	536

Multiply. Match each answer to a letter in the code.

1. 28
    $\times\ 6$
    168, m

2. 17
    $\times\ 8$

3. 56
    $\times\ 7$

4. 83
    $\times\ 5$

5. 94
    $\times\ 4$

6. 32
    $\times\ 6$

7. 67
    $\times\ 8$

8. 24
    $\times\ 8$

9. 19
    $\times\ 6$

10. 48
    $\times\ 4$

11. 72
    $\times\ 8$

12. 47
    $\times\ 8$

13. The highest point on earth is

___ ___ ___ ___ ___   ___ ___ ___ ___ ___ ___ ___
1. 2. 3. 4. 5.   6. 7. 8. 9. 10. 11. 12.

Multiplying Three Factors

First multiply any two factors.
Then multiply that product by the third factor.

$4 \times 8 \times 3$ $4 \times 8 \times 3$ $4 \times 8 \times 3$

$32 \times 3 = 96$ $4 \times 24 = 96$ $8 \times 12 = 96$

Multiply.

1. $2 \times 3 \times 4$ 24   2. $7 \times 6 \times 3$ 3. $4 \times 8 \times 1$

4. $9 \times 3 \times 3$ 5. $4 \times 2 \times 6$ 6. $5 \times 7 \times 2$

7. $8 \times 3 \times 5$ 8. $7 \times 6 \times 2$ 9. $2 \times 7 \times 7$

10. $7 \times 5 \times 4$ 11. $5 \times 3 \times 9$ 12. $4 \times 6 \times 7$

13. $3 \times 4 \times 5$ 14. $9 \times 5 \times 2$ 15. $4 \times 6 \times 8$

16. $2 \times 6 \times 9$ 17. $8 \times 4 \times 4$ 18. $7 \times 1 \times 8$

 Calculate

Find these products. Look for the pattern.

19a. 3×37
  b. 6×37
  c. 9×37
  d. 12×37
  e. Can you find 15×37 without multiplying?
  f. Write the next product in the pattern.

Multiplying Hundreds

413 + 413 + 413 = ☐
You can add **or** multiply
to solve this problem.

Add ones.
Add tens.
Add hundreds.

Multiply ones.
Multiply tens.
Multiply hundreds.

```
   413
   413
 + 413
 ─────
  1239
```

```
   413
 ×   3
 ─────
  1239
```

Multiply. Check the first row by adding.

1. 332
× 2
664

2. 221
× 4

3. 422
× 3

4. 123
× 3

5. 234
× 2

6. 412
× 3

7. 232
× 3

8. 312
× 3

9. 411
× 4

10. 323
× 3

11. 142
× 2

12. 213
× 3

13. 234
× 2

14. 423
× 3

15. 311
× 5

16. 132
× 3

17. 422
× 3

18. 324
× 2

19. 521
× 4

20. 233
× 3

21. 321
× 4

22. 212
× 4

23. 402
× 2

24. 312
× 4

25. 430
× 3

Trading Tens

$4 \times 168 = \boxed{?}$

Step 1
Multiply ones.
Trade ones.

$$\begin{array}{r} \overset{3}{16}8 \\ \times \quad 4 \\ \hline 2 \end{array}$$

Step 2
Multiply tens.
Add tens.
Trade tens.

$$\begin{array}{r} \overset{2\,3}{16}8 \\ \times \quad 4 \\ \hline 72 \end{array}$$

4×6 tens $= 24$ tens
24 tens $+ 3$ tens $= 27$ tens

Step 3
Multiply hundreds.
Add hundreds.

$$\begin{array}{r} \overset{2\,3}{16}8 \\ \times \quad 4 \\ \hline 672 \end{array}$$

Multiply. Check the first row by adding.

1. $\begin{array}{r} 567 \\ \times \quad 2 \\ \hline 1134 \end{array}$ $\begin{array}{r} 567 \\ + 567 \\ \hline 1134 \end{array}$

2. $\begin{array}{r} 539 \\ \times \quad 4 \\ \hline \end{array}$

3. $\begin{array}{r} 768 \\ \times \quad 3 \\ \hline \end{array}$

4. $\begin{array}{r} 946 \\ \times \quad 2 \\ \hline \end{array}$

5. $\begin{array}{r} 136 \\ \times \quad 3 \\ \hline \end{array}$

6. $\begin{array}{r} 238 \\ \times \quad 9 \\ \hline \end{array}$

7. $\begin{array}{r} 567 \\ \times \quad 4 \\ \hline \end{array}$

8. $\begin{array}{r} 839 \\ \times \quad 6 \\ \hline \end{array}$

9. $\begin{array}{r} 868 \\ \times \quad 9 \\ \hline \end{array}$

10. $\begin{array}{r} 475 \\ \times \quad 9 \\ \hline \end{array}$

11. $\begin{array}{r} 386 \\ \times \quad 4 \\ \hline \end{array}$

12. $\begin{array}{r} 277 \\ \times \quad 5 \\ \hline \end{array}$

13. $\begin{array}{r} 189 \\ \times \quad 9 \\ \hline \end{array}$

14. $\begin{array}{r} 728 \\ \times \quad 8 \\ \hline \end{array}$

15. $\begin{array}{r} 893 \\ \times \quad 7 \\ \hline \end{array}$

16. $\begin{array}{r} 443 \\ \times \quad 6 \\ \hline \end{array}$

17. $\begin{array}{r} 635 \\ \times \quad 3 \\ \hline \end{array}$

18. $\begin{array}{r} 248 \\ \times \quad 5 \\ \hline \end{array}$

19. $\begin{array}{r} 777 \\ \times \quad 7 \\ \hline \end{array}$

20. $\begin{array}{r} 393 \\ \times \quad 4 \\ \hline \end{array}$

21. $\begin{array}{r} 564 \\ \times \quad 3 \\ \hline \end{array}$

22. $\begin{array}{r} 485 \\ \times \quad 5 \\ \hline \end{array}$

23. $\begin{array}{r} 724 \\ \times \quad 6 \\ \hline \end{array}$

24. $\begin{array}{r} 843 \\ \times \quad 4 \\ \hline \end{array}$

25. $\begin{array}{r} 658 \\ \times \quad 7 \\ \hline \end{array}$

Zero in Multiplying

Any number times 0 is 0.
Remember zeros
when you multiply.

$$\begin{array}{r} \overset{1}{406} \\ \times\ \ \ 3 \\ \hline 1218 \end{array}$$

3 × 0 tens = 0 tens
0 tens + 1 ten = 1 ten

Multiply.

1. 200 × 5 1000	**2.** 507 × 4	**3.** 704 × 6	**4.** 600 × 3	**5.** 708 × 9
6. 507 × 8	**7.** 400 × 7	**8.** 908 × 6	**9.** 308 × 5	**10.** 200 × 4
11. 604 × 9	**12.** 209 × 6	**13.** 400 × 4	**14.** 507 × 3	**15.** 806 × 8

16. 500 × 4   **17.** 301 × 2   **18.** 100 × 7   **19.** 309 × 3

Review   (pp. 235–243)

1. 32 × 4	**2.** 56 × 4	**3.** 314 × 3	**4.** 839 × 6	**5.** 708 × 9

Practicing Multiplication

Do you remember these?

$$
\begin{array}{r}
72 \\
\times\ 3 \\
\hline
216
\end{array}
\qquad
\begin{array}{r}
{\scriptstyle 1} \\
24 \\
\times\ 3 \\
\hline
72
\end{array}
\qquad
\begin{array}{r}
413 \\
\times\ 3 \\
\hline
1239
\end{array}
\qquad
\begin{array}{r}
{\scriptstyle 2\ 3} \\
168 \\
\times\ 4 \\
\hline
672
\end{array}
$$

Find the products.

| 1. $\begin{array}{r}28\\ \times\ 3\\ \hline 84\end{array}$ | 2. $\begin{array}{r}62\\ \times\ 4\\ \hline\end{array}$ | 3. $\begin{array}{r}33\\ \times\ 2\\ \hline\end{array}$ | 4. $\begin{array}{r}87\\ \times\ 7\\ \hline\end{array}$ | 5. $\begin{array}{r}58\\ \times\ 4\\ \hline\end{array}$ | 6. $\begin{array}{r}49\\ \times\ 5\\ \hline\end{array}$ |

| 7. $\begin{array}{r}73\\ \times\ 5\\ \hline\end{array}$ | 8. $\begin{array}{r}50\\ \times\ 4\\ \hline\end{array}$ | 9. $\begin{array}{r}87\\ \times\ 3\\ \hline\end{array}$ | 10. $\begin{array}{r}59\\ \times\ 7\\ \hline\end{array}$ | 11. $\begin{array}{r}82\\ \times\ 4\\ \hline\end{array}$ | 12. $\begin{array}{r}18\\ \times\ 6\\ \hline\end{array}$ |

Multiply.

| 13. $\begin{array}{r}628\\ \times\ 4\\ \hline\end{array}$ | 14. $\begin{array}{r}509\\ \times\ 7\\ \hline\end{array}$ | 15. $\begin{array}{r}611\\ \times\ 3\\ \hline\end{array}$ | 16. $\begin{array}{r}209\\ \times\ 2\\ \hline\end{array}$ | 17. $\begin{array}{r}32\\ \times\ 4\\ \hline\end{array}$ |

| 18. $\begin{array}{r}390\\ \times\ 8\\ \hline\end{array}$ | 19. $\begin{array}{r}554\\ \times\ 5\\ \hline\end{array}$ | 20. $\begin{array}{r}982\\ \times\ 6\\ \hline\end{array}$ | 21. $\begin{array}{r}609\\ \times\ 3\\ \hline\end{array}$ | 22. $\begin{array}{r}811\\ \times\ 7\\ \hline\end{array}$ |

| 23. $\begin{array}{r}463\\ \times\ 3\\ \hline\end{array}$ | 24. $\begin{array}{r}304\\ \times\ 7\\ \hline\end{array}$ | 25. $\begin{array}{r}508\\ \times\ 5\\ \hline\end{array}$ | 26. $\begin{array}{r}623\\ \times\ 2\\ \hline\end{array}$ | 27. $\begin{array}{r}732\\ \times\ 3\\ \hline\end{array}$ |

Space Station Problems

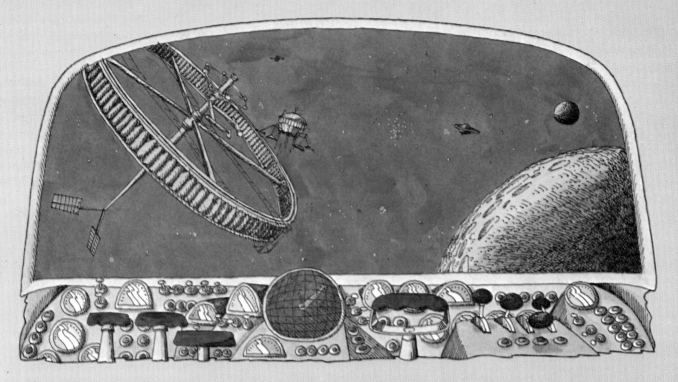

A space station is in orbit around a distant planet.

1. The space station can send 225 radio messages each week. How many messages in 4 weeks? 900

2. It takes 18 hours to make one orbit of the planet. How many hours for 7 orbits?

3. The crew can perform 43 experiments in one day. How many experiments can they perform in 5 days?

4. The space station library has 9 tape reels. There are 28 songs on each tape reel. How many songs altogether?

5. Each bottle of oxygen on the space station holds enough for 8 hours. There are 879 bottles. How many hours of oxygen do they have?

6. The computer checks equipment in the space station. It does 560 checks every minute. How many checks in 6 minutes?

Multiplying Thousands

$5386 + 5386 + 5386 = \boxed{?}$

You can add or multiply
to solve this problem.

```
  1 2 1
   5386
   5386
 + 5386
  16,158
```

```
  1 2 1
   5386
 ×    3
  16,158
```

Multiply. Check the first row by adding.

1. 4768
    ×   4
    19,072

2. 4596
    ×   3

3. 5867
    ×   3

4. 8249
    ×   4

5. 3466
    ×   2

6. 5836
    ×   8

7. 5236
    ×   5

8. 7423
    ×   9

9. 6837
    ×   6

10. 2543
     ×   4

11. 3869
     ×   5

12. 2463
     ×   6

13. 4813
     ×   7

14. 6234
     ×   5

15. 1782
     ×   3

16. 3784
     ×   2

17. 2113
     ×   7

18. 8426
     ×   3

19. 9141
     ×   8

20. 4280
     ×   5

Zero Again

Any number times 0 is 0.
Zero is important. It holds places.

Step 1
Multiply ones.
Trade.

$$\begin{array}{r} {}^{3} \\ 6008 \\ \times 4 \\ \hline 2 \end{array}$$

Step 2
Multiply tens.
Add.

$$\begin{array}{r} {}^{3} \\ 6008 \\ \times 4 \\ \hline 32 \end{array}$$

Step 3
Multiply
hundreds.

$$\begin{array}{r} {}^{3} \\ 6008 \\ \times 4 \\ \hline 032 \end{array}$$

Step 4
Multiply
thousands.

$$\begin{array}{r} {}^{3} \\ 6008 \\ \times 4 \\ \hline 24,032 \end{array}$$

Multiply.

1. 2020
    × 4
    8080

2. 7900
    × 3

3. 4093
    × 2

4. 5086
    × 4

5. 7031
    × 6

6. 2006
    × 8

7. 6100
    × 9

8. 5070
    × 8

9. 6073
    × 7

10. 3406
    × 3

11. 5089
    × 4

12. 4008
    × 6

13. 5706
    × 7

14. 6500
    × 8

15. 7013
    × 5

16. 7008
    × 9

17. 1005
    × 2

18. 2006
    × 3

19. 5020
    × 5

20. 6003
    × 6

21. An automobile has 4070 parts. How many parts in 5 automobiles?

22. The factory makes 1500 automobiles each day. How many are made in 2 days?

Bead Problems

Rosa is making necklaces with colored beads.
She is using four different beads.

288 green beads
make one necklace.

176 blue beads
make one necklace.

192 gold beads
make one necklace.

144 red beads
make one necklace.

Write a multiplication problem for each. Multiply.

1. How many gold beads in
   2 necklaces? 2 × 192 = 384

2. How many red beads in
   6 necklaces?

3. How many blue beads in
   7 necklaces?

4. How many green beads in
   6 necklaces?

5. How many gold beads in
   9 necklaces?

6. How many blue beads in
   5 necklaces?

7. How many red beads in
   8 necklaces?

8. How many green beads in
   9 necklaces?

9. How many gold beads in
   5 necklaces?

10. How many blue beads in
    4 necklaces?

Multiplying and Money

¹ ⁴
$0.18
×   6
──────
$1.08

¹ ⁴
$3.18
×   6
──────
$19.08

¹ ¹ ⁴
$13.18
×   6
──────
$79.08

Multiply. Remember to use . and $ in your answer.

1. $0.07
   ×   9
   ──────
   $0.63

2. $4.19
   ×   2
   ──────

3. $8.02
   ×   5
   ──────

4. $20.94
   ×   7
   ──────

5. $5.28
   ×   3
   ──────

6. $0.63
   ×   4
   ──────

7. $2.34
   ×   8
   ──────

8. $11.02
   ×   9
   ──────

9. $0.87
   ×   4
   ──────

10. $32.45
    ×   5
    ──────

11. $7.00
    ×   6
    ──────

12. $19.61
    ×   5
    ──────

13. $53.29
    ×   6
    ──────

14. $0.28
    ×   3
    ──────

15. $6.16
    ×   4
    ──────

16. $1.26
    ×   7
    ──────

17. $23.04
    ×   4
    ──────

18. $30.05
    ×   9
    ──────

19. $5.95
    ×   3
    ──────

20. $19.57
    ×   2
    ──────

 Challenge

21. A package of yarn costs $1.98. What is the cost of 5 packages of yarn?

22. A spool of thread costs $0.35. What is the cost of 3 spools of thread?

23. A package of buttons costs $1.10. What is the cost of 4 packages of buttons?

24. A package of needles costs $0.48. What is the cost of 7 packages of needles?

10 as a Factor

$10 \times 13 = ?$
To find the answer you can add or multiply.

Add 13 ten times, or multiply 13 by 10.

Multiply: 13
          $\times$ 10
           130

If **10** is a factor, the product has **0** in the ones place.

Write the products.

1. 320   2. 24   3. 920   4. 73   5. 330
  $\times$ 10 $\times$ 10 $\times$ 10 $\times$ 10 $\times$ 10
   3200

6. 89   7. 64   8. 242   9. 690   10. 525
  $\times$ 10 $\times$ 10 $\times$ 10 $\times$ 10 $\times$ 10

11. 90   12. 481   13. 12   14. 50   15. 500
  $\times$ 10 $\times$ 10 $\times$ 10 $\times$ 10 $\times$ 10

 Challenge

Use 10 as one factor.
Find one other factor for each product.

16. 420   17. 170   18. 640   19. 820   20. 730

100 as a Factor

13 + 13 + 13 + 13 + 13 + 13 + 13 + 13 + 13 + 13 +
13 + 13 + 13 + 13 + 13 + 13 + 13 + 13 + 13 + 13 +
13 + 13 + 13 + 13 + 13 + 13 + 13 + 13 + 13 + 13 +
13 + 13 + 13 + 13 + 13 + 13 + 13 + 13 + 13 + 13 +
13 + 13 + 13 + 13 + 13 + 13 + 13 + 13 + 13 + 13 +
13 + 13 + 13 + 13 + 13 + 13 + 13 + 13 + 13 + 13 +
13 + 13 + 13 + 13 + 13 + 13 + 13 + 13 + 13 + 13 +
13 + 13 + 13 + 13 + 13 + 13 + 13 + 13 + 13 + 13 +
13 + 13 + 13 + 13 + 13 + 13 + 13 + 13 + 13 + 13 +
13 + 13 + 13 + 13 + 13 + 13 + 13 + 13 + 13 + 13 = ?

$13 \times 100 = ?$
To find the answer
you can add or multiply.

Add 13 one hundred times,
or multiply 100 by 13.

Multiply:

$$\begin{array}{r} 100 \\ \times\ \ 13 \\ \hline 1300 \end{array}$$

If **100** is a factor, the product has **0** in
the tens place, and **0** in the ones place.

Multiply.

1. $\begin{array}{r} 200 \\ \times 100 \\ \hline 20{,}000 \end{array}$	**2.** $\begin{array}{r} 100 \\ \times\ \ 84 \\ \hline \end{array}$	**3.** $\begin{array}{r} 233 \\ \times 100 \\ \hline \end{array}$	**4.** $\begin{array}{r} 100 \\ \times\ \ 47 \\ \hline \end{array}$	**5.** $\begin{array}{r} 368 \\ \times 100 \\ \hline \end{array}$
6. $\begin{array}{r} 100 \\ \times\ \ 16 \\ \hline \end{array}$	**7.** $\begin{array}{r} 100 \\ \times\ \ 39 \\ \hline \end{array}$	**8.** $\begin{array}{r} 234 \\ \times 100 \\ \hline \end{array}$	**9.** $\begin{array}{r} 469 \\ \times 100 \\ \hline \end{array}$	**10.** $\begin{array}{r} 721 \\ \times 100 \\ \hline \end{array}$
11. $\begin{array}{r} 100 \\ \times\ \ 55 \\ \hline \end{array}$	**12.** $\begin{array}{r} 105 \\ \times 100 \\ \hline \end{array}$	**13.** $\begin{array}{r} 100 \\ \times 222 \\ \hline \end{array}$	**14.** $\begin{array}{r} 100 \\ \times\ \ 50 \\ \hline \end{array}$	**15.** $\begin{array}{r} 100 \\ \times 480 \\ \hline \end{array}$

16. 100×33 **17.** 100×60 **18.** 100×18

19. 409×100 **20.** 500×100 **21.** 270×100

1000 as a Factor

$$\begin{array}{r} 1000 \\ \times \quad 13 \\ \hline 13{,}000 \end{array}$$

$13 \times 1000 = \boxed{?}$

To find the answer, you can multiply like this:

$$\begin{array}{r} \mathbf{1000} \\ \times \quad \mathbf{13} \\ \hline \mathbf{13{,}000} \end{array}$$

If **1000** is a factor, the product has **0** in the hundreds, tens, and ones places.

Write the products.

1. $\begin{array}{r} 1000 \\ \times \quad 118 \\ \hline 118{,}000 \end{array}$
2. $\begin{array}{r} 1000 \\ \times \quad 23 \\ \hline \end{array}$
3. $\begin{array}{r} 1000 \\ \times \quad 46 \\ \hline \end{array}$
4. $\begin{array}{r} 1000 \\ \times \quad 237 \\ \hline \end{array}$
5. $\begin{array}{r} 1000 \\ \times \quad 60 \\ \hline \end{array}$

Multiply.

6. $\begin{array}{r} 100 \\ \times \quad 41 \\ \hline \end{array}$
7. $\begin{array}{r} 80 \\ \times \quad 10 \\ \hline \end{array}$
8. $\begin{array}{r} 1000 \\ \times \quad 64 \\ \hline \end{array}$
9. $\begin{array}{r} 10 \\ \times \quad 15 \\ \hline \end{array}$
10. $\begin{array}{r} 100 \\ \times \quad 99 \\ \hline \end{array}$

11. $\begin{array}{r} 1000 \\ \times \quad 600 \\ \hline \end{array}$
12. $\begin{array}{r} 106 \\ \times \quad 100 \\ \hline \end{array}$
13. $\begin{array}{r} 1061 \\ \times \quad 10 \\ \hline \end{array}$
14. $\begin{array}{r} 1000 \\ \times \quad 50 \\ \hline \end{array}$
15. $\begin{array}{r} 208 \\ \times \quad 100 \\ \hline \end{array}$

 Challenge

16. $\begin{array}{r} 10{,}000 \\ \times \quad 34 \\ \hline \end{array}$
17. $\begin{array}{r} 10{,}000 \\ \times \quad 241 \\ \hline \end{array}$
18. $\begin{array}{r} 10{,}000 \\ \times \quad 504 \\ \hline \end{array}$
19. $\begin{array}{r} 10{,}000 \\ \times \quad 760 \\ \hline \end{array}$

Practicing Multiplication

Look at some kinds of multiplication
you have learned to do.

$$
\begin{array}{r}
\overset{1}{24} \\
\times\ 3 \\
\hline
72
\end{array}
\qquad
\begin{array}{r}
413 \\
\times\ \ 3 \\
\hline
1239
\end{array}
\qquad
\begin{array}{r}
\overset{2\ 3}{168} \\
\times\ \ 4 \\
\hline
672
\end{array}
\qquad
\begin{array}{r}
\overset{3}{6008} \\
\times\ \ \ 4 \\
\hline
24{,}032
\end{array}
$$

Multiply.

1. $\begin{array}{r} 62 \\ \times\ 3 \\ \hline 186 \end{array}$

2. $\begin{array}{r} 17 \\ \times\ 4 \\ \hline \end{array}$

3. $\begin{array}{r} 412 \\ \times\ 2 \\ \hline \end{array}$

4. $\begin{array}{r} 603 \\ \times\ 4 \\ \hline \end{array}$

5. $\begin{array}{r} 13 \\ \times\ 6 \\ \hline \end{array}$

6. $\begin{array}{r} 58 \\ \times\ 7 \\ \hline \end{array}$

7. $\begin{array}{r} 40 \\ \times\ 3 \\ \hline \end{array}$

8. $\begin{array}{r} 583 \\ \times\ 7 \\ \hline \end{array}$

9. $\begin{array}{r} \overset{2\ 1}{4723} \\ \times\ \ \ 4 \\ \hline \end{array}$

10. $\begin{array}{r} 704 \\ \times\ 7 \\ \hline \end{array}$

11. $\begin{array}{r} \overset{4\ 3}{687} \\ \times\ 5 \\ \hline \end{array}$

12. $\begin{array}{r} 2671 \\ \times\ \ \ 3 \\ \hline \end{array}$

13. $\begin{array}{r} 18 \\ \times\ 6 \\ \hline \end{array}$

14. $\begin{array}{r} 804 \\ \times\ 9 \\ \hline \end{array}$

15. $\begin{array}{r} 94 \\ \times\ 7 \\ \hline \end{array}$

Find the products.

16. $\$2.35 \times 5$

17. 723×100

18. 1000×87

19. $\$6.57 \times 3$

20. 284×9

21. 506×4

22. 43×10

23. 750×6

24. 865×100

25. 270×4

26. 708×7

27. 1000×40

Summer Camp Problems

1. There are 29 cabins at Pine Mountain Camp. 6 people can share one cabin. How many people can stay at the camp?   174

2. A group of campers hikes 23 kilometers each day. How many kilometers do they hike in 4 days?

3. In a canoe race 10 people paddle each canoe. How many people in 10 canoes?

4. The swim class swims 575 meters each day. How many meters do they swim in 7 days?

5. The camp has a picnic each week. The campers eat 174 hamburgers at each picnic. How many hamburgers will they eat at 4 picnics?

6. The laundry at the summer camp washes 4500 pairs of socks each month. How many pairs do they wash in 3 months?

Product Puzzles

Find two numbers:
Their sum is 117.
Their product is 1700.

Try 100 as one number.

100 + 17 = 117
100 × 17 = 1700

Find two numbers for each puzzle.

1. Find two numbers:
   Their sum is 34.
   Their product is 240.   10, 24

2. Find two numbers:
   Their sum is 67.
   Their product is 570.

3. Find two numbers:
   Their sum is 168.
   Their product is 6800.

4. Find two numbers:
   Their sum is 1024.
   Their product is 24,000.

5. Find two numbers:
   Their sum is 93.
   Their product is 830.

 **Review**   (pp. 235–255)

| 1. | 317
× 8 | 2. | 971
× 10 | 3. | 5326
× 6 | 4. | 5074
× 3 | 5. | $7.05
× 5 |

6. 34 × 7   7. 205 × 4   8. 543 × 100   9. 1000 × 27

Multiplying Tens Times Tens

SPECIAL
CAT FOOD

tens × tens = hundreds

50	5 tens	50
× 70	× 7 tens	× 70
	35 hundreds	3500

Multiply.

1a. 8 tens
    × 3 tens
    24 hundreds

1b. 80
    × 30

2a. 5 tens
    × 9 tens

2b. 50
    × 90

3a. 4 tens
    × 7 tens

3b. 40
    × 70

4a. 9 tens
    × 4 tens

4b. 90
    × 40

5a. 6 tens
    × 8 tens

5b. 60
    × 80

Find the products.

6. 60
   × 10

7. 50
   × 30

8. 20
   × 40

9. 90
   × 50

10. 30
    × 60

11. 60
    × 20

12. 70
    × 30

13. 40
    × 40

14. 10
    × 80

15. 60
    × 90

16. 20
    × 70

17. 80
    × 90

18. 90
    × 90

19. 60
    × 40

20. 50
    × 80

21. 70
    × 60

22. 80
    × 80

23. 20
    × 40

Multiplying Tens Times Hundreds

tens × hundreds = thousands

$$
\begin{array}{r}
300 \\
\times\ 40 \\
\hline
\end{array}
\qquad
\begin{array}{r}
3 \text{ hundreds} \\
\times\ 4 \text{ tens} \\
\hline
12 \text{ thousands}
\end{array}
\qquad
\begin{array}{r}
300 \\
\times\ 40 \\
\hline
12,000
\end{array}
$$

Multiply.

1a. $\begin{array}{r} 4 \text{ hundreds} \\ \times\ 6 \text{ tens} \\ \hline 24 \text{ thousands} \end{array}$	**1b.** $\begin{array}{r} 400 \\ \times\ 60 \\ \hline \end{array}$	**2a.** $\begin{array}{r} 6 \text{ hundreds} \\ \times\ 8 \text{ tens} \\ \hline \end{array}$	**2b.** $\begin{array}{r} 600 \\ \times\ 80 \\ \hline \end{array}$

3. $\begin{array}{r} 700 \\ \times\ 80 \\ \hline \end{array}$	**4.** $\begin{array}{r} 900 \\ \times\ 50 \\ \hline \end{array}$	**5.** $\begin{array}{r} 300 \\ \times\ 70 \\ \hline \end{array}$	**6.** $\begin{array}{r} 400 \\ \times\ 70 \\ \hline \end{array}$	**7.** $\begin{array}{r} 600 \\ \times\ 90 \\ \hline \end{array}$
8. $\begin{array}{r} 600 \\ \times\ 70 \\ \hline \end{array}$	**9.** $\begin{array}{r} 300 \\ \times\ 50 \\ \hline \end{array}$	**10.** $\begin{array}{r} 300 \\ \times\ 90 \\ \hline \end{array}$	**11.** $\begin{array}{r} 800 \\ \times\ 30 \\ \hline \end{array}$	**12.** $\begin{array}{r} 600 \\ \times\ 50 \\ \hline \end{array}$

 Challenge

Find the missing factor.

13. $1800 = 20 \times \boxed{?}$

14. $4200 = 70 \times \boxed{?}$

15. $28,000 = 70 \times \boxed{?}$

16. $56,000 = 800 \times \boxed{?}$

17. $81,000 = 900 \times \boxed{?}$

Rounding

$4 \times 587 = $ ⬚

You can round to estimate the answer.

Round the large factor to the nearest ten.

$$
\begin{array}{r}
587 \\
\times \quad 4 \\
\hline
\end{array}
\qquad
\begin{array}{r}
590 \\
\times \quad 4 \\
\hline
2360
\end{array}
$$

Round the large factor to the nearest hundred.

$$
\begin{array}{r}
587 \\
\times \quad 4 \\
\hline
\end{array}
\qquad
\begin{array}{r}
600 \\
\times \quad 4 \\
\hline
2400
\end{array}
$$

Round the top number to the nearest ten. Multiply.

1. $\begin{array}{r} 783 \\ \times \quad 3 \\ \hline \end{array}$ $\begin{array}{r} 780 \\ \times \quad 3 \\ \hline 2340 \end{array}$

2. $\begin{array}{r} 417 \\ \times \quad 7 \\ \hline \end{array}$

3. $\begin{array}{r} 111 \\ \times \quad 8 \\ \hline \end{array}$

4. $\begin{array}{r} 929 \\ \times \quad 6 \\ \hline \end{array}$

5. $\begin{array}{r} 842 \\ \times \quad 5 \\ \hline \end{array}$

6. $\begin{array}{r} 198 \\ \times \quad 6 \\ \hline \end{array}$

7. $\begin{array}{r} 114 \\ \times \quad 8 \\ \hline \end{array}$

8. $\begin{array}{r} 146 \\ \times \quad 3 \\ \hline \end{array}$

9. $\begin{array}{r} 104 \\ \times \quad 9 \\ \hline \end{array}$

10. $\begin{array}{r} 215 \\ \times \quad 4 \\ \hline \end{array}$

11. $\begin{array}{r} 503 \\ \times \quad 2 \\ \hline \end{array}$

12. $\begin{array}{r} 384 \\ \times \quad 5 \\ \hline \end{array}$

13. $\begin{array}{r} 621 \\ \times \quad 6 \\ \hline \end{array}$

14. $\begin{array}{r} 455 \\ \times \quad 3 \\ \hline \end{array}$

Round the top number to the nearest hundred. Multiply.

15. $\begin{array}{r} 783 \\ \times \quad 3 \\ \hline \end{array}$ $\begin{array}{r} 800 \\ \times \quad 3 \\ \hline 2400 \end{array}$

16. $\begin{array}{r} 111 \\ \times \quad 8 \\ \hline \end{array}$

17. $\begin{array}{r} 929 \\ \times \quad 6 \\ \hline \end{array}$

18. $\begin{array}{r} 687 \\ \times \quad 4 \\ \hline \end{array}$

19. $\begin{array}{r} 842 \\ \times \quad 5 \\ \hline \end{array}$

20. $\begin{array}{r} 198 \\ \times \quad 8 \\ \hline \end{array}$

21. $\begin{array}{r} 115 \\ \times \quad 6 \\ \hline \end{array}$

22. $\begin{array}{r} 146 \\ \times \quad 3 \\ \hline \end{array}$

23. $\begin{array}{r} 102 \\ \times \quad 9 \\ \hline \end{array}$

Rounding and Money

Round to the nearest ten cents.   Round to the nearest dollar.

$6.49 rounds to **$6.50**   .**$6.49** rounds to **$6.00**

Round to the nearest ten cents. Multiply.

1. $1.53 $1.50
   ×   4   ×   4
           $6.00

2. $3.18
   ×   7

3. $6.75
   ×   5

4. $7.43
   ×   3

Round to the nearest dollar. Multiply.

5. $4.39
   ×   6

6. $0.89
   ×   5

7. $18.92
   ×   8

8. $10.43
   ×   2

9. $14.69
   ×   6

10. $9.89
    ×   5

11. $0.65
    ×   3

12. $25.98
    ×   4

13. $20.25
    ×   7

14. $14.50
    ×   2

 Challenge

Round to the nearest
dollar before finding the answers.

15. Ellen Garza and Ben Garza own
a bicycle shop. They charge
$2.85 to repair a tire. About
how much do they collect
for repairing 7 tires?

16. Bicycles cost $59.95.
About how much for 4 bicycles?

$59.95

Multiplying to Find Area

Area is always measured in square units.

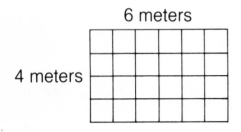

6 meters

4 meters

6 in a row,
4 rows.

$$\begin{array}{r} 6 \text{ meters} \\ \times\ 4 \text{ meters} \\ \hline 24 \text{ square meters} \end{array}$$

Multiply to find the area of these surfaces.

1. A square: one side is
   9 meters. 81 square meters

2. A square: one side is
   10 meters.

3. A rectangle: one side is 12
   meters, another is 7 meters.

4. A rectangle: one side is 49
   meters, another is 10 meters.

5. A rectangle: one side is 23
   meters, another is 1000 meters.

6. A rectangle: one side is 40
   meters, another is 30 meters.

 Challenge

7. One can of paint covers 25
   square meters. You have 8 cans
   of paint. Your wall measures
   225 square meters. Do you need
   more paint?

700 PUZZLE

A game for one player.

Get ready:
You need paper and a pencil.

To play:
Make four multiplication problems. Try to make
the sum of the products equal 700.

Box A

5
3
10   6

Box B

30   50
13   40

Use one number from Box A with one number from
Box B for each of the four problems.
Multiply. Add your products.

Here is one way to do it. You find another way.

$$5 \times 50 = 250 \qquad 250$$
$$3 \times 40 = 120 \qquad 120$$
$$5 \times 30 = 150 \qquad 150$$
$$6 \times 30 = 180 \qquad +\ 180$$
$$\overline{\hspace{2.2cm} 700}$$

Multiplying by Two Digits

$13 \times 17 = \boxed{?}$

Step 1
Multiply by
the ones.

$$
\begin{array}{r}
17 \\
\times\ 13 \\
\hline
51
\end{array}
\quad 3 \times 17
$$

Step 2
Multiply by
the tens.

$$
\begin{array}{r}
17 \\
\times\ 13 \\
\hline
51 \\
170
\end{array}
\quad 10 \times 17
$$

Step 3
Add the
products.

$$
\begin{array}{r}
17 \\
\times\ 13 \\
\hline
51 \\
+\ 170 \\
\hline
221
\end{array}
$$

Multiply.

1. $\begin{array}{r} 33 \\ \times\ 14 \\ \hline 462 \end{array}$
2. $\begin{array}{r} 34 \\ \times\ 16 \\ \hline \end{array}$
3. $\begin{array}{r} 53 \\ \times\ 18 \\ \hline \end{array}$
4. $\begin{array}{r} 72 \\ \times\ 19 \\ \hline \end{array}$
5. $\begin{array}{r} 84 \\ \times\ 13 \\ \hline \end{array}$
6. $\begin{array}{r} 29 \\ \times\ 12 \\ \hline \end{array}$

7. $\begin{array}{r} 67 \\ \times\ 12 \\ \hline \end{array}$
8. $\begin{array}{r} 94 \\ \times\ 17 \\ \hline \end{array}$
9. $\begin{array}{r} 48 \\ \times\ 16 \\ \hline \end{array}$
10. $\begin{array}{r} 72 \\ \times\ 18 \\ \hline \end{array}$
11. $\begin{array}{r} 58 \\ \times\ 15 \\ \hline \end{array}$
12. $\begin{array}{r} 36 \\ \times\ 13 \\ \hline \end{array}$

13. $\begin{array}{r} 42 \\ \times\ 14 \\ \hline \end{array}$
14. $\begin{array}{r} 37 \\ \times\ 15 \\ \hline \end{array}$
15. $\begin{array}{r} 53 \\ \times\ 19 \\ \hline \end{array}$
16. $\begin{array}{r} 46 \\ \times\ 17 \\ \hline \end{array}$
17. $\begin{array}{r} 87 \\ \times\ 12 \\ \hline \end{array}$
18. $\begin{array}{r} 28 \\ \times\ 16 \\ \hline \end{array}$

19. $\begin{array}{r} 39 \\ \times\ 19 \\ \hline \end{array}$
20. $\begin{array}{r} 96 \\ \times\ 12 \\ \hline \end{array}$
21. $\begin{array}{r} 44 \\ \times\ 13 \\ \hline \end{array}$
22. $\begin{array}{r} 57 \\ \times\ 18 \\ \hline \end{array}$
23. $\begin{array}{r} 89 \\ \times\ 16 \\ \hline \end{array}$
24. $\begin{array}{r} 15 \\ \times\ 15 \\ \hline \end{array}$

25. $\begin{array}{r} 35 \\ \times\ 15 \\ \hline \end{array}$
26. $\begin{array}{r} 86 \\ \times\ 14 \\ \hline \end{array}$
27. $\begin{array}{r} 50 \\ \times\ 17 \\ \hline \end{array}$
28. $\begin{array}{r} 71 \\ \times\ 12 \\ \hline \end{array}$
29. $\begin{array}{r} 95 \\ \times\ 11 \\ \hline \end{array}$
30. $\begin{array}{r} 81 \\ \times\ 19 \\ \hline \end{array}$

More Multiplying by Two Digits

43 × 27 is the sum of 3 × 27 and 40 × 27.

If you can do these,   you can do this!

```
   27        27           27
 ×  3      × 40         × 43
 ────      ────         ────
   81      1080           81
                      + 1080
                      ──────
                        1161
```

Multiply.

1. 48   2. 57   3. 63
  × 62   × 28   × 34
  ────
  2976

4. 86   5. 47   6. 76   7. 46   8. 82   9. 94
  × 54   × 29   × 33   × 27   × 42   × 37

10. 72   11. 35   12. 23   13. 44   14. 60   15. 86
   × 46   × 22   × 85   × 63   × 24   × 52

⭐ Challenge

16. What is the last digit in the product of 74 × 29?

17. Is the product of 56 × 37 nearer to 150 or to 1500?

18. What is the last digit in the product of 892 × 374?

19. Is the product of 41 × 29 nearer to 1200 or 120?

Practice Multiplying by Two Digits

Remember tens times tens? Multiply.

1.	70	2.	30	3.	50	4.	90	5.	80	6.	20
	× 40		× 80		× 50		× 20		× 60		× 70
	2800										

7.	80	8.	90	9.	70	10.	50	11.	40	12.	60
	× 50		× 90		× 80		× 20		× 30		× 90

Find the products.

13.	27	14.	53	15.	72	16.	59	17.	78	18.	58
	× 19		× 70		× 17		× 16		× 34		× 36

19.	47	20.	42	21.	63	22.	75	23.	49	24.	71
	× 30		× 23		× 57		× 64		× 12		× 24

25.	72	26.	86	27.	13	28.	22	29.	40	30.	57
	× 15		× 28		× 46		× 61		× 25		× 83

31.	60	32.	99	33.	32	34.	86	35.	59	36.	28
	× 40		× 11		× 76		× 14		× 20		× 92

Calculate

37. 324×56 38. 87×513 39. 620×66 40. 462×38

41. 921×13 42. 847×67 43. 82×773 44. 93×184

Multiplying with Four Factors

$4 \times 21 \times 30 \times 6 = \boxed{?}$

Step 1
Multiply the first
two factors.

Step 2
Multiply the product
by the third factor.

Step 3
Multiply that product
by the fourth factor.

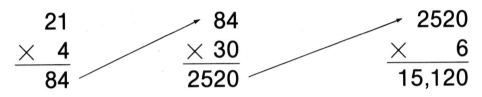

$$\begin{array}{r} 21 \\ \times\ \ 4 \\ \hline 84 \end{array} \qquad \begin{array}{r} 84 \\ \times\ 30 \\ \hline 2520 \end{array} \qquad \begin{array}{r} 2520 \\ \times\ \ \ \ 6 \\ \hline 15{,}120 \end{array}$$

Multiply.

1. $4 \times 20 \times 7 \times 5$ 2800

2. $15 \times 3 \times 6 \times 40$

3. $18 \times 2 \times 8 \times 4$

4. $5 \times 30 \times 4 \times 20$

5. $25 \times 3 \times 6 \times 21$

6. $3 \times 6 \times 4 \times 8$

7. $10 \times 2 \times 5 \times 7$

8. $3 \times 4 \times 16 \times 40$

9. $22 \times 5 \times 3 \times 6$

10. $4 \times 12 \times 8 \times 2$

11. $3 \times 30 \times 7 \times 2$

12. $50 \times 7 \times 1 \times 8$

13. $9 \times 6 \times 42 \times 3$

14. $4 \times 25 \times 8 \times 10$

 Challenge

15. $4 \times 21 \times 30 \times 6 = 15{,}120$.
How many different ways
can you find to multiply
these 4 factors?
Use trial and error.

Travel Problems

1. An airplane traveled 672 kilometers in an hour. How far did it travel in 5 hours? 3360 kilometers

2. A bus seats 58 people. How many people in 6 full buses?

3. A train car seats 88 people. How many people in 16 full cars?

4. 300 people each pay $70 for a train ticket. How much money is that?

5. 468 airplane passengers each have 2 suitcases. How many suitcases in all?

6. An ocean liner traveled 48 kilometers in an hour. How far did it travel in 17 hours?

7. The total cost of running a car is 8¢ for each kilometer. What is the cost for 4729 kilometers?

8. The taxi company charges $1.25 for each kilometer of a trip. How much do they charge for an 8-kilometer trip?

9. It costs $16.98 each day for vacation expenses. How much would a 6-day vacation cost?

10. A train trip lasts 21 hours. Each hour the train travels 60 kilometers. How many kilometers does the train travel during the whole trip?

11. Each centimeter on a map stands for 25 kilometers. If the distance between two cities on a map is 8 centimeters, how many kilometers are between them?

12. A travel agent planned a trip for a group of 82 people. She charged each of them $12. How much did she charge altogether?

13. Yoshie rode 48 kilometers a day on her bike trip. How far did she go in 13 days?

Chapter Review

Copy and complete. (ex. 1–3: p. 236)

1.

	× 7	+ 5
9		
6		

2.

	× 6	+ 2
3		
8		

3.

	× 5	+ 7
9		
7		

Find the products. (ex. 4–9: p. 237)

4.	72	**5.**	54	**6.**	92	**7.**	64	**8.**	35	**9.**	44
	× 8		× 6		× 4		× 7		× 4		× 9

Find the products. (ex. 10–13: p. 242), (ex. 14–17: p. 243),
(ex. 18, 19: p. 246), (ex. 20–22: p. 247)

10. 217×5 **11.** 672×8 **12.** 324×7 **13.** 723×6

14. 409×7 **15.** 900×6 **16.** 807×4 **17.** 500×3

18.	7896	**19.**	4523	**20.**	8009	**21.**	5046	**22.**	3205
	× 7		× 4		× 6		× 3		× 6

Multiply. (ex. 23: p. 249), (ex. 24: p. 250),
(ex. 25: p. 256), (ex. 26, 27: p. 263)

23.	$16.73	**24.**	47	**25.**	50	**26.**	17	**27.**	44
	× 4		× 10		× 70		× 19		× 34

Chapter Test

Copy and complete.

1.

	× 7	+ 5
2		
4		

2.

	× 9	+ 2
5		
3		

3.

	× 5	+ 7
8		
6		

Find the products.

4. 61
   × 3

5. 30
   × 4

6. 16
   × 2

7. 48
   × 6

8. 27
   × 5

9. 77
   × 8

10. 17
   × 4

11. 76
   × 3

12. 24
   × 8

13. 78
   × 5

14. 56
   × 4

15. 83
   × 7

Multiply.

16. 314
   × 5

17. 521
   × 8

18. 709
   × 7

19. 600
   × 6

20. 809
   × 5

21. 3423
   × 7

22. 1895
   × 5

23. 67
   × 10

24. 30
   × 40

25. 26
   × 21

Brush Up

Add, subtract, multiply, or divide.

1. 379 − 86   **2.** 362 + 545   **3.** 3457 + 278   **4.** 5003 − 1658

5. 9 × 5   **6.** 8 × 7   **7.** 6 × 9   **8.** 72 ÷ 9   **9.** 48 ÷ 8

Order from least to greatest.

10. 736, 673, 763, 376   **11.** 0.6, 0.3, 1.1, 0.4

Find equal fractions.

12. $\frac{1}{2} = \frac{?}{4}$ **13.** $\frac{2}{3} = \frac{4}{?}$ **14.** $\frac{1}{2} = \frac{8}{?}$ **15.** $\frac{3}{4} = \frac{?}{8}$ **16.** $\frac{1}{3} = \frac{?}{6}$

Find the sums or differences.

17. $\frac{3}{6} + \frac{2}{6}$ **18.** $\frac{9}{10} - \frac{5}{10}$ **19.** $\frac{7}{16} - \frac{3}{16}$ **20.** $\frac{9}{12} - \frac{7}{12}$ **21.** $\frac{4}{11} + \frac{3}{11}$

Write the letter.

22. Which is smaller than a right angle?   a   b   c

23. Which lines are parallel?   a   b   c

Multiply.

24. 6009 × 3   **25.** 654 × 9   **26.** 600 × 4   **27.** 53 × 86   **28.** 87 × 69

CHAPTER 11

Division

Using Division at Work

Bernadette Jeffers is a weather forecaster. On Saturday the high temperature was 82 degrees; on Sunday the high temperature was 78 degrees. To find the average high temperature for the 2 days, she adds both temperatures, then divides the sum by 2. The average high temperature was 80 degrees.

Reviewing Division Facts

Divide.

1. $2\overline{)8}$ $\overset{4}{}$
2. $2\overline{)18}$
3. $2\overline{)14}$
4. $2\overline{)6}$
5. $2\overline{)16}$

6. $3\overline{)18}$
7. $3\overline{)24}$
8. $3\overline{)12}$
9. $3\overline{)21}$
10. $3\overline{)27}$

11. $4\overline{)24}$
12. $4\overline{)16}$
13. $4\overline{)20}$
14. $4\overline{)36}$
15. $4\overline{)28}$

16. $5\overline{)20}$
17. $5\overline{)15}$
18. $5\overline{)35}$
19. $5\overline{)40}$
20. $5\overline{)45}$

21. $36 \div 6$
22. $18 \div 6$
23. $42 \div 6$
24. $54 \div 6$
25. $48 \div 6$

26. $56 \div 7$
27. $42 \div 7$
28. $63 \div 7$
29. $21 \div 7$
30. $49 \div 7$

31. $32 \div 8$
32. $72 \div 8$
33. $48 \div 8$
34. $64 \div 8$
35. $56 \div 8$

36. $27 \div 9$
37. $63 \div 9$
38. $45 \div 9$
39. $36 \div 9$
40. $81 \div 9$

41. The school building is 9 meters high. The office building is 36 meters high. How many times higher is the office building than the school?

Division with Remainders

$4\overline{)25}$ You cannot make 4 fair shares with 2 tens.

So trade tens for ones. Divide.

$$\overset{\text{6 r1}}{4\overline{)25}}$$

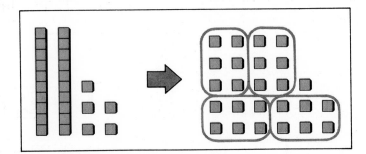

You get 6 ones in each share, and 1 left over.

**Take markers or pieces of paper.
Make fair shares. Write the division problem.**

1. Take 23 markers.
   Make 3 fair shares. $\overset{\text{7 r2}}{3\overline{)23}}$

2. Take 18 markers.
   Make 7 fair shares.

3. Take 13 markers.
   Make 4 fair shares.

4. Take 27 markers.
   Make 5 fair shares.

5. Take 17 markers.
   Make 3 fair shares.

6. Take 28 markers.
   Make 6 fair shares.

7. Take 9 markers.
   Make 4 fair shares.

8. Take 26 markers.
   Make 7 fair shares.

9. Take 19 markers.
   Make 6 fair shares.

10. Sharon has 27 colored pencils. She wants to
    make fair shares for 6 friends. How many pencils
    does each friend get?

More Remainders

×	1	2	3	4	5	6	7	8	9
5	5	10	15	20	25	30	35	40	45

Use the multiplication table to help you divide. Try $5\overline{)17}$.

$3 \times 5 = 15 \qquad 4 \times 5 = 20$
17 is between 15 and 20, so the quotient is 3 with a remainder.

$$\begin{array}{r} 3 \\ 5\overline{)17} \\ -15 \end{array} \quad 3 \times 5 = 15$$

Remember, the remainder must be less than the divisor.

quotient $\qquad$ **3** r**2** remainder
divisor $\;5\overline{)17}$
$$\begin{array}{r} -15 \\ \hline 2 \end{array}$$

Use the table. Divide.

1. $5\overline{)13}$ (2 r3)
2. $5\overline{)21}$
3. $5\overline{)49}$
4. $5\overline{)32}$
5. $5\overline{)19}$

6. $5\overline{)36}$
7. $5\overline{)29}$
8. $5\overline{)23}$
9. $5\overline{)43}$
10. $5\overline{)28}$

11. $5\overline{)17}$
12. $5\overline{)44}$
13. $5\overline{)27}$
14. $5\overline{)31}$
15. $5\overline{)48}$

16. 32 costumes are needed for the class play. 5 children each make an equal number of costumes. How many costumes does each child make? How many costumes left over?

17. The school play is 5 weeks away. It will take 28 hours of practice to get ready. How many hours should the class practice each week? How many hours left?

Dividing with a Table

×	1	2	3	4	5	6	7	8	9
6	6	12	18	24	30	36	42	48	54
7	7	14	21	28	35	42	49	56	63
8	8	16	24	32	40	48	56	64	72
9	9	18	27	36	45	54	63	72	81

This table will help you find the quotient. The remainder is up to you!

Use the table. Divide.

1. $6\overline{)20}$ (3 r2)
2. $7\overline{)11}$
3. $6\overline{)50}$
4. $8\overline{)12}$
5. $9\overline{)65}$

6. $9\overline{)44}$
7. $6\overline{)46}$
8. $8\overline{)10}$
9. $9\overline{)36}$
10. $7\overline{)51}$

11. $8\overline{)27}$
12. $8\overline{)29}$
13. $7\overline{)28}$
14. $9\overline{)43}$
15. $8\overline{)38}$

16. $7\overline{)39}$
17. $9\overline{)35}$
18. $8\overline{)56}$
19. $7\overline{)31}$
20. $8\overline{)54}$

21. $7\overline{)21}$
22. $9\overline{)71}$
23. $6\overline{)51}$
24. $8\overline{)16}$
25. $9\overline{)47}$

 Challenge

Write the numbers that can be remainders when you divide by each of these.

26. 2
27. 5
28. 6

29. 7
30. 8
31. 9

Practicing Division

$3\overline{)20}$

$3 \times 6 = 18$
$3 \times 7 = 21$

21 is more than 20, so 7 is too big.

Divide, multiply, subtract, bring down, write the remainder.

$$6\ r2$$
$$3\overline{)20}$$
$$\underline{-\ 18}\quad 6 \times 3 = 18$$
$$2$$

Divide.

1. $4\overline{)27}$ 6 r3

2. $8\overline{)35}$

3. $5\overline{)40}$

4. $7\overline{)47}$

5. $9\overline{)57}$

6. $7\overline{)28}$

7. $6\overline{)46}$

8. $2\overline{)17}$

9. $3\overline{)24}$

10. $4\overline{)18}$

11. $8\overline{)50}$

12. $5\overline{)45}$

13. $7\overline{)27}$

14. $9\overline{)70}$

15. $6\overline{)28}$

16. $2\overline{)11}$

17. $3\overline{)28}$

18. $4\overline{)28}$

19. $8\overline{)63}$

20. $5\overline{)43}$

 Challenge

21. Manny, Maureen, and Jack made $27 washing cars and divided the money equally. Manny spent $5 on a new bicycle tire. How much did he have left?

22. 5 books cost a total of $17. 4 books cost the same price, 1 book costs $2 more than the others. What is the price of the more expensive book?

Division Problems

Copy and complete each problem.

1. $3\overline{)26}$ ☐ r2 $3\overline{)26}$ 8 r2

2. $9\overline{)49}$ ☐ r4

3. $5\overline{)28}$ ☐ r3

4. $5\overline{)☐}$ 8 r1

5. $6\overline{)☐}$ 9 r0

6. $4\overline{)☐}$ 7 r3

7. $7\overline{)58}$ 8 r☐

8. $4\overline{)32}$ 8 r☐

9. $7\overline{)62}$ 8 r☐

10. $☐\overline{)39}$ 7 r4

11. $☐\overline{)23}$ 3 r2

12. $☐\overline{)43}$ 6 r1

13. $2\overline{)15}$ ☐ r1

14. $6\overline{)☐}$ 5 r5

15. $9\overline{)83}$ ☐ r2

16. $5\overline{)37}$ 7 r☐

 Calculate

17. Guess how many times you will need to subtract 5 from 100 before you reach zero. How close was your guess?

18. Guess how many times you will need to subtract 8 from 104 before you reach zero. How close was your guess?

278   SECTION 96   DIVISION PUZZLES

ODDBALL REMAINDER GAME

A game for one player.

Get ready:
Write each division problem on a slip of paper. You will need 18 slips. Make four Remainder Boxes like the ones below. Turn the slips over and mix them up.

To play:
Pick a slip from the pile. Divide and find the remainder. Then put your slip in the correct Remainder Box. Two slips do not belong in any of the Remainder Boxes. These are the Odd-Ball Remainders. Which ones are they?

$2\overline{)9}$	$7\overline{)22}$	$3\overline{)12}$
$6\overline{)22}$	$8\overline{)22}$	$7\overline{)34}$
$4\overline{)28}$	$5\overline{)19}$	$3\overline{)22}$
$6\overline{)29}$	$2\overline{)19}$	$7\overline{)32}$
$4\overline{)21}$	$6\overline{)12}$	$8\overline{)49}$
$6\overline{)36}$	$3\overline{)10}$	$9\overline{)56}$

Remainder 0	Remainder 1	Remainder 4	Remainder 6

Weekend Problems

1. Mandy Taylor has 15 packages of clay. She needs 2 packages of clay to make one pot. How many pots can she make? How much clay will she have left?   7 r1

2. Jessica has 43 light bulbs. She needs 5 light bulbs to make one lamp. How many lamps can she make? How many light bulbs will be left over?

3. A wagon has 4 wheels. Tony has 29 wheels. How many wagons can he make? How many wheels will he have left?

4. It takes 3 minutes to wrap a record album for a gift. How many record albums can Sheila wrap in 15 minutes?

5. Jill is making birdhouses. She needs 8 nails for each one. She has 13 nails. How many birdhouses can she make? How many nails are left over?

6. Jeff is planting seeds in a tray. He has 75 seeds. He puts 8 seeds in one row. How many rows can he make? How many seeds left over?

7. Peggy is making a photo album. She has 57 photos. She puts 6 pictures on each page. How many pages can she fill? How many photos will be left?

8. Jim Garcia needs 6 pieces of leather to make one braided belt. He has 21 pieces. How many belts can he make? How many pieces will be left?

10. Gary and Jonathan make ham sandwiches for their friends. They have 37 slices of ham. They put 5 slices of ham on each sandwich. How many sandwiches can they make? How much ham is left?

11. Jill and Paul are making peach jam. They have 33 peaches. It takes 4 peaches to make one full jar of jam. How many jars of jam can they make? How many peaches will be left?

12. Ann Watson is making kites. She needs 4 sheets of paper to make each one. She has 23 sheets of paper. How many kites can she make? How many sheets left over?

9. Greg Owens is writing invitations to a party. It takes 9 minutes to write each one. How many invitations can he write in 63 minutes?

13. Lily Lee is making a wooden box. She needs 6 pieces of wood for each box. How many boxes can she make with 44 pieces of wood?

 Review (pp. 273–281)

1. $8\overline{)35}$ 2. $5\overline{)43}$ 3. $7\overline{)27}$ 4. $9\overline{)70}$ 5. $4\overline{)39}$

Two-Digit Quotients

Step 1
Divide tens.

$$\begin{array}{r} 3 \\ 3\overline{)96} \\ -9 \\ \hline 0 \end{array}$$ 3 tens × 3 = 9 tens

Step 2
Bring down ones.

$$\begin{array}{r} 3 \\ 3\overline{)96} \\ -9\downarrow \\ \hline 06 \end{array}$$

Step 3
Divide ones.

$$\begin{array}{r} 32 \\ 3\overline{)96} \\ -9 \\ \hline 06 \\ -6 \\ \hline 0 \end{array}$$ 2 × 3 = 6

This is 9 tens and 6 ones divided into 3 equal groups.

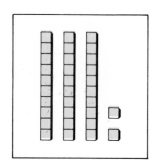 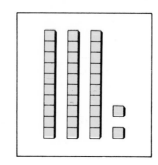 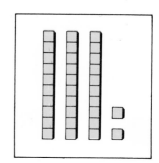

Divide.

1. $3\overline{)90}$ (30)   2. $2\overline{)84}$ 3. $3\overline{)66}$ 4. $5\overline{)55}$ 5. $6\overline{)60}$

6. $3\overline{)93}$ 7. $2\overline{)68}$ 8. $8\overline{)88}$ 9. $3\overline{)63}$ 10. $4\overline{)88}$

11. $2\overline{)60}$ 12. $4\overline{)84}$ 13. $3\overline{)69}$ 14. $2\overline{)82}$ 15. $7\overline{)77}$

More Two-Digit Quotients

Step 1
Divide tens.
Bring down ones.

```
      2
  3 )87
   - 6↓
    27
```

Step 2
Divide ones.

```
     29
  3 )87
   - 6
    27
  - 27
     0
```

Check.
Multiply the quotient
by the divisor.

```
    29  quotient
  ×  3  divisor
    87
```

Divide. Check the first row.

1. $4\overline{)96}$ (24)
2. $3\overline{)84}$
3. $5\overline{)85}$
4. $6\overline{)78}$
5. $2\overline{)50}$

6. $3\overline{)51}$
7. $4\overline{)76}$
8. $8\overline{)96}$
9. $5\overline{)95}$
10. $7\overline{)84}$

11. $3\overline{)54}$
12. $2\overline{)92}$
13. $5\overline{)80}$
14. $2\overline{)76}$
15. $6\overline{)96}$

16. $4\overline{)92}$
17. $5\overline{)75}$
18. $7\overline{)91}$
19. $6\overline{)84}$
20. $3\overline{)72}$

3 for 51¢   4 for 96¢   6 for 78¢

Quotients with Remainders

Step 1
Divide tens.
Divide ones.

$$\begin{array}{r} 26 \\ 3\overline{)79} \\ -6 \\ \hline 19 \\ -18 \\ \hline 1 \end{array}$$

Step 2
Write remainder.

$$\begin{array}{r} 26\ \text{r}1 \\ 3\overline{)79} \\ -6 \\ \hline 19 \\ -18 \\ \hline 1 \end{array}$$

Check.
Multiply quotient by
divisor. Add remainder.

$$\begin{array}{r} 26 \\ \times\ 3 \\ \hline 78 \\ +\ 1 \\ \hline 79 \end{array}$$

Divide. Check the first row.

1. $4\overline{)78}$ 19 r2

2. $3\overline{)85}$

3. $5\overline{)68}$

4. $6\overline{)76}$

5. $7\overline{)87}$

6. $2\overline{)55}$

7. $7\overline{)80}$

8. $4\overline{)67}$

9. $5\overline{)89}$

10. $6\overline{)93}$

11. $3\overline{)79}$

12. $4\overline{)51}$

13. $4\overline{)46}$

14. $4\overline{)50}$

15. $5\overline{)77}$

16. $2\overline{)37}$

17. $3\overline{)43}$

18. $5\overline{)62}$

19. $4\overline{)99}$

20. $8\overline{)94}$

21. $7\overline{)89}$

22. $6\overline{)71}$

23. $3\overline{)98}$

24. $3\overline{)40}$

25. $7\overline{)81}$

26. It takes 8 oranges to make a pitcher of orange juice. How many pitchers of orange juice can you make with 53 oranges? How many oranges left over?

Practicing Division with Remainders

Rewrite these problems using $\overline{)}$. Divide.

1. $97 \div 8$ $8\overline{)97}$ $\overset{12\ r1}{}$
    2. $86 \div 7$ 3. $92 \div 2$ 4. $95 \div 4$

5. $97 \div 7$ 6. $79 \div 3$ 7. $84 \div 5$ 8. $93 \div 6$ 9. $43 \div 3$

10. $84 \div 6$ 11. $73 \div 4$ 12. $92 \div 8$ 13. $72 \div 4$ 14. $79 \div 5$

15. $69 \div 4$ 16. $47 \div 3$ 17. $65 \div 5$ 18. $83 \div 7$ 19. $91 \div 6$

20. $81 \div 7$ 21. $72 \div 6$ 22. $95 \div 8$ 23. $31 \div 2$ 24. $85 \div 3$

 Challenge

25. Joan Rogers owns a pet store. She has 55 birds. She keeps 6 in each cage. How many cages does she need?

26. Joan has 49 hamsters. She keeps 3 in each cage. How many cages does she need?

27. Joan has 73 fish. If she puts 4 fish in each fishbowl, how many fishbowls does she need?

28. Joan puts 90 boxes of pet food in rows of 8 boxes. How many complete rows can she make?

Zero in Two-Digit Quotients

Step 1
Divide tens.
Bring down ones.

$$
\begin{array}{r}
2\\
4\overline{)83}\\
-8\\
\hline
03
\end{array}
$$

Step 2
Divide ones.
Write remainder.

$$
\begin{array}{r}
20\ r3\\
4\overline{)83}\\
-8\\
\hline
03\\
-\ 0\\
\hline
3
\end{array}
$$

Check.

$$4 \times 20 = 80$$
$$80 + 3 = 83$$

Divide. Check the first row.

1. $9\overline{)97}$ — 10 r7

2. $4\overline{)82}$

3. $2\overline{)61}$

4. $8\overline{)86}$

5. $7\overline{)75}$

6. $5\overline{)52}$

7. $3\overline{)31}$

8. $3\overline{)62}$

9. $7\overline{)79}$

10. $4\overline{)81}$

11. $3\overline{)92}$

12. $4\overline{)43}$

13. $6\overline{)64}$

14. $2\overline{)81}$

15. $9\overline{)98}$

16. $7\overline{)76}$

17. $65 \div 6$

18. $94 \div 9$

19. $42 \div 4$

20. $61 \div 6$

21. $41 \div 2$

22. $54 \div 5$

23. $21 \div 2$

24. $62 \div 6$

25. $49 \div 4$

26. $84 \div 8$

27. May has 61 strawberry plants. She makes 3 equal rows. How many plants in each row? How many plants left over?

28. Tom has 83 peaches. He divides them equally among 8 friends. How many peaches for each friend? How many left?

Reviewing Division

Remember these?

$$3 \overline{)20} \quad \text{6 r2}$$

$$3 \overline{)87} \quad \text{29}$$

$$3 \overline{)79} \quad \text{26 r1}$$

Divide.

1. $3 \overline{)95}$ 31 r2   2. $9 \overline{)56}$ 3. $7 \overline{)84}$ 4. $6 \overline{)41}$

5. $6 \overline{)53}$ 6. $7 \overline{)84}$ 7. $3 \overline{)86}$ 8. $5 \overline{)37}$

9. $7 \overline{)26}$ 10. $9 \overline{)47}$ 11. $8 \overline{)74}$ 12. $9 \overline{)86}$

13. $4 \overline{)34}$ 14. $5 \overline{)95}$ 15. $9 \overline{)73}$ 16. $8 \overline{)71}$

17. $3 \overline{)99}$ 18. $6 \overline{)19}$ 19. $4 \overline{)52}$ 20. $4 \overline{)74}$

21. $8 \overline{)85}$ 22. $5 \overline{)54}$ 23. $3 \overline{)72}$ 24. $8 \overline{)87}$

 Challenge

Copy and correct each problem.

25.
```
    6 r2
7 )43
  - 42
     1
```

26.
```
    9 r5
4 )43
  - 38
     5
```

27.
```
    2 r3
2 )83
  -  8
     3
```

28.
```
    9 r1
5 )36
  - 35
     1
```

Marching Band Problems

1. 62 drummers march in rows of 3. How many rows can they make? How many drummers left?   20 r2

2. 33 harmonica players march in rows of 4. How many rows can they make? How many harmonica players left?

3. 85 tuba players march in rows of 9. How many rows can they make? How many tuba players left?

4. 54 marching majorettes make rows of 6. How many rows can they make? How many majorettes left?

5. There are 96 flute players in the marching band. They march in rows of 7. How many rows can they make? How many flute players left?

6. There are 73 members in the Bagpipe Marching Band. They march in rows of 5. How many full rows of bagpipe players? How many players left?

7. 75 singers march in rows of 6. How many rows can they make? How many singers left?

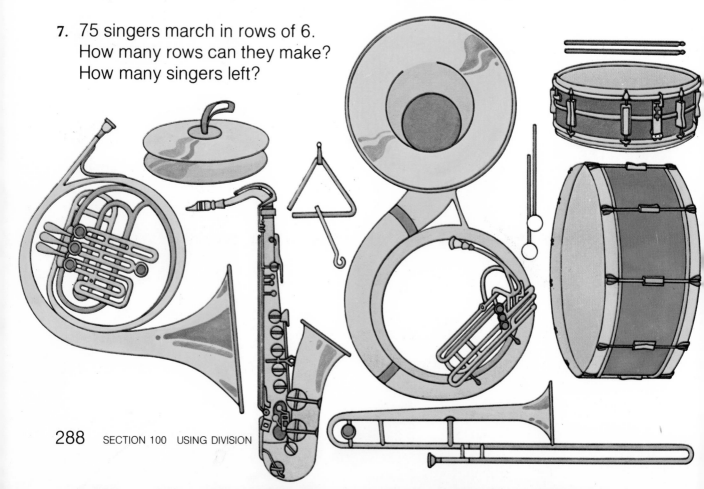

Dividing Hundreds

Step 1
Divide hundreds.
Bring down tens.

$$\begin{array}{r} 3 \\ 2\overline{)684} \\ -6 \\ \hline 08 \end{array}$$

Step 2
Divide tens.
Divide ones.

$$\begin{array}{r} 342 \\ 2\overline{)684} \\ -6 \\ \hline 08 \\ -8 \\ \hline 04 \\ -4 \\ \hline 0 \end{array}$$

Check.

$$\begin{array}{r} 342 \\ \times\quad 2 \\ \hline 684 \end{array}$$

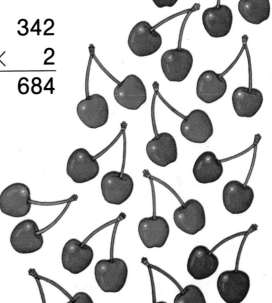

Divide. Check the first row.

1. $2\overline{)428}$ 214

2. $3\overline{)993}$

3. $4\overline{)848}$

4. $5\overline{)555}$

5. $3\overline{)639}$

6. $2\overline{)822}$

7. $3\overline{)696}$

8. $7\overline{)777}$

9. $4\overline{)884}$

10. $2\overline{)284}$

11. $3\overline{)969}$

12. $4\overline{)484}$

13. $2\overline{)688}$

14. $3\overline{)999}$

15. $4\overline{)888}$

16. $824 \div 2$

17. $336 \div 3$

18. $488 \div 4$

19. $444 \div 2$

20. $936 \div 3$

21. $686 \div 2$

22. $864 \div 2$

23. $848 \div 2$

24. $999 \div 9$

25. $844 \div 4$

26. $699 \div 3$

27. $666 \div 6$

More Dividing Hundreds

$2\overline{)135}$ There are not enough hundreds to divide.

Step 1
Divide tens.

$$
\begin{array}{r}
6 \\
2\overline{)135} \\
-12 \\
\hline
1
\end{array}
$$

1 hundred 3 tens
equal 13 tens.

Step 2
Divide ones.
Write remainder.

$$
\begin{array}{r}
67 \text{ r1} \\
2\overline{)135} \\
-12 \\
\hline
15 \\
-14 \\
\hline
1
\end{array}
$$

Divide. Check the first row.

1. $3\overline{)219}$ (73)
2. $4\overline{)309}$
3. $5\overline{)366}$
4. $2\overline{)149}$
5. $4\overline{)264}$

6. $6\overline{)537}$
7. $9\overline{)483}$
8. $7\overline{)347}$
9. $8\overline{)541}$
10. $3\overline{)238}$

11. $2\overline{)183}$
12. $6\overline{)381}$
13. $4\overline{)293}$
14. $7\overline{)441}$
15. $9\overline{)235}$

16. $345 \div 4$
17. $214 \div 6$
18. $168 \div 2$
19. $705 \div 9$

20. $441 \div 5$
21. $237 \div 3$
22. $513 \div 6$
23. $307 \div 8$

24. A year usually has 365 days. A week has 7 days. How many weeks in a year? How many days left over?

Placing the Quotient

$$8\overline{)23}$$

not enough tens
The quotient has
1 digit.

$$4\overline{)134}$$

not enough hundreds
The quotient has
2 digits.

$$6\overline{)714}$$

enough hundreds
The quotient has
3 digits.

Write the first digit for each quotient in the right place.

1. $8 \atop 6\overline{)538}$ 2. $8\overline{)119}$ 3. $4\overline{)463}$ 4. $7\overline{)92}$

5. $5\overline{)718}$ 6. $3\overline{)834}$ 7. $2\overline{)914}$ 8. $4\overline{)37}$

9. $9\overline{)814}$ 10. $4\overline{)802}$ 11. $6\overline{)84}$ 12. $6\overline{)34}$

How many digits in the quotient? Do not complete the problem.

13. $6\overline{)534}$ 14. $8\overline{)91}$ 15. $4\overline{)264}$ 16. $4\overline{)38}$

17. $8\overline{)769}$ 18. $7\overline{)777}$ 19. $6\overline{)57}$ 20. $3\overline{)90}$

21. $3\overline{)618}$ 22. $5\overline{)403}$ 23. $8\overline{)917}$ 24. $4\overline{)91}$

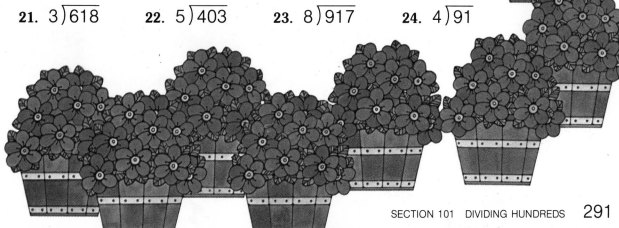

Practicing Division

Divide.

$$
\begin{array}{r}
195 \text{ r}3 \\
4\overline{)783} \\
-4 \\
\hline
38 \\
-36 \\
\hline
23 \\
-20 \\
\hline
3
\end{array}
$$

Check.

$$
\begin{array}{r}
195 \\
\times \quad 4 \\
\hline
780 \\
+ \quad 3 \\
\hline
783
\end{array}
$$

Divide. Check the first row.

1. $\overset{288}{3\overline{)864}}$
2. $7\overline{)938}$
3. $6\overline{)744}$
4. $3\overline{)496}$
5. $4\overline{)573}$

6. $8\overline{)911}$
7. $6\overline{)944}$
8. $4\overline{)686}$
9. $2\overline{)937}$
10. $3\overline{)815}$

11. $5\overline{)763}$
12. $6\overline{)848}$
13. $3\overline{)419}$
14. $7\overline{)817}$
15. $4\overline{)946}$

16. $844 \div 4$
17. $677 \div 2$
18. $493 \div 3$
19. $715 \div 5$

20. $949 \div 6$
21. $737 \div 3$
22. $663 \div 6$
23. $249 \div 2$

24. Miranda has 145 melons. She packs 4 in each crate. How many full crates? How many melons left?

25. Walter has 293 apples. He packs 6 in each bag. How many full bags? How many apples left?

Zero in Three-Digit Quotients

Step 1
Divide hundreds.
Bring down tens.

$$\begin{array}{r} 2 \\ 4\overline{)837} \\ -8 \\ \hline 03 \end{array}$$

Step 2
Divide tens.
Bring down ones.

$$\begin{array}{r} 20 \\ 4\overline{)837} \\ -8 \\ \hline 03 \\ -0 \\ \hline 37 \end{array}$$

0 tens $\times$ 4 = 0 tens

Step 3
Divide ones.

$$\begin{array}{r} 209 \text{ r1} \\ 4\overline{)837} \\ -8 \\ \hline 03 \\ -0 \\ \hline 37 \\ -36 \\ \hline 1 \end{array}$$

Divide. Check the first row.

1. $6\overline{)964}$ 160 r4
2. $4\overline{)523}$
3. $5\overline{)506}$
4. $6\overline{)616}$
5. $2\overline{)209}$

6. $2\overline{)807}$
7. $3\overline{)721}$
8. $7\overline{)767}$
9. $3\overline{)901}$
10. $9\overline{)940}$

11. $5\overline{)505}$
12. $6\overline{)784}$
13. $5\overline{)508}$
14. $3\overline{)620}$
15. $4\overline{)832}$

16. $7\overline{)740}$
17. $8\overline{)804}$
18. $6\overline{)656}$
19. $4\overline{)809}$
20. $3\overline{)613}$

21. $2\overline{)219}$
22. $9\overline{)977}$
23. $4\overline{)683}$
24. $3\overline{)451}$
25. $6\overline{)665}$

Collector Problems

1. Alice and Adam have collected 102 toy trucks. They place 7 trucks on each shelf. How many full shelves do they have? How many trucks are left over?
14 r4

2. Sarah puts 6 postcards on each page of her album. She has 246 postcards. How many pages can she fill? How many postcards will she have left over?

3. Matt Ryan collects old colored bottles. He can fit 6 bottles on a shelf. He has 107 bottles. How many shelves are filled? How many bottles are left?

4. Tom collects plant leaves and puts them in a book. He can fit 3 leaves on each page. He has 304 leaves. How many pages does he fill? How many leaves are left?

5. Laura Martinez has collected 172 old pennies. She puts 8 on each page of an album. How many pages does she fill? How many pennies are left?

6. Paul has collected 146 old keys. He keeps 4 on each key ring. How many full key rings does he have? How many keys left over?

Division and Money

3 models cost $5.07.
How much does each model cost?

```
      $1.69
  3 ) $5.07
    - 3
      20
    - 18
      27
    - 27
       0
```

Remember to
line up decimals.

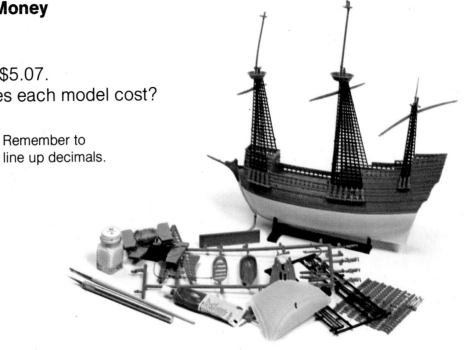

Divide. Remember . and $ in your answer.

1.
```
      $0.93
  6 ) $5.58
```

2. 9) $2.16

3. 8) $4.16

4. 4) $9.72

5. 5) $5.80

6. 7) $9.31

7. 2) $9.96

8. 3) $4.68

9. 4) $5.20

10. 5) $9.45

11. 6) $7.56

12. 3) $3.69

13. 4) $7.80

14. 9) $2.43

15. 7) $7.56

16. 2) $3.98

 Calculate

17a. Divide 603,729 by 777. Were you surprised?
  b. Make up a problem like this one.

Work Problems

Friends get together after school.
They find small jobs and divide their money equally.

1. Linda, Don, and Beth are paid $6.75 for raking leaves. How much does each one earn?
$2.25

2. 5 children wash cars on the weekend. Together they earn $9.50. How much does each child earn?

3. Franco and Elena receive $7.10 for cleaning out a neighbor's garage. How much does each one receive?

4. Bill Wong pays 4 children $6 for washing windows. How much is each child paid?

5. 3 children make $8.40 selling lemonade. What is the fair share for each of them?

6. After a snowstorm 8 children make $8 shovelling snow. How much money does each child earn?

⭐ **Challenge**

7. Joyce Wilson pays a total of $3.75 an hour for planting a garden. 3 children take the job and work for 5 hours. How much does each one earn?

Practicing Division

$$\begin{array}{r} 6 \text{ r2} \\ 3\overline{)20} \end{array}$$

not enough tens
Start with ones.

$$\begin{array}{r} 168 \text{ r2} \\ 5\overline{)842} \end{array}$$

enough hundreds
Start with hundreds.

$$\begin{array}{r} 67 \text{ r1} \\ 2\overline{)135} \end{array}$$

not enough hundreds
Start with tens.

Divide. Check the first row.

1. $\begin{array}{r} 153 \\ 5\overline{)765} \end{array}$
2. $6\overline{)864}$
3. $4\overline{)739}$
4. $8\overline{)986}$
5. $5\overline{)938}$

6. $9\overline{)117}$
7. $7\overline{)869}$
8. $2\overline{)936}$
9. $3\overline{)855}$
10. $6\overline{)93}$

11. $7\overline{)84}$
12. $5\overline{)496}$
13. $8\overline{)897}$
14. $2\overline{)79}$
15. $5\overline{)525}$

16. $61 \div 9$
17. $848 \div 4$
18. $998 \div 6$
19. $747 \div 3$

20. $705 \div 5$
21. $71 \div 8$
22. $857 \div 7$
23. $103 \div 6$

24. $67 \div 7$
25. $653 \div 4$

26. $168 \div 2$
27. $207 \div 3$

28. $595 \div 6$
29. $680 \div 9$

 Review (pp. 273–297)

1. $5\overline{)29}$
2. $6\overline{)84}$
3. $3\overline{)95}$
4. $4\overline{)209}$
5. $7\overline{)767}$

Finding Averages

Find the average number of people in a family.

Family	Number of People
Williams	3
Peterson	5
Lazar	4

Step 1
Find the total number of people in all the families.

$$3 + 5 + 4 = 12$$

Step 2
Divide the total number of people by the number of families.

$$12 \div 3 = 4$$

The average is
4 people in a family.

Find the average number of people in these families.

1.

Family	Number of People
Jones	5
Yip	3
Schmitt	7
Belinsky	5

2.

Family	Number of People
Shapiro	4
Walker	3
Shea	5
Pierce	4

5

3.

Family	Number of People
Carter	8
O'Malley	4
Dix	5
Adams	6
Martin	7

4.

Family	Number of People
Mills	5
Dehler	6
Ford	3
Ortiz	2
Jacobs	4

Find the average number of hours spent doing jobs around the house.

5.

Family	Hours
Taylor	22
Miller	29
Weston	26
Brooks	23

6.

Family	Hours
Rogers	35
Owens	31
Potter	34
Jones	36

Find the average amount spent on meat for a meal.

7.

Family	Amount Spent
Cruz	$3.00
Madison	3.92
White	2.65

8.

Family	Amount Spent
Jackson	$2.00
Vanelli	3.66
Simpson	2.26

Weather Problems

Use what you know about averages
to solve these.

	Sunny Days	Cloudy Days	Rainy Days
Week 1	3	3	1
Week 2	4	1	2
Week 3	5	2	0

1. Use the chart. Find the average of sunny days for each week.   4

2. Use the chart. Find the average of days that are not sunny for each week.

3. In Newbridge it rains 6 centimeters in March, 11 centimeters in April, and 7 centimeters in May. What is the average rainfall for each month?

4. During the 5 years from 1976 through 1980, 45 centimeters of snow fell in North Glen. What is the average snowfall for each year?

5. Every year the lifeguard counts the number of days that are warm enough for swimming. She finds that in 3 years, there are 372 days that are warm enough for swimming. What is the average for each year?

6. Temperatures for 4 days:
Monday: 18 degrees
Tuesday: 19 degrees
Wednesday: 20 degrees
Thursday: 19 degrees
What is the average daily temperature?

Dividing by Tens

Step 1
Divide tens.

$$\begin{array}{r} 2 \\ 40\overline{)987} \\ -\ 80 \\ \hline 18 \end{array}$$

2 times 40 is near 98.

Step 2
Bring down ones.

$$\begin{array}{r} 2 \\ 40\overline{)987} \\ -\ 80 \\ \hline 187 \end{array}$$

Step 3
Divide.

$$\begin{array}{r} 24\ \text{r}27 \\ 40\overline{)987} \\ -\ 80 \\ \hline 187 \\ -\ 160 \\ \hline 27 \end{array}$$

Divide. Check the first row.

1. $\begin{array}{r} 31\ \text{r}21 \\ 30\overline{)951} \end{array}$ 2. $20\overline{)684}$ 3. $40\overline{)900}$ 4. $30\overline{)726}$

5. $20\overline{)947}$ 6. $60\overline{)790}$ 7. $40\overline{)723}$ 8. $70\overline{)813}$

9. $20\overline{)814}$ 10. $30\overline{)995}$ 11. $20\overline{)630}$ 12. $50\overline{)714}$

13. $70\overline{)800}$ 14. $80\overline{)998}$ 15. $40\overline{)663}$ 16. $60\overline{)712}$

17. $50\overline{)574}$ 18. $30\overline{)700}$ 19. $70\overline{)927}$ 20. $20\overline{)983}$

Dividing by Two Digits

Step 1
Round the divisor.
Guess the first digit
of the quotient. Divide.

$$\begin{array}{r} 2 \\ 26\overline{)794} \\ -52 \\ \hline 27 \end{array}$$

26 rounds to 30.
$79 \div 30$ is about 2.
Guess 2.

27 is larger than 26.
Your guess is too small.
Try 3.

Step 2
If your guess is
too large or too small,
guess again. Divide.

$$\begin{array}{r} 30 \text{ r}14 \\ 26\overline{)794} \\ -78 \\ \hline 14 \end{array}$$

Divide.

1. $23\overline{)781}$ 33 r22

2. $38\overline{)538}$

3. $45\overline{)982}$

4. $17\overline{)548}$

5. $52\overline{)592}$

6. $21\overline{)678}$

7. $62\overline{)820}$

8. $31\overline{)976}$

9. $35\overline{)680}$

10. $12\overline{)826}$

11. $18\overline{)193}$

12. $24\overline{)484}$

13. $674 \div 13$

14. $914 \div 29$

15. $843 \div 44$

16. $816 \div 36$

17. $286 \div 25$

18. $854 \div 56$

19. $471 \div 19$

20. $963 \div 82$

21. Paul Palmer picked
465 peppers. He packed
24 peppers into each pot. How
many pots did he pack? How
many peppers left?

More Two-Digit Divisors

Step 1
Make as many guesses as you need to find the first digit of the quotient.

$$40\overline{)357}$$?

Think:
$40 \times 7 = 280$ Too small.
$40 \times 8 = 320$ Just right!
$40 \times 9 = 360$ Too large.

Step 2
Divide.

$$
\begin{array}{r}
8 \text{ r}37 \\
40\overline{)357} \\
-320 \\
\hline
37
\end{array}
$$

Divide. Check the first row.

1. $20\overline{)184}$ 9 r4
2. $40\overline{)293}$

3. $30\overline{)126}$
4. $20\overline{)147}$

5. $40\overline{)323}$
6. $60\overline{)484}$

7. $70\overline{)513}$
8. $20\overline{)114}$

9. $30\overline{)295}$
10. $40\overline{)217}$
11. $20\overline{)117}$
12. $30\overline{)291}$

13. $50\overline{)384}$
14. $80\overline{)195}$
15. $60\overline{)818}$
16. $40\overline{)535}$

17. $199 \div 30$
18. $306 \div 50$
19. $431 \div 60$
20. $705 \div 80$

21. $133 \div 30$
22. $375 \div 40$
23. $346 \div 50$
24. $829 \div 90$

25. $646 \div 70$
26. $192 \div 20$
27. $329 \div 60$
28. $687 \div 80$

Guessing the Quotient

Step 1
Round the divisor.
Guess the first digit.

$$\begin{array}{r} 7 \\ 32\overline{)218} \\ -224 \\ \hline \end{array}$$

32 rounds to 30.
218 ÷ 30 is about 7.

7 × 32 = 224
Your guess is
too large.
Guess lower.

Step 2
Divide.

$$\begin{array}{r} 6\ r26 \\ 32\overline{)218} \\ -192 \\ \hline 26 \end{array}$$

Divide. Check the first row.

1. $33\overline{)265}$ (8 r1)

2. $91\overline{)283}$

3. $42\overline{)178}$

4. $84\overline{)377}$

5. $28\overline{)143}$

6. $63\overline{)531}$

7. $13\overline{)127}$

8. $25\overline{)165}$

9. $53\overline{)381}$

10. $28\overline{)213}$

11. $17\overline{)121}$

12. $14\overline{)123}$

13. $587 \div 63$

14. $123 \div 17$

15. $224 \div 41$

16. $185 \div 27$

17. $645 \div 76$

18. $159 \div 16$

19. $432 \div 51$

20. $276 \div 37$

21. $361 \div 42$

22. $105 \div 34$

23. $150 \div 25$

24. $364 \div 58$

25. There are 12 students in each sailing class. There are 104 students in all. How many full sailing classes. How many students left?

26. A boat trip to the island and back takes 45 minutes. How many trips can be made in 120 minutes?

Practicing with Two-Digit Divisors

Divide. Check the first row by multiplying.

1. $\overset{17\ r53}{54\overline{)971}}$

2. $33\overline{)228}$

3. $49\overline{)373}$

4. $16\overline{)637}$

5. $72\overline{)581}$

6. $20\overline{)723}$

7. $13\overline{)461}$

8. $36\overline{)168}$

9. $40\overline{)370}$

10. $24\overline{)803}$

11. $62\overline{)482}$

12. $18\overline{)582}$

13. $90\overline{)823}$

14. $28\overline{)734}$

15. $56\overline{)171}$

16. $30\overline{)918}$

17. $55\overline{)431}$

18. $26\overline{)264}$

19. $60\overline{)582}$

20. $40\overline{)912}$

21. $32\overline{)124}$

22. $70\overline{)914}$

23. $82\overline{)228}$

24. $25\overline{)804}$

 Challenge

25. It takes 192 hours to build a sailboat from a kit. Sara spends 32 hours each week building the sailboat. How many weeks does it take?

Chapter Review

Divide. (ex. 1–5: p. 277), (ex. 6–10: p. 283),
(ex. 11–13: p. 285), (ex. 14, 15: p. 286)

1. $3\overline{)23}$ 2. $8\overline{)63}$ 3. $7\overline{)47}$ 4. $5\overline{)38}$ 5. $9\overline{)70}$

6. $8\overline{)96}$ 7. $3\overline{)51}$ 8. $5\overline{)85}$ 9. $4\overline{)76}$ 10. $2\overline{)50}$

11. $47 \div 3$ 12. $85 \div 7$ 13. $83 \div 5$ 14. $62 \div 6$ 15. $42 \div 4$

Divide. (ex. 16, 17: p. 289), (ex. 18, 19: p. 290),
(ex. 20, 21: p. 292), (ex. 22, 23: p. 293)

16. $4\overline{)848}$ 17. $3\overline{)969}$ 18. $2\overline{)147}$ 19. $6\overline{)537}$

20. $815 \div 3$ 21. $686 \div 5$ 22. $605 \div 2$ 23. $730 \div 7$

Find the average height. (ex. 24, 25: p. 298)

24.

Bill	105 cm
Helen	109 cm
Anne	116 cm
Mark	126 cm

25.

Beth	150 cm
Charlie	133 cm
Don	146 cm
Martha	135 cm

Divide. (ex. 26, 27: p. 301), (ex. 28, 29: p. 302)

26. $20\overline{)947}$ 27. $50\overline{)714}$ 28. $62\overline{)453}$ 29. $84\overline{)377}$

Chapter Test

Divide.

1. $7 \overline{)30}$

2. $8 \overline{)17}$

3. $9 \overline{)29}$

4. $6 \overline{)26}$

5. $6 \overline{)32}$

6. $7 \overline{)37}$

7. $8 \overline{)42}$

8. $9 \overline{)47}$

9. $46 \div 6$

10. $28 \div 8$

11. $30 \div 9$

12. $40 \div 6$

Divide.

13. $4 \overline{)88}$

14. $7 \overline{)84}$

15. $3 \overline{)92}$

16. $4 \overline{)80}$

17. $129 \div 6$

18. $288 \div 9$

19. $246 \div 8$

20. $490 \div 7$

Find the average age.

21.

Peter	10 years old
Tomas	14 years old
Jenny	15 years old
Pam	17 years old

22.

Maria	21 years old
Barbara	27 years old
Jack	18 years old
Peter	26 years old

Divide.

23. $30 \overline{)995}$

24. $70 \overline{)846}$

25. $20 \overline{)694}$

26. $70 \overline{)923}$

Brush Up

Multiply or divide.

1. $\begin{array}{r} 10 \\ \times\ 5 \end{array}$ **2.** $\begin{array}{r} 100 \\ \times\ 3 \end{array}$ **3.** $\begin{array}{r} 10 \\ \times\ 6 \end{array}$ **4.** $\begin{array}{r} 1000 \\ \times\ 7 \end{array}$ **5.** $\begin{array}{r} 100 \\ \times\ 9 \end{array}$

6. $\begin{array}{r} 64 \\ \times\ 10 \end{array}$ **7.** $\begin{array}{r} 10 \\ \times\ 15 \end{array}$ **8.** $\begin{array}{r} 100 \\ \times\ 31 \end{array}$ **9.** $\begin{array}{r} 100 \\ \times\ 70 \end{array}$ **10.** $\begin{array}{r} 100 \\ \times\ 10 \end{array}$

11. $10\overline{)30}$ **12.** $10\overline{)80}$ **13.** $10\overline{)120}$ **14.** $10\overline{)270}$

15. $10\overline{)73}$ **16.** $10\overline{)95}$ **17.** $10\overline{)184}$ **18.** $10\overline{)347}$

Multiply or divide.

19. $\begin{array}{r} 3 \\ \times\ 4 \end{array}$ **20.** $\begin{array}{r} 8 \\ \times\ 2 \end{array}$ **21.** $\begin{array}{r} 4 \\ \times\ 5 \end{array}$ **22.** $\begin{array}{r} 7 \\ \times\ 3 \end{array}$ **23.** $\begin{array}{r} 7 \\ \times\ 8 \end{array}$ **24.** $\begin{array}{r} 4 \\ \times\ 8 \end{array}$

25. $\begin{array}{r} 12 \\ \times\ 8 \end{array}$ **26.** $\begin{array}{r} 12 \\ \times\ 5 \end{array}$ **27.** $\begin{array}{r} 36 \\ \times\ 2 \end{array}$ **28.** $\begin{array}{r} 16 \\ \times\ 4 \end{array}$ **29.** $\begin{array}{r} 36 \\ \times\ 3 \end{array}$ **30.** $\begin{array}{r} 60 \\ \times\ 7 \end{array}$

31. $\begin{array}{r} 16 \\ \times\ 5 \end{array}$ **32.** $\begin{array}{r} 2000 \\ \times\ 4 \end{array}$ **33.** $\begin{array}{r} 16 \\ \times\ 8 \end{array}$ **34.** $\begin{array}{r} 2000 \\ \times\ 6 \end{array}$ **35.** $\begin{array}{r} 16 \\ \times\ 10 \end{array}$

36. $4\overline{)10}$ **37.** $3\overline{)49}$ **38.** $7\overline{)43}$ **39.** $7\overline{)365}$

40. $16\overline{)48}$ **41.** $12\overline{)52}$ **42.** $16\overline{)79}$ **43.** $12\overline{)88}$

44. $3\overline{)11}$ **45.** $12\overline{)25}$ **46.** $8\overline{)58}$ **47.** $9\overline{)60}$

CHAPTER 12

Measurement and Graphing

Using Measurement at Work

Carlos Estrada owns a cheese shop. A customer wants
to buy 2 pieces of cheese that weigh a total of 1 kilogram.
Carlos cuts one piece that weighs 540 grams. He wants to
find the weight of the other piece. Carlos knows that
1 kilogram equals 1000 grams. He subtracts 540 from
1000. The other piece of cheese should weigh 460 grams.

Length and Time

Length
100 centimeters (cm) = 1 meter (m)
1000 meters = 1 kilometer (km)

Time
60 seconds (s) = 1 minute (min)
60 minutes = 1 hour (h)
24 hours = 1 day
7 days = 1 week
365 days = 1 year
52 weeks = 1 year
12 months = 1 year

Use the charts to find the missing numbers.

1. 200 cm = ▢ m   2 m

2. 3 m = ▢ cm

3. 500 cm = ▢ m

4. 1 km = ▢ m

5. 4000 m = ▢ km

6. 7000 m = ▢ km

7. 9 weeks = ▢ days

8. 125 minutes = ▢ hours ▢ minutes

9. 3 days = ▢ hours

10. 24 months = ▢ years

11. 3 years = ▢ months

12. 395 days = ▢ year ▢ days

13. 3 km = ▢ m

14. 4 m = ▢ cm

15. 800 cm = ▢ m

16. 360 minutes = ▢ hours ▢ minutes

Grams

Weights in **grams (g)**

paper clip
1 g

button
2 g

nickel
5 g

Use the pictures to do these.

1. How much do 12 paper clips weigh?   12 g

2. How much do 10 buttons weigh?

3. How many nickels weigh 20 g?

4. 48 buttons weigh ▢ g.

5. How many paper clips weigh the same as one button?

6. A new piece of chalk weighs about 2 nickels or ▢ g.

7. A tea bag and a button weigh the same. 4 tea bags weigh ▢ g.

8. 3 raisins weigh about the same as a paper clip. 6 raisins weigh about ▢ g.

 Challenge

9. How many buttons weigh as much as 2 nickels?

10. How many nickels weigh as much as 20 buttons?

11. How many nickels weigh as much as 100 paper clips?

12. How many paper clips weigh as much as 50 nickels?

Gram Problems

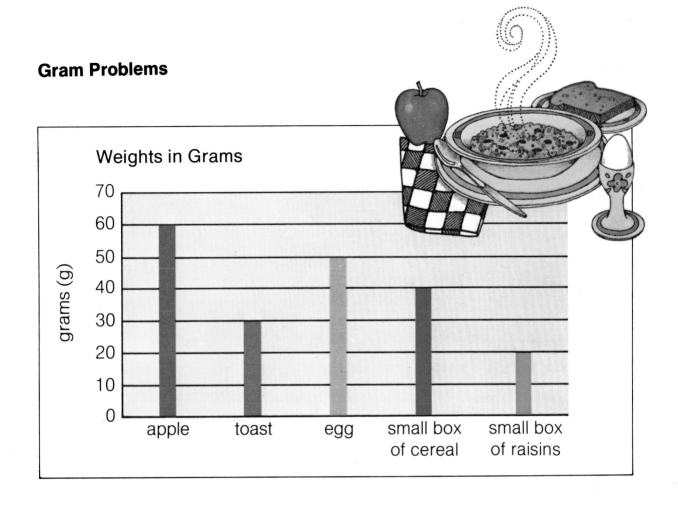

Weights in Grams

grams (g)

70
60
50
40
30
20
10
0

apple   toast   egg   small box of cereal   small box of raisins

Use the bar graph to do these.

1. The apple weighs about ⬚ g. 60

2. The scale on this bar graph shows weight from ⬚ to ⬚ g.

3. 10 apples weigh about ⬚ g.

4. The egg weighs about ⬚ g.

5. 12 eggs weigh about ⬚ g.

6. The toast weighs about ⬚ g.

7. How much more does the apple weigh than the egg?

8. How much more does the egg weigh than the toast?

9. Bill bought 6 eggs, 2 small boxes of cereal, and 1 small box of raisins. What was the total weight?

Kilograms

1000 g = 1 **kilogram (kg)**

book	telephone	cat
1 kg	2 kg	5 kg

Use the pictures to do these.

1. The cat weighs ⬚ g.   5000

2. The telephone weighs ⬚ g.

3. How many books weigh as much as the cat?

4. A new piece of chalk weighs 10 g. How many pieces of chalk weigh a kilogram?

5. A nickel weighs 5 g. How many nickels weigh a kilogram?

6. A paper clip weighs 1 g. How many paper clips in a kilogram?

 Calculate

Multiply to find the total weight.

7. 14 desks

8. 25 chairs

9. 500 lamps

lamp 850 g

chair 15 kg

desk 40 kg

Kilogram Problems

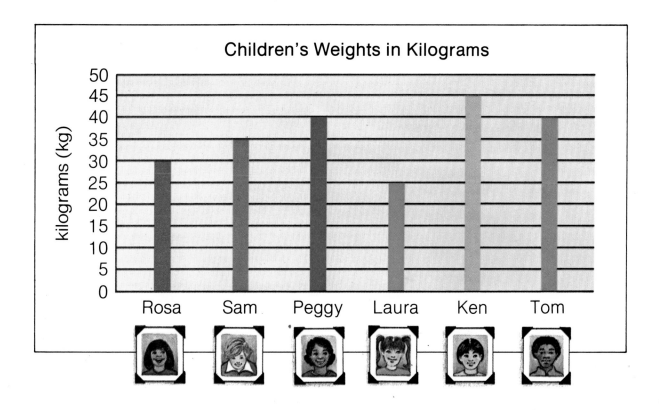

Children's Weights in Kilograms

Use the bar graph to do these.

1. The scale on this bar graph shows weight from ⬚ kg to ⬚ kg.
   0 kg to 50 kg

2. About how much does Rosa weigh?

3. About how much does Sam weigh?

4. About how much does Laura weigh?

5. Which two children weigh the same?

6. How much more does Peggy weigh than Laura?

7. What is the weight of the three girls altogether?

8. What is the weight of the three boys altogether?

Liters and Milliliters

A cubic centimeter holds 1 **milliliter (ml)** of liquid.
There are 1000 milliliters in a **liter (ℓ)**.

mug
125 ml

drinking glass

small paper cup
60 ml

paint bottle

soup spoon 7 ml

1 cm

1 cm

1 cm

Use the pictures to answer these questions.

1. How many milliliters of fruit juice would you need to fill the mug 3 times? 375 ml

2. How many milliliters of milk in 4 small paper cups?

3. About how many milliliters would the drinking glass hold, 150 ml or 15 ml?

4. About how many milliliters would the paint bottle hold, 14 ml or 140 ml?

Write the answers.

5. $2\,\ell = \text{?}\ \text{ml}$ 6. $3000\ \text{ml} = \text{?}\ \ell$ 7. $4\,\ell = \text{?}\ \text{ml}$ 8. $5\,\ell = \text{?}\ \text{ml}$

9. A pail holds 10 ℓ of water. How many milliliters is that?

10. How many milliliters of milk would you drink at one time, 2000 ml or 200 ml?

Liter Problems

A cubic centimeter holds
1 milliliter of liquid.

A cube 10 centimeters on each
side has a volume of 1000
cubic centimeters.
It can hold 1 liter of liquid.

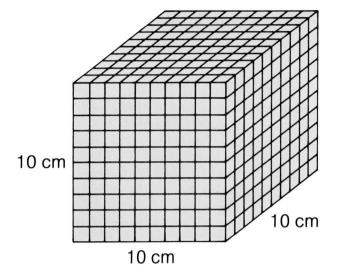

10 cm

10 cm

10 cm

How many milliliters in each of these containers?

1.
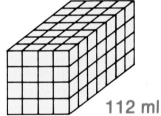
112 ml

2.
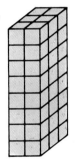

3.
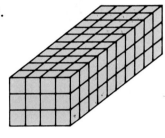

4.
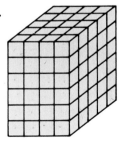

5.

6.
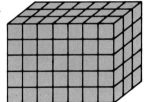

 Review (pp. 311–317)
Find the answers.

1. 2000 g = ? kg   **2.** 3 kg = ? g   **3.** 7 ℓ = ? ml   **4.** 5000 ml = ? ℓ

Temperature in Degrees Celsius

Temperature can be measured in **degrees Celsius (°C)**. Each mark on the thermometer stands for 2 degrees.

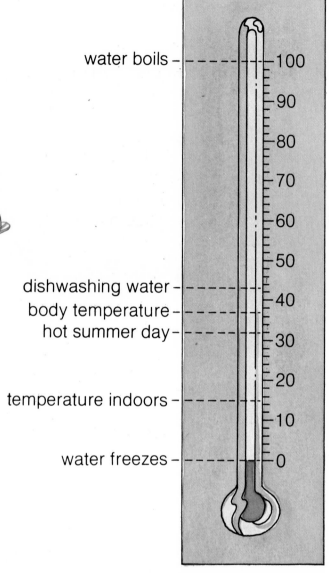

water boils — 100
90
80
70
60
50
dishwashing water — 40
body temperature — 40
hot summer day — 30
20
temperature indoors — 10
water freezes — 0

Use the thermometer.
What temperature is shown for each of these?

1. hot summer day   32°C

2. dishwashing water

3. water freezes

4. temperature indoors

5. water boils

6. body temperature

7. How much warmer is the temperature of boiling water than the temperature of dishwashing water?

8. How much cooler is the temperature of a hot summer day than body temperature?

9. A cold winter day would be about what temperature?

10. A nice spring day would be about what temperature?

Measurement Problems

Add, subtract, multiply, or divide to solve these.

1. The temperature in Chicago is 18°C. The temperature in Miami is 30°C. How much warmer is it in Miami?   12°C

2. Anna's apple weighed 85 g. She did not eat the core which weighed 5 g. How many grams of apple did she eat?

3. An orange weighs 200 g. How many oranges weigh a kilogram?

4. A tank holds 240 ℓ. It has a leak and loses 500 ml each hour. How many hours before the tank is empty?

 Challenge

5. At 8:00 A.M. the temperature is 16°C. The temperature increases 2°C every hour. What is the temperature at 2:00 P.M.?

6. Jack Barker weighed 84 kg. He went on a diet and lost 2 kg each month. What was his weight in 6 months?

Measuring to the Nearest Inch

The line is 1 **inch** long.
You can write **in.** for inch.

in.

The screw is about 1 in. long.

To the nearest inch, the screwdriver is 4 in. long.

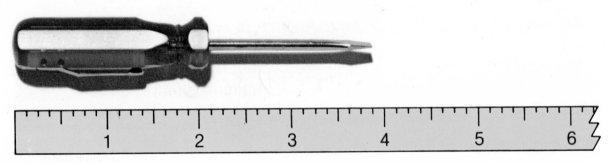

Measure each length to the nearest inch.

1. 1 in.

2.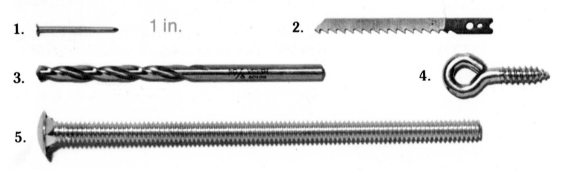

3.

4.

5.

Use a tape measure. Measure to the nearest half-inch.

6. How many inches tall are you?

7. How high is the top of your desk from the floor?

8. How far is it from your desk to the desk next to yours?

9. Start at the wall and take 4 steps. How many inches did you walk?

Inches, Feet, Yards, and Miles

These units are also used
to measure length.

1 foot (ft) = 12 inches
1 yard (yd) = 3 feet
1 yard = 36 inches
1 mile (mi) = 1760 yards
1 mile = 5280 feet

To change larger units
to smaller units, multiply.

4 yards = ⬚ feet
Think: 1 yard = 3 feet
$4 \times 3 = 12$
4 yards = 12 feet

Find the number of units.

1. 2 miles = ⬚ yards   3520

2. 2 yards = ⬚ inches

3. 4 feet = ⬚ inches

4. 6 yards = ⬚ feet

5. 10 yards = ⬚ feet

6. 8 yards = ⬚ inches

7. 3 miles = ⬚ feet

8. 2 miles = ⬚ feet

Write the best answer.

9. Would you measure the length
of a car in feet or miles?

10. Would you measure the width
of a stamp in feet or inches?

11. Would you measure the
perimeter of your city in inches
or miles?

12. Would you measure the length
of your room in feet or miles?

Area

Sylvia and Janet have rented an apartment. Find the answers to these problems. Remember, to find area, multiply length times width.

1. Their apartment is about 50 feet long and 30 feet wide. What is the area in square feet?
   50 × 30 = 1500
   Area is 1500 square feet.

2. Janet is putting shelf paper on 10 shelves. Each shelf is 1 foot wide and 4 feet long. How many square feet of paper does she need?

3. One room needs a new carpet. The room is 5 yards long and 5 yards wide. How many square yards of carpet are needed?

4. The kitchen floor needs new floor tiles. Each tile is 1 foot square. The floor is 12 feet wide and 14 feet long. How many tiles are needed?

 Challenge

5. One room is 18 feet long and 12 feet wide. How many square yards of carpet are needed?

Volume

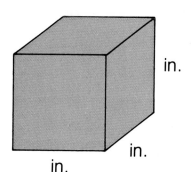

This is a **cubic inch (cubic in.)**.
You can use it to measure volume.

Find the volume of each shape in cubic inches.
The shapes are shown smaller than actual size.

1.

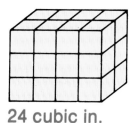

24 cubic in.

2.

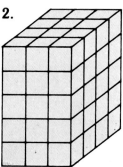

3.

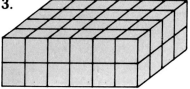

4.

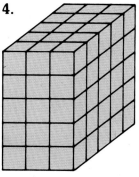

5.

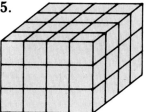

6.

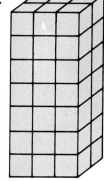

 Review (pp. 311–323)

1. 2500 ml = ⬚ ℓ ⬚ ml

2. Is 40°C hot or cold?

3. 4 feet = ⬚ inches

4. 1 mile = ⬚ feet

Cups, Pints, and Quarts

You can use these units to measure liquids.

2 cups = 1 pint (pt)
2 pints = 1 quart (qt)
4 cups = 1 quart

1 cup   1 pint   1 quart

Find the number of units.

1. 4 quarts = ▢ pints   8
2. 8 cups = ▢ quarts
3. 3 pints = ▢ cups

4. 1 quart = ▢ pints
5. 2 quarts = ▢ cups
6. 6 cups = ▢ pints

7. 5 pints = ▢ cups
8. 7 pints = ▢ cups
9. 2 quarts = ▢ pints

10. 12 cups = ▢ quarts
11. 12 pints = ▢ quarts

12. 5 quarts = ▢ cups
13. 16 cups = ▢ pints

 Challenge

14. A recipe for potato soup asks for 3 cups of chopped potatoes, $\frac{1}{4}$ cup of onion, $4\frac{1}{2}$ cups of milk, $1\frac{1}{4}$ cups of cream, and 4 cups of chicken broth. About how much soup will the recipe make?

Cups, Pints, Quarts, and Gallons

Gallons are also used to measure liquids.

4 quarts = 1 gallon (gal)
8 pints = 1 gallon
16 cups = 1 gallon

To change smaller units to larger units, you can divide.

11 quarts = ⬚ gallons ⬚ quarts
Think: 4 quarts in a gallon.

$$\begin{array}{r} 2\ r3 \\ 4\overline{)11} \end{array}$$

11 quarts = 2 gallons 3 quarts

Copy and complete each sentence.

1. 5 cups = ⬚ quarts ⬚ cups   5 cups = 1 quart 1 cup

2. 9 pints = ⬚ gallons ⬚ pints

3. 14 cups = ⬚ quarts ⬚ cups

4. 5 cups = ⬚ quarts ⬚ cups

5. 3 pints = ⬚ quarts ⬚ pints

6. 6 quarts = ⬚ gallons ⬚ quarts

7. 10 quarts = ⬚ gallons ⬚ quarts

 Calculate

8. There are about 7.5 gallons in 1 cubic foot. How many gallons in 950 cubic feet?

Ounces, Pounds, and Tons

Ounces, **pounds**, and **tons** can be used as measurements for weight.

I pound (lb) = 16 ounces (oz)
1 ton (T) = 2000 pounds

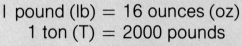

mouse: 7 ounces   person: 140 pounds   elephant: 2 tons

Multiply to find the number of units.

1. 3 pounds = ⬚ ounces 48

2. 5 pounds = ⬚ ounces

3. 2 tons = ⬚ pounds

4. 6 pounds = ⬚ ounces

5. 5 tons = ⬚ pounds

6. 10 tons = ⬚ pounds

7. 7 pounds = ⬚ ounces

8. 4 pounds = ⬚ ounces

Copy and complete.

9. 18 ounces = ⬚ pound ⬚ ounces

10. 4000 pounds = ⬚ tons

11. 3000 pounds = ⬚ ton ⬚ pounds

12. 32 ounces = ⬚ pounds

13. 36 ounces = ⬚ pounds ⬚ ounces

14. 96 ounces = ⬚ pounds

Temperature in Degrees Fahrenheit

Temperature can be measured in
degrees Fahrenheit (°F).
Each mark on the thermometer
stands for 2 degrees.

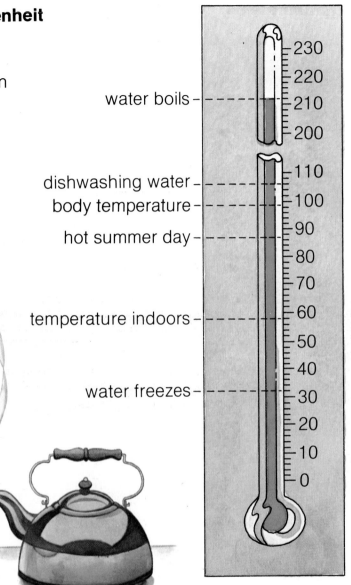

**Use the thermometer.
What temperature is shown
for each of these?**

1. hot summer day   87°F

2. dishwashing water

3. water freezes

4. temperature indoors

5. water boils

6. body temperature

7. How much warmer is the
   temperature of boiling water
   than the temperature of
   dishwashing water?

8. How much cooler is the
   temperature of the hot summer
   day than body temperature?

9. A cold winter day would be
   about what temperature?

10. A nice spring day would be
    about what temperature?

Reading a Bar Graph

Graphs can help you solve problems.

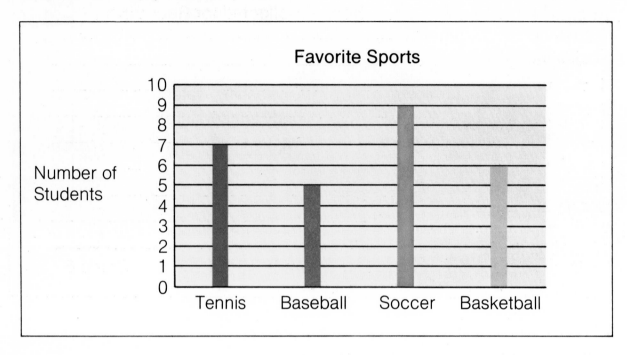

Favorite Sports

Use the graph to answer these questions.

1. The scale on the graph is from
   ⬚ students to ⬚ students.
   0 students to 10 students

2. How many more students like
   soccer than like basketball?

3. How many students like tennis
   best?

4. How many students like soccer
   best?

5. How many students like
   baseball best?

6. How many students like
   basketball best?

7. How many more students like
   tennis than baseball?

8. How many students were asked
   about their favorite sport?

Using a Bar Graph

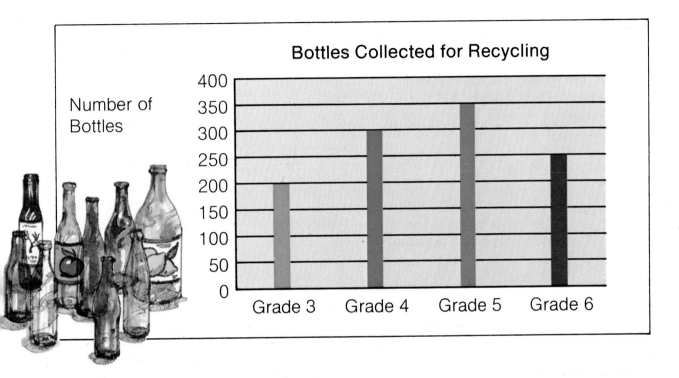

Bottles Collected for Recycling

Number of Bottles

Use the graph to answer these questions.

1. The scale on the graph is from ⬚ bottles to ⬚ bottles.
   0 bottles to 400 bottles

2. How many more bottles did grade 4 collect than grade 3?

3. How many fewer bottles did grade 6 collect than grade 5?

4. Which grade collected the most bottles?

5. How many bottles did grades 5 and 6 collect in all?

6. How many bottles collected by grades 3, 4, 5, and 6 in all?

7. Grade 8 collected as many bottles as grade 6 and grade 3 together. How many bottles did grade 8 collect?

8. Grade 7 collected 100 fewer bottles than the total collected by grades 3 and 4. How many bottles for grade 7?

Reading a Line Graph

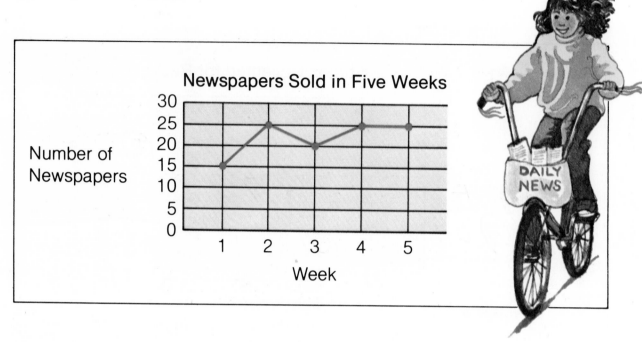

Newspapers Sold in Five Weeks

Number of Newspapers

Use the graph to answer the questions.

1. How many newspapers were sold during week 1? **15**

2. How many newspapers were sold altogether?

3. How many newspapers were sold altogether in the first three weeks?

4. How many more newspapers were sold during week 4 than during week 3?

5. Were more newspapers sold the first two weeks or the second two weeks?

6. During which two weeks were the same number of newspapers sold?

 Calculate

7. Use the graph. 43 newspapers were sold for 15¢ each. The rest were 45¢ each. How much money was taken in?

Reading a Picture Graph

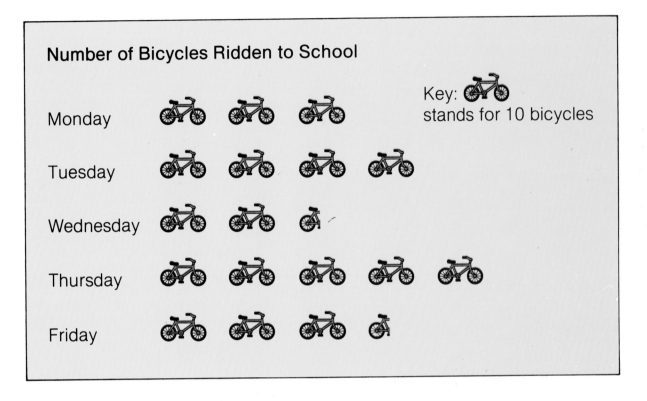

Number of Bicycles Ridden to School

Monday

Tuesday

Wednesday

Thursday

Friday

Key: stands for 10 bicycles

Use the graph to answer the questions.

1. What does 🚲 stand for?
   5 bicycles

2. How many bicycles were ridden to school on Monday?

3. How many bicycles were ridden to school on Tuesday?

4. How many bicycles were ridden to school on Friday?

5. How many more bicycles were ridden on Friday than on Monday?

6. How many fewer bicycles were ridden on Tuesday than on Thursday?

7. How many bicycles were ridden to school during the week?

8. Make a drawing to show 35 bicycles.

Chapter Review

Find the answers.   (ex. 1: p. 312), (ex. 2–6: p. 314), (ex. 7–10: p. 316)

1a. How many nickels weigh as much as 15 paper clips?

1 g   5 g

  b. How many paper clips weigh as much as 2 nickels?

2. 1000 g = ☐ kg   **3.** 2 kg = ☐ g   **4.** 6 kg = ☐ g

5. 7000 g = ☐ kg   **6.** 3000 g = ☐ kg   **7.** 5 ℓ = ☐ ml

8. 6000 ml = ☐ ℓ **9.** 4 ℓ = ☐ ml   **10.** 8000 ml = ☐ ℓ

Write the answers.   (ex. 11, 12: p. 318)

11. Which temperature is more comfortable, 15°C or 40°C?

12. How much warmer is 40°C than 15°C?

Find the number of units.   (ex. 13–16: p. 321)

                               (ex. 17–20: p. 325), (ex. 19–22: p. 326)

13. 3 yards = ☐ feet   **14.** 6 feet = ☐ yards

15. 2 feet = ☐ inches   **16.** 2 yards = ☐ feet

17. 8 quarts = ☐ gallons   **18.** 2 quarts = ☐ cups

19. 3 gallons = ☐ quarts   **20.** 3 quarts = ☐ pints

21. 4000 pounds = ☐ tons   **22.** 1 pound = ☐ ounces

Chapter Test

Find the answers.

1a. How many buttons weigh as much as 1 piece of chalk?

b. How many pieces of chalk weigh as much as 20 buttons?

2 g

10g

2. 1 kg = ⯑ g

3. 7000 g = ⯑ kg

4. 3 kg = ⯑ g

5. 6 ℓ = ⯑ ml

6. 4000 ml = ⯑ ℓ

7. 3000 ml = ⯑ ℓ

8. 2000 ml = ⯑ ℓ

9. 8 ℓ = ⯑ ml

10. 2000 g = ⯑ kg

11. Which temperature is best for swimming, 10°C or 31°C?

12. How much cooler is 17°C than 31°C?

Find the number of units.

13. 12 yards = ⯑ feet

14. 24 inches = ⯑ feet

15. 7 feet = ⯑ yards ⯑ foot

16. 2 yards = ⯑ inches

17. 2 gallons = ⯑ quarts

18. 2 gallons = ⯑ pints

19. 8 pints = ⯑ cups

20. 4 cups = ⯑ quart

21. 2 pounds = ⯑ ounces

22. 48 ounces = ⯑ pounds

Brush Up

Add, subtract, multiply, or divide.

1. $9\overline{)35}$ 2. $7\overline{)60}$ 3. $8\overline{)74}$ 4. $9\overline{)62}$ 5. $6\overline{)47}$

6. $8\overline{)54}$ 7. $4\overline{)936}$ 8. $7\overline{)987}$ 9. $3\overline{)699}$ 10. $7\overline{)301}$

11. $\begin{array}{r} 181 \\ \times\ \ 9 \\ \hline \end{array}$
12. $\begin{array}{r} 246 \\ \times\ \ 7 \\ \hline \end{array}$
13. $\begin{array}{r} 137 \\ \times\ \ 6 \\ \hline \end{array}$
14. $\begin{array}{r} 270 \\ \times\ \ 8 \\ \hline \end{array}$
15. $\begin{array}{r} 339 \\ \times\ \ 6 \\ \hline \end{array}$

16. $\begin{array}{r} 650 \\ \times\ \ 9 \\ \hline \end{array}$
17. $\begin{array}{r} 581 \\ \times\ \ 7 \\ \hline \end{array}$
18. $\begin{array}{r} 697 \\ \times\ \ 4 \\ \hline \end{array}$
19. $\begin{array}{r} 768 \\ \times\ \ 3 \\ \hline \end{array}$
20. $\begin{array}{r} 879 \\ \times\ \ 5 \\ \hline \end{array}$

21. $\begin{array}{r} \$57.96 \\ 0.79 \\ +\ \ 85.36 \\ \hline \end{array}$
22. $\begin{array}{r} \$5.00 \\ -\ \ 3.85 \\ \hline \end{array}$
23. $\begin{array}{r} \$7.13 \\ -\ \ 4.28 \\ \hline \end{array}$
24. $\begin{array}{r} \$5.43 \\ -\ \ 5.37 \\ \hline \end{array}$
25. $\begin{array}{r} \$6.67 \\ 0.89 \\ +\ \ 9.73 \\ \hline \end{array}$

26. $\frac{4}{7} + \frac{2}{7}$ 27. $\frac{8}{10} - \frac{3}{10}$ 28. $\frac{12}{16} - \frac{10}{16}$ 29. $\frac{8}{9} - \frac{1}{9}$

Write the answers.

30.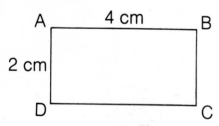

30a. Find the perimeter of shape ABCD.

b. Find the area of shape ABCD.

31. Are the lines parallel?
Write **yes** or **no**.

31a.   31b. 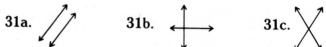 31c.

Extra Practice

Set 1   For use after pages 3–11.
Add or subtract.

1. 4   2. 8   3. 12   4. 13   5. 9   6. 11   7. 6
  + 8   + 8   − 7   − 5   + 2   − 9   + 7

8. 3   9. 15   10. 1   11. 17   12. 9   13. 5   14. 16
  + 4   − 8   + 7   − 9   + 0   + 3   − 7

15. $2 + 9$ 16. $1 - 0$ 17. $7 + 7$ 18. $3 + 9$ 19. $0 + 4$ 20. $7 - 6$

21. $4 - 2$ 22. $8 + 7$ 23. $4 + 3$ 24. $1 + 8$ 25. $6 + 6$ 26. $10 - 5$

27. $2 + 3$ 28. $6 + 8$ 29. $12 - 3$ 30. $9 + 6$ 31. $7 + 5$ 32. $2 - 2$

Set 2   For use after pages 12–14.
Add or subtract.

1. 3   2. 8   3. 5   4. 3   5. 6   6. 2   7. 5
    4   1   3   9   1   5   4
  + 6   + 0   + 2   + 4   + 5   + 7   + 5

8. $(6 + 2) - 5$ 9. $8 + (6 - 1)$ 10. $(9 + 2) + 4$ 11. $(0 + 1) + 8$

Set 3   For use after pages 19–23.
Add or subtract.

1. 72   2. 7384   3. 369   4. 5728   5. 7235
  + 13   + 1511   + 230   + 4270   − 6215

6. 563   7. 8485   8. 65   9. 3658   10. 1492
  − 341   − 6273   − 51   − 1135   + 8306

Set 4　For use after pages 29–34.
Add.

1. $\begin{array}{r} 26 \\ + 8 \\ \hline \end{array}$
2. $\begin{array}{r} 43 \\ + 9 \\ \hline \end{array}$
3. $\begin{array}{r} 51 \\ + 19 \\ \hline \end{array}$
4. $\begin{array}{r} 76 \\ + 14 \\ \hline \end{array}$
5. $\begin{array}{r} 62 \\ + 29 \\ \hline \end{array}$
6. $\begin{array}{r} 57 \\ + 24 \\ \hline \end{array}$

7. $\begin{array}{r} 182 \\ + 444 \\ \hline \end{array}$
8. $\begin{array}{r} 525 \\ + 193 \\ \hline \end{array}$
9. $\begin{array}{r} 269 \\ + 640 \\ \hline \end{array}$
10. $\begin{array}{r} 158 \\ + 91 \\ \hline \end{array}$
11. $\begin{array}{r} 743 \\ + 84 \\ \hline \end{array}$
12. $\begin{array}{r} 343 \\ + 276 \\ \hline \end{array}$

13. $\begin{array}{r} 208 \\ + 455 \\ \hline \end{array}$
14. $\begin{array}{r} 534 \\ + 37 \\ \hline \end{array}$
15. $\begin{array}{r} 827 \\ + 45 \\ \hline \end{array}$
16. $\begin{array}{r} 265 \\ + 406 \\ \hline \end{array}$
17. $\begin{array}{r} 436 \\ + 129 \\ \hline \end{array}$
18. $\begin{array}{r} 543 \\ + 218 \\ \hline \end{array}$

19. $\begin{array}{r} 85 \\ 341 \\ + 653 \\ \hline \end{array}$
20. $\begin{array}{r} 65 \\ 180 \\ + 754 \\ \hline \end{array}$
21. $\begin{array}{r} 540 \\ 261 \\ + 38 \\ \hline \end{array}$
22. $\begin{array}{r} 772 \\ 305 \\ + 127 \\ \hline \end{array}$
23. $\begin{array}{r} 659 \\ 406 \\ + 332 \\ \hline \end{array}$
24. $\begin{array}{r} 271 \\ 722 \\ + 19 \\ \hline \end{array}$

25. $34 + 17 + 48$
26. $46 + 45 + 7$
27. $65 + 18 + 27$
28. $14 + 13 + 9$
29. $63 + 42 + 17$
30. $77 + 50 + 18$
31. $461 + 12 + 5$
32. $109 + 65 + 32$
33. $995 + 71 + 11$

Set 5　For use after pages 35–41.
Add.

1. $\begin{array}{r} 448 \\ + 166 \\ \hline \end{array}$
2. $\begin{array}{r} 384 \\ + 127 \\ \hline \end{array}$
3. $\begin{array}{r} 716 \\ + 92 \\ \hline \end{array}$
4. $\begin{array}{r} 636 \\ + 188 \\ \hline \end{array}$
5. $\begin{array}{r} 277 \\ + 529 \\ \hline \end{array}$
6. $\begin{array}{r} 195 \\ + 62 \\ \hline \end{array}$

7. $\begin{array}{r} 767 \\ + 66 \\ \hline \end{array}$
8. $\begin{array}{r} 436 \\ + 189 \\ \hline \end{array}$
9. $\begin{array}{r} 543 \\ + 278 \\ \hline \end{array}$
10. $\begin{array}{r} 185 \\ + 199 \\ \hline \end{array}$
11. $\begin{array}{r} 326 \\ + 485 \\ \hline \end{array}$
12. $\begin{array}{r} 579 \\ + 177 \\ \hline \end{array}$

13. $\begin{array}{r} 2469 \\ + 3522 \\ \hline \end{array}$
14. $\begin{array}{r} 1989 \\ + 465 \\ \hline \end{array}$
15. $\begin{array}{r} 5447 \\ + 2165 \\ \hline \end{array}$
16. $\begin{array}{r} 4439 \\ + 6563 \\ \hline \end{array}$
17. $\begin{array}{r} 1967 \\ + 2068 \\ \hline \end{array}$

18. $1861 + 989$
19. $3054 + 6565$
20. $7872 + 849$
21. $3528 + 558$
22. $1749 + 602$
23. $2877 + 365$
24. $429 + 4362$
25. $1859 + 2665$

Set 6   For use after pages 42–49.
Subtract.

1.	18 − 9	2.	14 − 6	3.	59 − 24	4.	165 − 32	5.	574 − 362	6.	899 − 146

7.	94 − 65	8.	31 − 12	9.	64 − 25	10.	83 − 74	11.	45 − 39	12.	94 − 18

13.	345 − 84	14.	576 − 82	15.	842 − 61	16.	433 − 72	17.	403 − 283	18.	226 − 135

19. $237 - 155$ 20. $539 - 243$ 21. $522 - 341$ 22. $774 - 82$

Set 7   For use after pages 52–57.
Subtract.

1.	622 − 435	2.	571 − 382	3.	620 − 334	4.	575 − 186	5.	643 − 594	6.	400 − 265

7.	275 − 188	8.	306 − 39	9.	411 − 262	10.	564 − 375	11.	560 − 95	12.	723 − 432

13.	7301 − 4623	14.	2000 − 645	15.	4915 − 2866	16.	8000 − 6103	17.	1598 − 499	18.	7715 − 3826

Set 8   For use after pages 58–61.
Add or subtract.

1.	$5.14 − 1.23	2.	$6.22 + 5.10	3.	$7.08 − 3.28	4.	$9.56 − 4.93	5.	$6.00 − 2.98	6.	$4.88 + 6.35

7.	$2.30 − 1.84	8.	$1.75 + 0.90	9.	$7.68 − 3.99	10.	$5.90 − 2.46	11.	$8.05 − 5.18	12.	$6.26 + 3.59

Set 9 For use after pages 70–78.
Multiply.

1. 7×2
2. 6×5
3. 3×2
4. 6×2
5. 5×5
6. 8×2
7. 3×5

8. 4×3
9. 7×4
10. 8×3
11. 3×3
12. 5×4
13. 2×4
14. 9×3

15. 8×1
16. 7×0
17. 4×1
18. 6×0
19. 3×1
20. 10×2
21. 10×6

22. 9×2 23. 5×3 24. 7×5 25. 2×2 26. 5×9 27. 5×1

28. 7×3 29. 8×4 30. 5×2 31. 10×9 32. 1×4 33. 6×4

34. 5×4 35. 2×1 36. 4×0 37. 3×2 38. 10×5 39. 10×3

Set 10 For use after pages 79–84.
Multiply.

1. 3×6
2. 6×6
3. 4×7
4. 7×6
5. 1×7
6. 5×7
7. 8×6

8. 5×6
9. 2×7
10. 7×7
11. 0×6
12. 3×7
13. 9×7
14. 8×7

15. 8×9
16. 5×8
17. 9×9
18. 3×9
19. 4×8
20. 5×9
21. 1×8

22. 4×9
23. 6×9
24. 0×9
25. 2×9
26. 3×8
27. 6×8
28. 8×8

29. 1×6 30. 4×7 31. 9×6 32. 2×6 33. 6×7 34. 7×0

35. 2×8 36. 1×9 37. 7×8 38. 3×9 39. 9×8 40. 7×9

41. 8×0 42. 5×3 43. 6×4 44. 7×9 45. 5×5 46. 8×7

Set 11 For use after pages 93–97.

Copy and complete.

1. $3 \text{ m} = \square \text{ cm}$ 2. $900 \text{ cm} = \square \text{ m}$ 3. $5 \text{ m} = \square \text{ cm}$ 4. $200 \text{ cm} = \square \text{ m}$

5. $1 \text{ m} = \square \text{ cm}$ 6. $300 \text{ cm} = \square \text{ m}$ 7. $6 \text{ m} = \square \text{ cm}$ 8. $800 \text{ cm} = \square \text{ m}$

9. $2 \text{ m} = \square \text{ cm}$ 10. $9 \text{ m} = \square \text{ cm}$ 11. $1 \text{ km} = \square \text{ m}$ 12. $1000 \text{ m} = \square \text{ km}$

Set 12 For use after pages 98–101.

Find the perimeter and the area of each shape.

1. 5 m, 5 m (square)

2. 10 m, 4 m (rectangle)

3. 3 m, 12 m (rectangle)

4. 9 m, 2 m (rectangle)

5. 4 m, 4 m (square)

Set 13 For use after pages 104–111.

Write the times in numbers.

1. two-thirty

2. eight-fifteen

3. five to nine

4. quarter to ten

5. twenty after six

6. twenty to one

Copy and complete.

7. $180 \text{ s} = \square \text{ min}$

8. $24 \text{ months} = \square \text{ years}$

9. $1 \text{ year} = \square \text{ weeks}$

10. $3 \text{ weeks} = \square \text{ days}$

11. $48 \text{ h} = \square \text{ days}$

12. $35 \text{ days} = \square \text{ weeks}$

13. $1 \text{ year} = \square \text{ days}$

14. $3 \text{ h} = \square \text{ min}$

15. $60 \text{ s} = \square \text{ min}$

Set 14 For use after pages 120–127.
Divide.

1. $3\overline{)24}$ 2. $4\overline{)16}$ 3. $3\overline{)18}$ 4. $4\overline{)20}$ 5. $3\overline{)15}$

6. $5\overline{)15}$ 7. $4\overline{)12}$ 8. $4\overline{)28}$ 9. $5\overline{)45}$ 10. $3\overline{)6}$

11. $6\overline{)42}$ 12. $6\overline{)30}$ 13. $7\overline{)14}$ 14. $5\overline{)20}$ 15. $4\overline{)24}$

16. $7\overline{)42}$ 17. $6\overline{)36}$ 18. $7\overline{)21}$ 19. $5\overline{)10}$ 20. $7\overline{)49}$

21. $6\overline{)18}$ 22. $5\overline{)35}$ 23. $7\overline{)28}$ 24. $8\overline{)8}$ 25. $9\overline{)63}$

26. $8 \div 2$ 27. $27 \div 3$ 28. $0 \div 6$ 29. $6 \div 3$ 30. $72 \div 9$

31. $2 \div 1$ 32. $48 \div 8$ 33. $12 \div 2$ 34. $45 \div 9$ 35. $56 \div 8$

36. $72 \div 8$ 37. $81 \div 9$ 38. $6 \div 6$ 39. $0 \div 9$ 40. $14 \div 2$

Set 15 For use after pages 128–131.
Divide.

1. $5\overline{)37}$ 2. $7\overline{)30}$ 3. $2\overline{)11}$ 4. $4\overline{)27}$ 5. $2\overline{)17}$

6. $3\overline{)20}$ 7. $8\overline{)23}$ 8. $4\overline{)21}$ 9. $6\overline{)38}$ 10. $7\overline{)20}$

11. $5\overline{)41}$ 12. $9\overline{)19}$ 13. $6\overline{)22}$ 14. $8\overline{)42}$ 15. $4\overline{)15}$

16. $3\overline{)11}$ 17. $7\overline{)37}$ 18. $8\overline{)20}$ 19. $5\overline{)27}$ 20. $4\overline{)33}$

21. $3\overline{)19}$ 22. $6\overline{)52}$ 23. $7\overline{)44}$ 24. $9\overline{)70}$ 25. $8\overline{)65}$

26. $2\overline{)17}$ 27. $3\overline{)11}$ 28. $9\overline{)80}$ 29. $6\overline{)55}$ 30. $6\overline{)87}$

31. $4\overline{)18}$ 32. $6\overline{)51}$ 33. $2\overline{)25}$ 34. $8\overline{)51}$ 35. $7\overline{)51}$

36. $5\overline{)46}$ 37. $7\overline{)23}$ 38. $3\overline{)26}$ 39. $6\overline{)50}$ 40. $8\overline{)67}$

Set 16 For use after pages 137–143.

Read each problem. Answer the questions.

1. You have $5.00. You buy a plant for $2.95. How much do you have left?
   a. What is the question?
   b. What are the important facts?

2. Clay pots cost $2 each. How much do 8 clay pots cost?
   a. What is the question?
   b. What are the important facts?

3. You run ■ hours a day for ▲ days. How many hours do you run in all?
   a. Will you add, subtract, multiply, or divide?

4. You have ■ to spend on pencils. You pay ▲ . How much money do you have left?
   a. Will you add, subtract, multiply, or divide?

5. A poster costs $2.99 and 100 staples cost 59¢. How much for the poster and the staples?
   a. What numbers do you need?
   b. What number is not needed?
   c. Solve the problem.

6. You have 25 magazines. Each one costs 85¢. You buy 7 more. How many magazines now?
   a. What numbers do you need?
   b. What number is not needed?
   c. Solve the problem.

7. Staplers cost $4 each. How many staplers can you buy?
   a. What do you need to know before you can solve the problem?

8. You buy 3 scarves for $3 each. How much change do you get?
   a. What do you need to know before you can solve the problem?

Set 17 For use after pages 144–145.

Solve these two-step problems.

1. You have $10.00 to spend on groceries. You spend $4.50 on meat and $2.75 on vegetables. How much do you have left?

2. You buy a camera for $18.50 and 2 rolls of film for $2 each. How much do you spend in all?

Set 18   For use after pages 153–155.

Write letters to answer the questions.

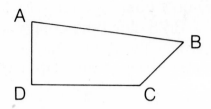

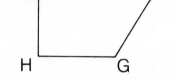

1a. Which angle is a right angle?
 b. Which angles are less than
    a right angle?
 c. Which angle is greater than
    a right angle?

2a. Which angles are right angles?
 b. Which angle is less than
    a right angle?
 c. Which angle is greater than
    a right angle?

Set 19   For use after pages 156–159.

Tell whether each shape is a square, a rectangle, or both.

1.    2.   3.    4.

Set 20   For use after pages 156–159.

Write intersecting or parallel for each pair of lines.

1.   2.   3.   4.

Set 21   For use after pages 164–166.

Write congruent, similar, or not similar for each pair.

1.   2.   3.

Set 22 For use after pages 180–181.

Which fraction is greater?

1. $\frac{1}{6}$ or $\frac{1}{5}$ 2. $\frac{3}{8}$ or $\frac{5}{8}$ 3. $\frac{2}{7}$ or $\frac{5}{7}$ 4. $\frac{7}{9}$ or $\frac{4}{9}$ 5. $\frac{1}{2}$ or $\frac{1}{3}$

6. $\frac{3}{5}$ or $\frac{2}{5}$ 7. $\frac{1}{8}$ or $\frac{1}{9}$ 8. $\frac{6}{9}$ or $\frac{2}{9}$ 9. $\frac{3}{4}$ or $\frac{2}{4}$ 10. $\frac{1}{8}$ or $\frac{1}{5}$

Set 23 For use after pages 182–185.

Add or subtract.

1. $\frac{2}{5} + \frac{2}{5}$ 2. $\frac{1}{6} + \frac{4}{6}$ 3. $\frac{5}{6} - \frac{3}{6}$ 4. $\frac{2}{5} + \frac{3}{5}$ 5. $\frac{7}{8} + \frac{2}{8}$

6. $\frac{5}{9} + \frac{1}{9}$ 7. $\frac{3}{4} - \frac{1}{4}$ 8. $\frac{4}{5} - \frac{2}{5}$ 9. $\frac{3}{5} + \frac{1}{5}$ 10. $\frac{6}{7} - \frac{3}{7}$

11. $\begin{array}{r} \frac{1}{3} \\ + \frac{1}{3} \\ \hline \end{array}$ 12. $\begin{array}{r} \frac{3}{7} \\ + \frac{3}{7} \\ \hline \end{array}$ 13. $\begin{array}{r} \frac{1}{3} \\ + \frac{1}{3} \\ \hline \end{array}$ 14. $\begin{array}{r} \frac{8}{9} \\ - \frac{5}{9} \\ \hline \end{array}$ 15. $\begin{array}{r} \frac{6}{8} \\ + \frac{1}{8} \\ \hline \end{array}$ 16. $\begin{array}{r} \frac{4}{7} \\ - \frac{2}{7} \\ \hline \end{array}$

Set 24 For use after pages 186–189.

Change these mixed numbers to fractions.

1. $1\frac{2}{3}$ 2. $2\frac{1}{2}$ 3. $1\frac{2}{5}$ 4. $2\frac{2}{3}$ 5. $1\frac{1}{5}$ 6. $2\frac{1}{3}$

7. $4\frac{1}{2}$ 8. $1\frac{3}{4}$ 9. $1\frac{5}{6}$ 10. $2\frac{1}{4}$ 11. $2\frac{1}{8}$ 12. $1\frac{2}{7}$

Change these fractions to mixed numbers.

13. $\frac{5}{4}$ 14. $\frac{8}{5}$ 15. $\frac{4}{3}$ 16. $\frac{8}{6}$ 17. $\frac{10}{7}$ 18. $\frac{9}{8}$

19. $\frac{9}{5}$ 20. $\frac{12}{5}$ 21. $\frac{8}{7}$ 22. $\frac{13}{6}$ 23. $\frac{12}{8}$ 24. $\frac{10}{6}$

Set 25 For use after pages 186–189.

Add or subtract.

1. $6\frac{2}{5}$
$+\ 2\frac{1}{5}$

2. $3\frac{3}{7}$
$+\ 4\frac{2}{7}$

3. $6\frac{4}{5}$
$-\ 2\frac{2}{5}$

4. $8\frac{6}{7}$
$-\ 2\frac{4}{7}$

5. $5\frac{1}{4}$
$+\ 1\frac{2}{4}$

6. $4\frac{7}{9}$
$-\ 3\frac{3}{9}$

7. $2\frac{1}{6}$
$+\ 7\frac{2}{6}$

8. $7\frac{5}{8}$
$-\ 5\frac{3}{8}$

9. $1\frac{4}{9}$
$+\ 6\frac{2}{9}$

10. $9\frac{4}{6}$
$-\ 6\frac{3}{6}$

11. $4\frac{2}{8}$
$+\ 1\frac{3}{8}$

12. $7\frac{8}{9}$
$-\ 4\frac{5}{9}$

13. $5\frac{3}{9}$
$+\ 3\frac{4}{9}$

14. $5\frac{5}{9}$
$-\ 2\frac{2}{9}$

15. $3\frac{4}{8}$
$+\ 6\frac{1}{8}$

16. $4\frac{3}{4}$
$-\ 2\frac{1}{4}$

17. $4\frac{2}{6}$
$+\ 4\frac{2}{6}$

18. $6\frac{4}{7}$
$-\ 5\frac{3}{7}$

Set 26 For use after pages 190–191.

Copy and complete to find equal fractions.

1. $\frac{1}{2} = \frac{?}{10}$

2. $\frac{2}{3} = \frac{?}{6}$

3. $\frac{1}{2} = \frac{?}{8}$

4. $\frac{1}{3} = \frac{?}{9}$

5. $\frac{2}{3} = \frac{?}{12}$

6. $\frac{1}{5} = \frac{?}{10}$

7. $\frac{1}{4} = \frac{?}{16}$

8. $\frac{1}{3} = \frac{?}{6}$

9. $\frac{3}{4} = \frac{?}{12}$

10. $\frac{4}{9} = \frac{?}{18}$

Set 27 For use after pages 192–195.

Find a common denominator. Then add or subtract.

1. $\frac{1}{3} + \frac{1}{6}$

2. $\frac{4}{10} - \frac{1}{5}$

3. $\frac{1}{2} + \frac{3}{8}$

4. $\frac{10}{12} - \frac{2}{6}$

5. $\frac{1}{2} + \frac{4}{4}$

6. $\frac{3}{4} - \frac{3}{8}$

7. $\frac{3}{4} + \frac{1}{12}$

8. $\frac{6}{7} - \frac{5}{14}$

9. $\frac{3}{5} + \frac{2}{6}$

10. $\frac{8}{9} - \frac{2}{3}$

11. $\frac{3}{10}$
$+\ \frac{1}{5}$

12. $\frac{5}{6}$
$-\ \frac{1}{3}$

13. $\frac{2}{3}$
$+\ \frac{3}{9}$

14. $\frac{2}{5}$
$+\ \frac{3}{10}$

15. $\frac{9}{10}$
$-\ \frac{2}{5}$

16. $\frac{15}{16}$
$-\ \frac{3}{8}$

Set 28 For use after pages 196–197.
Multiply.

1. $\frac{1}{2} \times 6$
2. $\frac{1}{4} \times 8$
3. $\frac{1}{3} \times 3$
4. $\frac{1}{3} \times 6$
5. $\frac{1}{5} \times 10$

6. $\frac{1}{4} \times 12$
7. $\frac{1}{8} \times 16$
8. $\frac{1}{15} \times 15$
9. $\frac{1}{2} \times 10$
10. $\frac{1}{3} \times 9$

Set 29 For use after pages 201–202.
Add or subtract.

1. $\begin{array}{r} 6.2 \\ + 3.5 \\ \hline \end{array}$
2. $\begin{array}{r} 8.6 \\ - 3.4 \\ \hline \end{array}$
3. $\begin{array}{r} 14.4 \\ + 6.3 \\ \hline \end{array}$
4. $\begin{array}{r} 4.5 \\ - 2.6 \\ \hline \end{array}$
5. $\begin{array}{r} 3.9 \\ + 1.1 \\ \hline \end{array}$
6. $\begin{array}{r} 12.3 \\ - 9.2 \\ \hline \end{array}$

7. $5.5 + 2.8$
8. $31.4 - 1.5$
9. $16.8 + 4.5$
10. $5.7 - 3.6$

11. $12.1 + 9.7$
12. $8.9 - 2.1$
13. $105.3 + 84.1$
14. $77.5 + 301.2$

Set 30 For use after pages 203–204.
Write a decimal for each.

1. $\frac{3}{10}$
2. $\frac{5}{10}$
3. $2\frac{4}{10}$
4. $5\frac{2}{10}$
5. $3\frac{6}{10}$
6. $\frac{1}{10}$

7. $\frac{41}{100}$
8. $\frac{12}{100}$
9. $\frac{34}{100}$
10. $\frac{67}{100}$
11. $\frac{5}{100}$
12. $\frac{39}{100}$

Set 31 For use after pages 205–207.
Add or subtract.

1. $\begin{array}{r} 6.45 \\ + 1.34 \\ \hline \end{array}$
2. $\begin{array}{r} 5.62 \\ - 1.44 \\ \hline \end{array}$
3. $\begin{array}{r} 9.89 \\ + 2.64 \\ \hline \end{array}$
4. $\begin{array}{r} 7.75 \\ - 3.56 \\ \hline \end{array}$
5. $\begin{array}{r} 3.12 \\ + 4.69 \\ \hline \end{array}$
6. $\begin{array}{r} 1.88 \\ - 0.49 \\ \hline \end{array}$

7. $\begin{array}{r} \$3.81 \\ + 4.17 \\ \hline \end{array}$
8. $\begin{array}{r} \$6.65 \\ + 3.32 \\ \hline \end{array}$
9. $\begin{array}{r} \$4.45 \\ - 2.54 \\ \hline \end{array}$
10. $\begin{array}{r} \$5.98 \\ - 3.69 \\ \hline \end{array}$
11. $\begin{array}{r} \$7.00 \\ + 0.87 \\ \hline \end{array}$
12. $\begin{array}{r} \$4.02 \\ - 1.65 \\ \hline \end{array}$

Set 32   For use after pages 213–215.
Write the sums.

1. $70,000 + 2000 + 400 + 10 + 1$ 2. $300,000 + 60,000 + 5000$

3. $50,000 + 2000 + 400 + 60 + 5$ 4. $20,000 + 5000 + 900 + 50 + 4$

5. $30,000 + 1000 + 800 + 60$ 6. $800,000 + 90,000 + 4000$

Set 33   For use after pages 213–215.
Copy. Put in the commas.

1. 16843   2. 146899   3. 645602   4. 741552   5. 183643

6. 986143   7. 71360   8. 242891   9. 11035   10. 12002

11. 12976   12. 21521   13. 546113   14. 33619   15. 503011

Set 34   For use after pages 216–218.
Write the numbers.

1. twenty thousand, thirty

2. one hundred ten thousand, five

3. two million, four hundred one

4. five hundred sixty-six million

5. nine hundred seventy thousand

6. five million, two hundred

7. eighty million, six hundred thousand, twenty-three

8. four hundred twenty-six thousand, one hundred forty-three

Set 35   For use after pages 216–218.
Order these numbers.

1. 14,501 ◯ 14,591   2. 453,258 ◯ 467,258   3. 790,361 ◯ 690,361

4. 124,585 ◯ 124,995   5. 707,264 ◯ 507,264   6. 23,023 ◯ 42,323

7. 754,909 ◯ 754,907   8. 60,684 ◯ 60,640   9. 526,652 ◯ 563,226

Set 36   For use after pages 219–223.

Round to the nearest ten.

1. 85   2. 14   3. 31   4. 11   5. 87   6. 54

7. 28   8. 73   9. 25   10. 14   11. 61   12. 39

13. 84   14. 51   15. 46   16. 22   17. 77   18. 43

Round to the nearest hundred.

19. 338   20. 812   21. 652   22. 741   23. 455   24. 108

25. 150   26. 779   27. 943   28. 175   29. 241   30. 803

31. 1665   32. 14,896   33. 7732   34. 4116   35. 28,362

Set 37   For use after pages 224–225.

Write the sums.

1. 6 + 0.9 + 0.01

2. 6000 + 300 + 40 + 3 + 0.2

3. 70 + 3 + 0.5 + 0.05

4. 300 + 40 + 6 + 0.2 + 0.09

5. 5 + 0.6 + 0.02

6. 1000 + 100 + 10 + 1 + 0.1

7. 500 + 30 + 5 + 0.1 + 0.06

8. 10 + 0.6 + 0.07

9. 300 + 90 + 7 + 0.5 + 0.05

10. 5000 + 400 + 80 + 8 + 0.6

11. 200 + 80 + 1 + 0.4 + 0.03

12. 3000 + 200 + 70 + 5 + 0.1

Set 38   For use after pages 226–227.

Write the numbers.

1. six hundred forty-one and five-tenths

2. eighty-three and fourteen-hundredths

3. fifty thousand, twenty and sixteen-hundredths

4. twenty-two thousand, one hundred twelve and five-tenths

Set 39 For use after pages 235–237.
Multiply.

1. 14×2	2. 23×3	3. 22×4	4. 13×3	5. 42×2	6. 62×4
7. 42×2	8. 21×4	9. 12×3	10. 74×2	11. 44×2	12. 23×3
13. 11×2	14. 51×4	15. 72×3	16. 61×5	17. 91×4	18. 24×2

Set 40 For use after pages 238–240.
Multiply.

1. 36×5	2. 65×6	3. 48×4	4. 29×2	5. 62×7	6. 74×3
7. 35×4	8. 54×4	9. 47×3	10. 19×6	11. 27×2	12. 39×5
13. 75×3	14. 83×6	15. 38×4	16. 52×6	17. 67×3	18. 43×5

Set 41 For use after pages 241–245.
Multiply.

1. 233×3	2. 214×6	3. 141×2	4. 327×3	5. 100×4	6. 455×3
7. 306×3	8. 511×5	9. 486×2	10. 616×3	11. 523×3	12. 678×4

13. 302×4 14. 465×2 15. 524×2 16. 502×3 17. 631×8

18. 421×5 19. 324×4 20. 621×6 21. 243×3 22. 514×7

Set 42   For use after pages 246–249.
Multiply.

1. 6815×3

2. 968×4

3. 2647×5

4. 1606×7

5. 8714×4

6. 1202×8

7. 8565×6

8. 7206×3

9. $\$26.62 \times 4$

10. $\$30.94 \times 5$

Set 43   For use after pages 250–255.
Multiply.

1. 56×10

2. 35×100

3. 260×10

4. 106×1000

5. 59×100

6. 349×100

7. 205×100

8. 517×1000

9. 994×1000

Set 44   For use after pages 256–261.
Multiply.

1. 40×30

2. 70×40

3. 50×50

4. 400×20

5. 30×80

6. 500×60

7. 60×20

8. 20×70

9. 90×40

10. 400×80

11. 600×60

12. 800×80

Set 45   For use after pages 262–263.
Multiply.

1. 52×63

2. 24×15

3. 76×27

4. 34×23

5. 21×54

6. 18×16

7. 31×33

8. 94×11

9. 59×42

10. 22×63

11. 41×52

12. 25×13

Set 46 For use after pages 273–279.
Divide.

1. $9\overline{)81}$ 2. $4\overline{)36}$ 3. $9\overline{)45}$ 4. $7\overline{)42}$ 5. $6\overline{)18}$

6. $7\overline{)49}$ 7. $7\overline{)63}$ 8. $8\overline{)32}$ 9. $7\overline{)21}$ 10. $8\overline{)56}$

11. $5\overline{)43}$ 12. $5\overline{)36}$ 13. $6\overline{)26}$ 14. $8\overline{)15}$ 15. $7\overline{)41}$

16. $6\overline{)51}$ 17. $2\overline{)15}$ 18. $9\overline{)60}$ 19. $8\overline{)45}$ 20. $7\overline{)37}$

21. $4\overline{)21}$ 22. $9\overline{)33}$ 23. $7\overline{)61}$ 24. $4\overline{)35}$ 25. $8\overline{)19}$

Set 47 For use after pages 282–283.
Divide.

1. $3\overline{)84}$ 2. $7\overline{)98}$ 3. $4\overline{)64}$ 4. $5\overline{)75}$ 5. $6\overline{)78}$

6. $8\overline{)96}$ 7. $2\overline{)48}$ 8. $4\overline{)52}$ 9. $6\overline{)84}$ 10. $7\overline{)91}$

11. $3\overline{)63}$ 12. $5\overline{)70}$ 13. $6\overline{)96}$ 14. $6\overline{)72}$ 15. $7\overline{)77}$

16. $3\overline{)54}$ 17. $4\overline{)56}$ 18. $3\overline{)96}$ 19. $2\overline{)68}$ 20. $4\overline{)72}$

Set 48 For use after pages 284–288.
Divide.

1. $4\overline{)97}$ 2. $4\overline{)43}$ 3. $3\overline{)85}$ 4. $4\overline{)78}$ 5. $6\overline{)61}$

6. $6\overline{)93}$ 7. $5\overline{)74}$ 8. $2\overline{)49}$ 9. $7\overline{)93}$ 10. $3\overline{)67}$

11. $64 \div 5$ 12. $71 \div 2$ 13. $46 \div 3$ 14. $88 \div 7$ 15. $55 \div 4$

16. $76 \div 6$ 17. $92 \div 8$ 18. $58 \div 3$ 19. $69 \div 5$ 20. $74 \div 6$

Set 49 For use after pages 289–294.
Divide.

1. $4\overline{)872}$ 2. $7\overline{)935}$ 3. $4\overline{)264}$ 4. $3\overline{)882}$ 5. $9\overline{)692}$

6. $3\overline{)965}$ 7. $6\overline{)458}$ 8. $8\overline{)896}$ 9. $6\overline{)721}$ 10. $4\overline{)124}$

11. $728 \div 6$ 12. $682 \div 9$ 13. $388 \div 7$ 14. $550 \div 5$ 15. $984 \div 3$

16. $725 \div 5$ 17. $735 \div 7$ 18. $469 \div 5$ 19. $583 \div 3$ 20. $419 \div 8$

Set 50 For use after pages 295–296.
Divide.

1. $3\overline{)\$7.56}$ 2. $8\overline{)\$5.68}$ 3. $3\overline{)\$1.23}$ 4. $5\overline{)\$3.55}$

5. $\$8.16 \div 4$ 6. $\$6.75 \div 5$ 7. $\$9.16 \div 2$ 8. $\$4.55 \div 7$

Set 51 For use after pages 298–300.
Find the averages.

1. 27, 43, 44   2. 7, 15, 23, 3   3. 56, 17, 26

4. 4, 19, 20, 1   5. 61, 74, 24   6. 11, 16, 44, 5

Set 52 For use after pages 301–305.
Divide.

1. $20\overline{)614}$ 2. $60\overline{)804}$ 3. $30\overline{)654}$ 4. $12\overline{)350}$ 5. $16\overline{)129}$

6. $22\overline{)739}$ 7. $55\overline{)655}$ 8. $80\overline{)604}$ 9. $90\overline{)741}$ 10. $21\overline{)119}$

11. $462 \div 23$ 12. $500 \div 41$ 13. $264 \div 41$ 14. $432 \div 53$ 15. $284 \div 31$

Set 53   For use after pages 314–317.

Copy and complete.

1. 2 kg = ⬚ g

2. 1000 g = ⬚ kg

3. 2800 g = ⬚ kg ⬚ g

4. 3000 g = ⬚ kg

5. 5 kg = ⬚ g

6. 3500 g = ⬚ kg ⬚ g

7. 5 ℓ = ⬚ ml

8. 1000 ml = ⬚ ℓ

9. 1850 ml = ⬚ ℓ ⬚ ml

Set 54   For use after pages 320–327.

Copy and complete.

1. 24 inches = ⬚ feet

2. 9 feet = ⬚ yards

3. 2 yards = ⬚ inches

4. 3 feet = ⬚ inches

5. 36 inches = ⬚ yard

6. 1 mile = ⬚ feet

7. 8 cups = ⬚ quarts

8. 3 pints = ⬚ cups

9. 3 quarts = ⬚ pints

Set 55   For use after pages 328–331.

Use each graph to answer the questions.

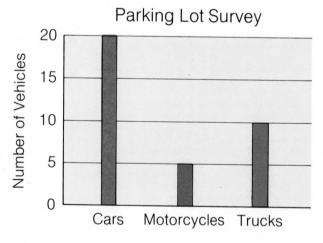

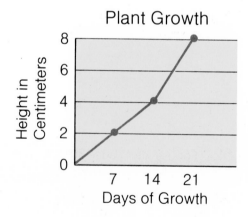

1a. How many cars in the parking lot?

b. How many trucks?

c. How many motorcycles?

2a. How tall was the plant on day 14?

b. How tall on day 7?

c. How tall on day 21?

Enrichment

Set 1   For use after page 8.

In a magic square, the sum of each row, column, and diagonal is the same. In this magic square, all the sums are 9.

2	3	4
5	3	1
2	3	4

Copy and complete the squares below.

1.
4		7
	3	
		8

2.
4		
	5	
3		6

3.
2		
7		1
3		

Set 2   For use after page 14.

Use the magic squares above to answer these questions.

1. Subtract 1 from each number in the first magic square. Is the result a magic square?

2. Subtract 2 from each number in the second magic square. Is the result a magic square?

Set 3   For use after page 21.

Solve these problems.

1. $(8753 - 5322) + 2367$

2. $555 + (7389 - 167)$

3. $(4653 + 2234) - 5673$

4. $5598 - (2353 + 31)$

Set 4   For use after page 34.

What is the pattern? What number comes next?

1. 7, 15, 23, ▢

2. 307, 311, 315, ▢

3. 762, 769, 776, ▢

Set 5 For use after page 41.

What is the pattern? What number comes next?

1. 86, 84, 82, □

2. 108, 104, 100, □

3. 40, 35, 30, □

4. 722, 720, 718, □

5. 90, 80, 70, □

6. 447, 440, 433, □

Set 6 For use after page 54.

The □ in each problem stands for the same digit. Find the digit.

1.
```
   93
 -□□
   5
```

2.
```
  □1
- 5□
  14
```

3.
```
  4□9
-10□
 □□6
```

4.
```
 □5□
- □9
 □05
```

5.
```
 □4□
-1□5
 208
```

6.
```
 □□9
- □□
 □02
```

7.
```
 □47
- □5
 □□□
```

8.
```
 □6□
- □0
 □□□
```

9.
```
 □12
-435
 2□□
```

10.
```
 □18
-  □
 □0□
```

Set 7 For use after 59.

Copy and complete these magic squares.

1.

7		9
12	10	
	6	13

2.

234	63	
	140	
157	217	

3.

		40
	55	90
70		

Set 8 For use after page 73.

Complete these facts.

1. $3 \times □ = 27$

2. $5 \times □ = 40$

3. $4 \times □ = 16$

4. $5 \times □ = 20$

5. $2 \times □ = 16$

6. $4 \times □ = 36$

7. $5 \times □ = 45$

8. $5 \times □ = 25$

Set 9   For use after page 82.

Find a pair of numbers for each sum and product.

1.

Numbers	Sum	Product
2, 4	6	8
	12	35
	11	30

2.

Numbers	Sum	Product
	15	56
	17	72
	12	32

Set 10   For use after page 101.

1. The perimeter of a rectangle is 20 cm. One side is 4 cm. What is the area?

2. The area of a rectangle is 30 square m. One side is 5 m. What is the perimeter?

Set 11   For use after page 103.

Find the volume of each box.

Box	Length	Width	Height
1. A	2 cm	3 cm	2 cm
2. B	2 cm	4 cm	3 cm
3. C	5 cm	2 cm	6 cm

Set 12   For use after page 111.

Copy and complete.

1. 2 wk 42 d = ⬚ d

2. 7 h 6 min = ⬚ min

3. 3 yr 17 wk = ⬚ wk

4. 46 h 120 min = ⬚ d

5. 2 min 6 s = ⬚ s

6. 19 d 48 h = ⬚ wk

7. 23 h 60 min = ⬚ d

8. 6 d 24 h = ⬚ wk

9. 51 wk 7 d = ⬚ yr

Set 13 For use after page 124.

Use ÷ and − to complete these number sentences.

1. 15 ◯ 3 ◯ 2 = 3

2. 27 ◯ 6 ◯ 7 = 3

3. 36 ◯ 9 ◯ 1 = 3

4. 15 ◯ 3 ◯ 3 = 4

5. 77 ◯ 5 ◯ 8 = 9

6. 63 ◯ 7 ◯ 3 = 6

Set 14 For use after page 129.

The ? in each problem stands for the same digit. Find the digit.

1. $4 \overline{)\smash{?5}}$ 8 r?

2. $6 \overline{)\smash{4?}}$? r5

3. $3 \overline{)\smash{2?}}$? r2

4. $? \overline{)\smash{5?}}$ 7 r2

Set 15 For use after page 140.

Tell how you would solve these problems. Which two would you use, +, −, ×, or ÷?

1. Wood School has 8 baseballs, 6 soccer balls, 2 pianos, and 6 drums. How many more balls than musical instruments?

2. Paint brushes cost $1.50. The Bears Club bought 10 paint brushes. There are 5 members in the club. How much did each member pay?

Set 16 For use after page 145.

Solve these problems.

1. Mr. Hom took a $20.00 bill to the shopping mall. He spent $11.25 for paint and $6.95 for meat. He gave equal amounts of the change to his 3 children. How much money did each child get?

2. Carol, Jose, and Kim earned $10.00 raking leaves. They spent $4.50 at a movie and $3.40 for food. They shared the change equally. How much change did each one get?

Set 17 For use after page 147.

Write a word problem for each number sentence.

1. $8 \div 4 = 2$ 2. $4 \times \$1.00 = \$4.00$ 3. $17 + 6 = 23$

4. $234 + 68 = 302$ 5. $\$5.00 \div 4 = \$1.25$ 6. $21 \div 3 = 7$

Set 18 For use after page 157.

Copy and complete this chart.

	Name	Shape	Number of Angles	Number of Sides
1.	Triangle	△		
2.	Square	□		
3.	Pentagon	⬠		
4.	Hexagon	⬡		
5.	Octagon	⯃		

Set 19 For use after page 161.

Copy the graph on page 161. Leave off the letters and dots on that graph.

1. Mark dots for each of these ordered pairs. Letter the dots in order. Then connect the dots. What shape did you draw?

A (2,1)   B (6, 1)   C (6,5)
D (2,5)   E (2,1)

2. Copy the graph again. Now use these ordered pairs. What did you draw?

A (1,1)   B (2,1)   C (2,3)
D (3,3)   E (3,1)   F (6,1)
G (6,4)   H (5,6)   I (2,6)
J (1,4)   K (1,1)

Set 20 For use after page 181.
Which fraction is greater?

1. $\frac{3}{4}$ or $\frac{3}{5}$
2. $\frac{2}{7}$ or $\frac{1}{7}$
3. $\frac{2}{9}$ or $\frac{2}{8}$
4. $\frac{3}{7}$ or $\frac{4}{7}$
5. $\frac{1}{8}$ or $\frac{1}{9}$

Set 21 For use after page 185.
Make a fraction strip to show these number sentences. If you do not remember what a fraction strip is, turn first to page 178.

1. $\frac{3}{10} + \frac{7}{10}$
2. $\frac{5}{11} + \frac{3}{11}$
3. $\frac{1}{12} + \frac{5}{12}$
4. $\frac{3}{5} + \frac{1}{5}$

Set 22 For use after page 195.

1. Denise has a bag of 20 marbles. $\frac{1}{5}$ are blue. $\frac{3}{10}$ are green. $\frac{1}{10}$ are clear. The rest are red. How many are red?

2. Bill has a collection of toy cars and trucks. $\frac{1}{4}$ are sports cars. $\frac{2}{5}$ are station wagons. The rest are trucks. What part are trucks?

Set 23 For use after page 202.
Copy and complete these magic squares.

1.

1.5		2.7
	1.9	
1.1		2.3

2.

	4.4	
0.4	3.8	
	3.2	2.4

3.

	8.5	12.3
		21.3
		7.2

4. Add 7.5 to each number in the first magic square. Is the result a magic square?

5. Subtract 4.8 from each number in the third magic square. Is the result a magic square?

Set 24 For use after page 215.

For each number, decide which digit is in the thousands place, the hundreds place, and the ones place.

1. seven hundred thousand, fifteen

2. two thousand forty-five

3. eighty-five thousand, two hundred twenty-four

4. forty-seven thousand, eight hundred thirty-nine

5. one hundred one thousand, four hundred ten

6. eight hundred forty-four thousand, thirty-eight

7. nine hundred sixty-five thousand, three hundred sixteen

8. two hundred ninety-eight thousand, seven hundred fifty-six

Set 25 For use after page 221.

1. Start with the number 7. Multiply by 8. Round to the nearest 10. Divide by 5. Subtract 5. What number do you find?

2. Start with the number 81. Add 145. Round to the nearest hundred. Subtract 128. Divide by 8. Multiply by 9. What number do you find?

Set 26 For use after page 223.

1. The distance from Ada to Logan is 52 kilometers. Jorge and Anita made three round trips. How many kilometers did they go? Round your answer to the nearest ten kilometers.

2. Bill flew 1053 kilometers from Akron, Ohio, to Boston, Massachusetts. Ann flew 6850 kilometers from New York City to Rome, Italy. How many kilometers did they fly in all? Round your answer to the nearest hundred kilometers.

Set 27 For use after page 227.

For each number, decide which digit is in the hundreds place, the ones place, the tenths place, and the hundredths place.

1. three hundred twenty-eight and twenty-three hundredths

2. four hundred nine and eighty-eight hundredths

3. eight thousand forty-two and sixteen-hundredths

4. one thousand and eight-hundredths

Set 28 For use after page 242.
Multiplication is related to division as shown.

$18 \div 3 = 6$	$18 \div 6 = 3$
$3 \times 6 = 18$	$6 \times 3 = 18$

Write another division fact and two multiplication facts for each division fact.

1. $36 \div 9 = 4$

2. $56 \div 7 = 8$

3. $42 \div 6 = 7$

4. $710 \div 5 = 142$

5. $276 \div 12 = 23$

6. $255 \div 15 = 17$

Set 29 For use after page 253.
Solve each problem two ways.

1. Kim buys 7 notebooks for $1.95 each and 7 pens for $0.55 each. How much money does she spend? Hint: try $7 \times (\$1.95 + \$0.55)$ and $(7 \times \$1.95) + (7 \times \$0.55)$.

2. Jess buys 2 boxes of erasers and 3 boxes of paper clips. Each box contains 1500 items. How many erasers and paper clips does he buy?

3. Manuel buys 3 books for $2.95 each and 3 pads of paper for $0.75 each. How much money does he spend?

4. Suzy buys 10 boxes of pencils. Each box contains 12 blue pencils and 24 red pencils. How many pencils does she buy?

Set 30   For use after page 265.

Find all the different ways to multiply these factors.
Does changing the way the factors are grouped change
the product?

1. $26 \times 9 \times 4 \times 10$

2. $38 \times 15 \times 9 \times 20$

Set 31   For use after page 277.

Score these problems. If an answer is right give it
10 points. If the quotient is right but the remainder is
wrong give it 5 points. Give a wrong answer 0 points.
Check your answers. The score is 60 points.

1. $2\overline{)15}$ 7 r2

2. $9\overline{)86}$ 8 r5

3. $8\overline{)73}$ 9 r1

4. $5\overline{)42}$ 8 r2

5. $7\overline{)44}$ 6 r2

6. $6\overline{)38}$ 6 r3

7. $3\overline{)29}$ 9 r2

8. $9\overline{)32}$ 3 r5

Set 32   For use after page 281.

The ▢ in each problem stands for the same digit. Find
the digit.

1. $▢\overline{)8▢}$ ▢ r8

2. $▢\overline{)6▢}$ ▢ r4

3. $5\overline{)▢9}$ 9 r▢

4. $▢\overline{)4▢}$ 6 r5

Set 33   For use after page 286.

The ▢ in each problem stands for the same digit. Find
the digit.

1. $▢\overline{)99}$ 1▢ r3

2. $▢\overline{)91}$ ▢0 r1

3. $▢\overline{)57}$ 1▢ r1

4. $▢\overline{)▢5}$ 1▢ r1

5. $▢\overline{)6▢}$ 8 r4

6. $3\overline{)▢3}$ 7 r▢

7. $▢\overline{)▢8}$ 11 r1

8. $8\overline{)7▢}$ ▢ r7

Set 34 For use after page 291.

In each problem, the ▨ stands for the same digit. Find the digit.

1.
$$7\overline{)53▨} \quad \text{7▨ r4}$$

2.
$$8\overline{)5▨5} \quad \text{▨1 r▨}$$

3.
$$5\overline{)4▨▨} \quad \text{86 r▨}$$

4.
$$6\overline{)▨7▨} \quad \text{9▨ r▨}$$

Set 35 For use after page 296.

1. Alan, Manuel, Lisa, and Jolie earned $7.00. They spent $2.67 on lunch, $3.90 for skating, and $0.23 for stamps. They shared the change equally. How much change did each one get?

2. Maria earned $1.50 per hour for 3 hours. Erik earned $1.25 per hour for 4 hours. Paul earned $1.30. They shared what they earned equally. How much did each one get?

Set 36 For use after page 313.

Make a bar graph like the one on page 313. Use the information in this table.

Food	Potato	Tomato	Grape	Carrot	Plum
Weight in Grams (g)	70	50	5	30	20

Set 37 For use after page 319.

This table shows the highest temperature recorded in five different cities on one day. Use this information to make a bar graph.

City	Anchorage	Buffalo	Honolulu	Las Vegas	Philadelphia
Temperature	10°C	15°C	30°C	35°C	20°C

Measurement Tables

Metric System

Length
10 millimeters (mm) = 1 centimeter (cm)
10 centimeters = 1 decimeter (dm)
$\left. \begin{array}{l} 1000 \text{ millimeters} \\ 100 \text{ centimeters} \\ 10 \text{ decimeters} \end{array} \right\}$ = 1 meter (m)
1000 meters = 1 kilometer (km)

Area
100 square millimeters (mm²) =
   1 square centimeter (cm²)
10,000 square centimeters =
   1 square meter (m²)

Volume
1000 cubic millimeters (mm³) =
   1 cubic centimeter (cm³)
1,000,000 cubic centimeters =
   1 cubic meter (m³)

Capacity
1000 milliliters (ml) = 1 liter (ℓ)
1000 liters = 1 kiloliter (kl)

Mass
1000 milligrams (mg) = 1 gram (g)
1000 grams = 1 kilogram (kg)
1000 kilograms = 1 metric ton (t)

Time
60 seconds (s) = 1 minute (min)
60 minutes = 1 hour (h)
24 hours = 1 day (d)
7 days = 1 week (wk)
28 to 31 days = 1 month (mo)
12 months = 1 year (yr)

Customary System

Length
12 inches (in.) = 1 foot (ft)
3 feet = 1 yard (yd)
1760 yards = 1 mile (mi)

Area
144 square inches (in.²) =
   1 square foot (ft²)
9 square feet = 1 square yard (yd²)

Volume
1728 cubic inches (in.³) =
   1 cubic foot (ft³)
27 cubic feet = 1 cubic yard (yd³)

Capacity
2 cups = 1 pint (pt)
2 pints = 1 quart (qt)
4 quarts = 1 gallon (gal)

Weight
16 ounces (oz) = 1 pound (lb)
2000 pounds = 1 ton (T)

Symbol List

+	plus
−	minus
×	times
⌐ *or* ÷	divided by
=	equals *or* is equal to
≠	is not equal to
>	is greater than
<	is less than
( )	do the operation inside parentheses first
. . .	pattern continues without end
8 r2	eight remainder two
20.7	twenty and seven-tenths (decimal point)
∟	right angle
∠ ABC	angle ABC
°C	degree Celsius
°F	degree Fahrenheit
50¢	fifty cents
$1.25	one dollar and twenty-five cents
3:45	three forty-five (time)

Glossary

acute angle   An angle that measures less than a right angle.

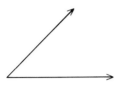

addend   A number that is added.
   Example $5 + 8 = 13$ The addends are 5 and 8.

addition (+)   An operation on two numbers to find how many in all or how much in all.
   Example $7 + 9 = 16$ 7 and 9 are **addends**. 16 is the **sum**.

angle   A shape formed by two lines that meet.

area   The number of units, usually square, needed to cover a surface.
   Example   The area of this rectangle is 6 square units.

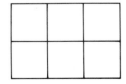

associative property of addition   The way in which addends are grouped does not change the sum.
   Example $(3 + 2) + 4 = 3 + (2 + 4)$

associative property of multiplication   The way in which factors are grouped does not change the product.
   Example $(5 \times 3) \times 2 = 5 \times (3 \times 2)$

average (mean)   The quotient found by dividing a sum by the number of addends.
   Example   5 is the average of 7, 6, and 2 because $7 + 6 + 2 = 15$ and $15 \div 3 = 5$.

bar graph   A graph with bars of different lengths to show and compare information.

capacity   The amount a container will hold when filled.

circle   A closed curve with all points an equal distance from a center point.

circle graph   A graph that can be used to show parts of a whole.

common denominator   A number used as a denominator to make two or more equal fractions.
   Example   12 is a common denominator for $\frac{2}{3}$ and $\frac{1}{4}$ because $\frac{2}{3}$ equals $\frac{8}{12}$ and $\frac{1}{4}$ equals $\frac{3}{12}$.

commutative property of addition   The order in which addends are added does not change the sum.
   Example $7 + 5 = 5 + 7$

commutative property of multiplication
The order in which factors are multiplied does not change the product.
Example $3 \times 7 = 7 \times 3$

cone A solid with one circular face.

congruent Having the same size and shape.

coordinate graph A drawing of numbered lines that cross at right angles and are used to name the positions of points. The names of the positions are written as **ordered pairs.**

count To name numbers in order, matching each number with an object, to find how many objects in all.

corner (vertex) Three or more edges of a solid meet in a corner.

cube A solid with six congruent square faces.

customary measurement system A measurement system that uses inches, feet, yards, and miles as units of length; cups, pints, quarts, and gallons as units of capacity; ounces, pounds, and tons as units of weight; and degrees Fahrenheit as units of temperature.

cylinder A solid with two congruent circular faces.

decimal A number that uses place value and a decimal point to show tenths and hundredths.
Example 5.75 Read *five and seventy-five hundredths.*

degree Celsius (°C) A standard unit for measuring temperature in the metric system.
Example Water freezes at 0°C and boils at 100°C.

degree Fahrenheit (°F) A standard unit for measuring temperature in the customary measurement system.
Example Water freezes at 32°F and boils at 212°F.

denominator The numeral below the bar in a fraction.
Example $\frac{2}{5}$ The denominator is 5.

difference The answer to a subtraction problem.
Example $8 - 3 = 5$ The difference is 5.

digit Any one of the ten symbols 0, 1, 2, 3, 4, 5, 6, 7, 8, or 9.

dividend The number that is divided in a division problem.
Example $3\overline{)18}$ *or* $18 \div 3$ The dividend is 18.

division ($\overline{)}$ *or* $\div$) An operation on two numbers that tells the number of equal groups and the number left over, or the number in each group and the number left over.

Example
$$5\overline{)37}\ \ ^{7\,r2}$$
5 is the **divisor**, 37 is the **dividend**, 7 is the **quotient**, and 2 is the **remainder**.

divisor The number by which the dividend is divided.
Example $4\overline{)36}$ *or* $36 \div 4$ The divisor is 4.

edge Two faces of a solid meet in an edge.

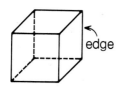

equal fractions (equivalent fractions)
Fractions that name the same number.
Example $\frac{1}{2}$ and $\frac{2}{4}$ are equal fractions.

equals *or* **is equal to** (=) Have the same value.
Example $5 + 7 = 12$ Read *five plus seven equals twelve* or *five plus seven is equal to twelve.*

equation A number sentence with an equals sign (=).
Examples $6 + 4 = 10$
$8 - 7 = 1$

estimate To guess a likely answer. One way to estimate an answer is to round the numbers before doing the problem.

even number A whole number with 0, 2, 4, 6, or 8 in the ones place.
Examples 6, 78, 112

face A flat surface of a solid.

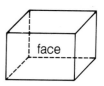

factor A number that is multiplied.
Example $6 \times 7 = 42$ The factors are 6 and 7.

fraction A number that names part of a whole or group.
Examples $\frac{1}{3}, \frac{3}{4}$

graph A drawing used to show and compare information. Some types of graphs are bar graphs, circle graphs, line graphs, and picture graphs.

identity property for addition If one of two addends is 0, the sum is the same as the other addend.
Example $57 + 0 = 57$

identity property for multiplication If one of two factors is 1, the product is the same as the other factor.
Example $17 \times 1 = 17$

intersecting lines Lines that meet or cross.

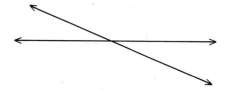

length The measurement of an object from end to end.

like fractions Fractions with the same denominator.
Example $\frac{1}{4}$ and $\frac{3}{4}$ are like fractions.

line graph   A graph in which a line is used to show change.

line of symmetry   If a shape can be folded along a line so that each half is the same size and shape, the fold line is a line of symmetry.

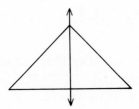

metric system   A measurement system that uses centimeters, meters, and kilometers as units of length; milliliters and liters as units of capacity; grams and kilograms as units of mass; and degrees Celsius as units of temperature.

minus (−)   A symbol that shows subtraction.
   Example $11 - 3 = 8$ Read *eleven minus three equals eight.*

mixed number   The sum of a whole number and a fraction.
   Example $2\frac{1}{3} = 2 + \frac{1}{3}$

multiplication (×)   An operation on two numbers, called **factors**. If one factor is the number of groups, the other factor is the number in each group.
   Example $7 \times 8 = 56$ 7 and 8 are factors. 56 is the **product.**

number line   A line with equally spaced points named by numbers.

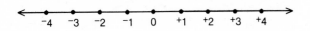

numeral   A name or symbol for a number.
   Examples $\frac{1}{3}$, 2.3, 5, $15\frac{3}{4}$

numerator   The numeral above the bar in a fraction.
   Example $\frac{2}{5}$ The numerator is 2.

obtuse angle   An angle that measures greater than a right angle.

odd number   A whole number with 1, 3, 5, 7, or 9 in the ones place.
   Examples   9, 21, 243

parallel lines   Lines that do not intersect. Parallel lines are always the same distance apart.

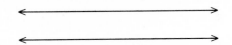

parentheses ( )   Symbols of grouping. Parentheses tell which part or parts of a problem to do first.
   Example $(6 - 4) + 1$ Do $(6 - 4)$ first.

perimeter   The distance around a shape. The perimeter of a shape is the sum of the lengths of the sides.

period   A group of three digits set off by a comma in a numeral.
   Example   342,674,408   From right to left, the periods are the ones period, the thousands period, and the millions period.

perpendicular lines Lines that intersect at right angles.

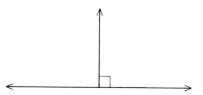

place value The value given to the place in which a digit appears in a numeral.
Example 32 The place value of 3 is tens. The place value of 2 is ones.

plus (+) A symbol that shows addition.
Example 7 + 8 = 15 Read *seven plus eight equals fifteen.*

probability The chance of an event occurring, written as a fraction between 0 (the event cannot occur) and 1 (the event must occur).
Example You toss a coin. The probability of it landing heads up is 1 out of 2, or $\frac{1}{2}$.

product The answer to a multiplication problem.
Example 4 × 12 = 48 The product is 48.

pyramid A solid. One face is a triangle, rectangle, or other shape with angles. The other faces are triangles.

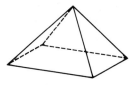

quotient The answer to a division problem.
Example 16 ÷ 8 = 2 The quotient is 2.

rectangle A shape with four sides and four right angles.

rectangular prism A solid with six faces that are rectangles.

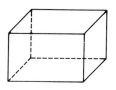

remainder The number left over in a division problem. The remainder must be less than the divisor.
Example 5)‾17 3 r2 The remainder is 2.

right angle An angle with the same shape as the corner of a square.

Roman numerals Symbols used by the Romans to name numbers.
Examples I V X L C D
            1 5 10 50 100 500

rounding Writing a number to the nearest ten or hundred.
Example 134 rounded to the nearest hundred is 100.

similar   Having the same shape.

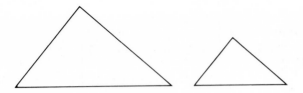

solve   To find the answer to a problem.

sphere   A solid with all points the same distance from a center point.

square   A shape with four equal sides and four right angles.

subtraction (−)   An operation on two numbers to find how many are left or how much greater one number is than the other.
   Example $12 - 7 = 5$ 5 is the **difference.**

sum   The answer to an addition problem.
   Example $11 + 7 = 18$ The sum is 18.

times (×)   A symbol that shows multiplication.
   Example $4 \times 5 = 20$ Read *four times five equals twenty.*

trade   In addition, subtraction, and multiplication, to make one group of ten out of ten ones or ten ones out of one group of ten.
   Example $14 = 1$ ten $+ 4$ ones

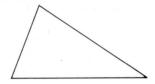

Also, to make one hundred from ten tens, one thousand from ten hundreds, and so on.

triangle   A shape with three sides and three angles.

unlike fractions   Fractions with different denominators.
   Example $\frac{1}{3}$ and $\frac{1}{4}$ are unlike fractions.

volume   The number of cubic units needed to fill a solid.
   Example   The volume of this cube is 8 units.

whole number   Any one of the numbers 0, 1, 2, 3, 4, 5, and so on.

zero property for multiplication   If 0 is a factor, the product is 0.
   Example $17 \times 0 = 0$

Index

C 2
D 3
E 4
F 5
G 6
H 7
I 8
J 9